CLOSE UP ■ 02

MOVIES AND TONE • READING ROHMER • VOICES IN FILM

First published in Great Britain in 2007 by
Wallflower Press
6a Middleton Place, Langham Street, London W1W 7TE
www.wallflowerpress.co.uk

A catalogue for this book is available from the British Library.

ISBN 978-1-905674-06-0 (pbk)
ISBN 978-1-905674-07-7 (hbk)

Printed by Replika Press Pvt Ltd (India)

CLOSE UP ■ 02

MOVIES AND TONE • READING ROHMER • VOICES IN FILM

edited by

JOHN GIBBS & DOUGLAS PYE

WALLFLOWER

LONDON & NEW YORK

CONTENTS

Editors' introduction

The title of this series signals its major intentions: to engage with the detail of films and television programmes and to make analysis of detailed decision-making central to the arguments being advanced in each individual study. These are modest objectives at one level, since it should be self-evident that any worthwhile study of the arts must engage closely with its objects. But even with the widespread institutionalisation of film and media studies and with a plurality of approaches to the subject being made available through an ever-expanding literature, studies that genuinely focus on the material complexity of films and make this detail fundamental to their enquiries are rare. The magnetic field of powerful concepts and approaches that dominated film theory from the early 1970s, and which often seemed to discourage engagement with the individual and specific, has weakened but it is still common to find, especially in texts designed for students, films being presented as little more than illustrations of wider concepts or approaches. 'Top down' ways of thinking, in which the general framework takes precedence over the particular text, still pervade the literature and much teaching about film. Yet, if 'top down' approaches can become programmatic, too often finding only examples of their own paradigms, the corrective cannot be to abandon informing frameworks. Theory and concept are required to channel and focus analysis, but investigation of the texture of filmmaking and of the dramatised world, informed by awareness of history and convention, must be able to question and re-shape concept and theory. There is still a huge challenge in understanding what films are and how they work to create meaning and affect. The objective of the *Close-Up* series comes to seem less modest when we begin to wrestle with the rich intersection of material elements in any moment of a film or television drama, attempting to find ways of capturing in language the nuances of action, performance and setting, the degrees of emphasis created by the selection of light, framing and editing, the grading of music, dialogue and other sound. *Close-Up* will engage with many different areas of cinema and television drama and individual contributions will be written from a variety of critical and theoretical positions. What they will all share is a strong sense of the particular, the choices that make films distinctive and on which arguments for significance and value must rest.

John Gibbs and Douglas Pye
Close-up series editors
May 2007

2.1 MOVIES AND TONE
Douglas Pye

ACKNOWLEDGEMENTS

I should like to thank all the members of The Sewing Circle, the informal film analysis seminar for postgraduates and staff in the Department of Film, Theatre & Television, University of Reading, and especially the participants in a series of seminars held some years ago on the topic of tone. I am very grateful to John Gibbs for his unfailing support, invaluable suggestions and his sympathetic but firm editorial guidance, and to Lib Taylor and Michael Walker for responding generously to specific questions.

1. A missing concept

The first hunting sequence in *The Deer Hunter* (Michael Cimino, 1979) follows Michael (Robert De Niro) and Nick (Christopher Walken) leaving a mountain cabin in the dawn light to hunt deer. We watch them as they climb and clamber over the rocky terrain. Quite early in the 25-shot sequence Michael moves well ahead of Nick (we do not see them together in the frame after shot 3) and we then largely follow Michael (there are only two shots of Nick between shot 4 and shot 25) in his single-minded focus on the hunt until he kills a stag with a single round, in accordance with the 'one-shot' philosophy he has so emphatically expounded earlier in the film. What we are shown both illustrates Michael's skill and confirms the moral seriousness with which he imbues the act of hunting. The absence of the other members of the hunting party intensifies the focus on Michael's values. He is, it seems clear, The Deer Hunter, and the allusion to James Fenimore Cooper's *The Deerslayer*, together with Michael's insistence on the significance of the one-shot kill, evoke a long-standing tradition in American fiction, given potent initial form by Cooper's 'Leatherstocking' novels, in which the experience of men with guns in the wilderness can take on transcendent value.

The images alone, in their context, would have carried meanings and associations of this kind. But Cimino accompanies the sequence with non-diegetic music. Beginning very softly as the men leave the cabin, choral singing builds in volume and intensity as the hunt develops, ceasing abruptly with Michael's shot which echoes unaccompanied across the landscape. This is the second use of religious choral music in the film, paralleling that of the earlier Russian Orthodox marriage ceremony (though here the choir seems entirely male) and therefore implicitly inviting linkage of the two sequences. The music is so assertive that it can seem to convey unambiguously the film's valuation of Michael's hunt as sacred ritual – music as direct editorial comment. This is certainly the way in which a number of the early accounts of the film understood it.

> The hunting scenes are framed in Olympian terms – long-shots of snow-capped mountains in the background, the morning frost on the ground, the soundtrack bursting with religious choral music, and Michael seen in a meticulously edited pursuit of the deer. The whole sequence self-consciously strains for transcendence, and though its operatic quality ... is visually exciting, on an intellectual level it borders on the banal and laughable. (Auster & Quart 1979: 7)

> When Michael climbs a mountain to hunt, it's a Holy Mountain, a mystical aerie straight out of Leni Riefenstahl's *The Blue Light*. Russian choral singing underscores his unhurried pursuit of a kingly stag, which he fells according to his code, with one clean shot. (Dempsey 1979: 16)

When Cimino sends his Pennsylvania steelworker out to hunt, he transports him to sublime mountain peaks which are emphatically not in Pennsylvania, and accompanies the action with an embarrassingly lush and obvious score. (Axeen 1979: 18)

And what of the hunting of the deer? It is hard for me to take these sequences seriously, and not only because of the heavenly choirs with which Cimino accompanies the action … The sequences are doubtless intended to establish the dignity of the hunter, and his pride in the exercise of his predatory skills … I don't find this a dismal objective, but the point is bungled through grandiosity and vagueness. (Callenbach 1979: 21)

All these critics were responding to the challenge for criticism posed by what many saw as a difficult and enigmatic film. In wrenching the quotations from their contexts I do not wish to belittle their arguments but to establish interpretations of the hunt sequence that seemed widely shared among early commentators. It is easy to see why these views were held. The music is emphatically editorial but, unless it was read ironically (and the context made such a reading unlikely), there seemed little alternative but to take it as intending affirmation of the spiritual mystique of hunting. All the writers quoted believe the sequence to be reaching for this kind of significance but failing to achieve it. At the very least they experience a disparity between ends and means, a striving for effect and meaning by way of a heightened rhetoric that risks seeming banal, embarrassing, grandiose, clichéd.

In a somewhat later account, Robin Wood develops a different view of the sequence, within an intricate revaluation of the film:

The *mise-en-scène* of the hunt – grandiose landscapes, choir, hero against the skyline – is clearly a critical crux: your response to the entire film will be coloured by how you read it. It seems to me further evidence of Cimino's audacity. On the one hand, it certainly cannot be taken ironically; on the other, the stylisation, the break with realistic effect, is much too extreme and much too foregrounded for it simply to be read straight, the 'standard emblems of romantic uplift' (Britton) being clearly placed, as it were within quotation marks. The mode within which the sequence operates is, it seems to me, the mode of the archaic: the stylistic archaism at once embodies and places a concept of nobility and heroism that belongs to a past (perhaps a purely mythic one). (1986: 285)

Wood responds to the same elements as the earlier writers but, on the basis of a prior argument which identifies in the film's presentation of Clairton a breakdown of tradition, a community 'eroded beyond repair' (1986: 284), trusts the film to be deploying the rhetoric of the hunt with self-conscious analytical intent. Wood's methodology is significant: he first establishes a context; he dismisses the idea of irony, then argues that the 'extreme' and 'foregrounded' nature of Cimino's decision-making should be understood – in its difference from the prevailing style – as a sign that we are not to read the sequence 'straight'. The very fact that the rhetorical choices might be seen as 'standard devices' points for Wood not to an unsuccessful striving for effect but to the conscious evocation of a specific 'mode' of address ('the archaic') which can simultaneously evoke and critically place values which belong to the past. To crystalise his argument about the status of the sequence he uses a vivid analogy with the ways in which a speaker or writer can signal different levels of address in language: '"the standard emblems of romantic uplift" (Britton) being clearly placed, as it were within quotation marks'. It is as though, in this sequence, the film adopts a significantly different 'voice' from that used before.

Although the concept does not figure explicitly in these accounts of the sequence, what is at issue in the opposed interpretations can be seen as an understanding of tone. That is to say that the questions being probed by these critics are not simply about what is being signified in the dramatic material of the film but about the ways in which the film addresses its spectator and implicitly invites us to understand its attitude to its material and the stylistic register it employs. As Wood's analogy of 'quotation marks' suggests, we are familiar with the various means by which mode of address and attitude can be signalled in language – matters that we can think of, loosely, as to do with 'tone of voice'. As a critical concept, though, tone has been out of favour for many years.[1]

In fact, it is a concept which has had a very limited place in film theory and criticism. This is at one level surprising, given the crucial role tone plays in enabling us to orientate ourselves to any film. We seem, more often than not, to respond almost instinctively to the various elements in a film's opening that in combination signal its tone – part of the complex but seemingly automatic process which enables us to understand the kind of film we are watching and how it wants us to take it. When these habitual processes are disturbed, as they sometimes are when we watch films from a culture other than our own, or when a film makes it difficult immediately to say what kind of thing it is, it can be an uncomfortable or disorientating experience. And even movies that seem to establish their tone straightforwardly can hold all sorts of tonal surprises in store. In these respects, responding to or trying to make out the tone of a film has much in common with the even more habitual processes by which we try to gauge tone when we are involved in conversation. The obvious centrality of tone of voice for our response to film and theatre should not need stressing: dialogue and its performance are at the heart of our experiences of movies and plays. But they are also contained within frameworks of production which in turn add many potential dimensions to the manipulation of tone.

The very limited discussion of tone in film criticism and theory may well be linked to the history of the concept in twentieth-century literary criticism from I. A. Richards onwards. In this tradition it was central to the understanding of how the words of the poem or story addressed the reader, the tone of voice that could be adduced from the words on the page. This included not just tone in the narrow sense of implied emotion or attitude (angry, forceful, gentle, ironic, sarcastic, patronising) but wider issues of class location, educational level, implied intelligence, sensitivity, moral sense, and so on. Tone here, as M. H. Abrams indicates, shades into 'voice' conceived as the whole ethos of the work, the 'sense of a distinctive authorial presence' (1971: 125). These considerations in turn mutate into concepts such as 'authorial voice' and 'implied author'. In the appropriation of narratology by film theory, questions about the appropriate ways of describing narrative levels such as 'narrator' and 'implied filmmaker' have been much debated, but on the whole questions about tone and voice that were so central in the literary tradition from Richards to Wayne C. Booth and beyond slipped out of sight or were abandoned in the pursuit of other registers of meaning and forms of analysis.

But in our experience of movies, as in our day-to-day lives, tone stubbornly refuses to go away, however much we choose to ignore or work around it. Like 'point of view', to which it is intimately linked, it is a term that does not comfortably fit the hybrid dramatic medium of film (it is rooted in 'voice' in the way that point of view is rooted in perspective representation). Yet as a concept it gestures towards some of the most crucial issues for film analysis: the relationships of a film to its material, its traditions and its spectator. Like point of view, of course, tone is not present in a film as, say, patterns of angle/reverse-angle editing might be. In conversation tone is implicit in the speaker's manner, the effect of multiple variants such as timbre, linguistic register, volume, pace, cadence and rhythm, together with facial and bodily expression, and is subject to the interplay of intention, utterance and reception within a specific context. In a parallel way the tone of a film is implied by the various interrelated modes of the film's address and our response to them.

The centrality of tone to our experience of films is indisputable. The question I want to explore in this study is whether it can become a functional critical concept. As a means of focusing on the film's address to the spectator it feels as though it should be indispensable to film criticism. Indeed, the potential for tonal complexity is at the heart of film as a dramatic and narrative art and we ignore it at the risk of impoverishing our understanding of films. At the same time, because tone is implicit, not declared, it is inevitably slippery and subject to ambiguity and misunderstanding, which is also to imply that an understanding of tone can always be contested. Tone and interpretation are inseparable.

Nevertheless, significant problems are embedded in the history of the concept within literary criticism. For I. A. Richards, tone was rooted in norms of social intercourse.[2] Understanding and deploying tone appropriately could be seen as dependent on discrimination born of the right education and social experience. With the challenges to such social hierarchies in the last century critical approaches that seemed based in old class assumptions were rightly suspect. Can tone become a useable concept, free of such assumptions? Certainly nothing in the concept itself implies discrimination inherently based on social class or background. But it is a fact of everyday social interaction that understanding any discourse depends on knowledge and experience: of language and its various registers; of manners and mores; of social situations; of people and professions, and so on. We learn how to employ tone as we develop our use of language and respond to the tone of others. So with novels or films: our understanding of their modes of address can deepen and expand as our experience grows and our discrimination develops.

The Deer Hunter is a valuable case study in this context because it is characterised by an unusually non-discursive approach that makes a reading of tone especially challenging. This means that on the one hand its concerns are not spelt out in dialogue: the characters are unusually inarticulate or at least uncomfortable with expressing themselves in language. This is comically exemplified by Axel's (Chuck Aspegren) constant refrain of 'Fuckin' A' and more problematically by a number of Michael's enigmatic utterances, which puzzle his friends as much as they puzzle us ('This is this', as he holds up a bullet towards Stanley (John Cazale), is one such utterance). But more significant in this respect are two of the film's methods: on the one hand the creation of episodes or moments which take on an evidently metaphorical or even symbolic resonance; and on the other the juxtaposition of scenes with relatively little concern for linear narrative or cause/effect logic. The film foregrounds its metaphorical rhetoric but we are left to make sense of what we see and hear with much less rhetorical help than is common in movies. These methods undoubtedly contributed to the controversy the film provoked and the divergent readings it generated.

The first hunt is, as Wood indicates, a key sequence in terms of how we understand the film, but it is one of many that pose similar problems for the viewer and critic. It is as though Cimino and his collaborators disclaim the possibility of a clear explanatory framework or an authoritative level of narration which would enable us to orientate our reading. We might compare *The Deer Hunter* in these respects with strategies in other 1970s Vietnam movies: the words of the opening soundtrack song, including 'You're out of touch, my baby', over our first images of Bruce Dern's character, Bob Hyde, in *Coming Home* (Hal Ashby, 1978); the vision of the war as absurd in the voice-over that opens *Who'll Stop the Rain* (Karel Reisz, 1978); or Willard's (Martin Sheen) voice-over in the first sequence of *Apocalypse Now* (Francis Ford Coppola, 1979). Although the two uses of voice-over cited are carefully placed, and their authority in some ways later qualified by the films, they provide a level of narration which gives us some bearings and an initial statement of themes. *The Deer Hunter* provides no such help. As Wood's argument implies, we therefore have to orientate ourselves by gradually accumulating a sense of the kind of world presented, and intuiting, as sequence follows sequence, how the film's strategies of drama and narration are intended – how in fact the film is addressing us.

At the level of detailed realisation, too, the film sets in place networks of decision-making which accumulate meaning in the overall context of sequence and/or film. Three small-scale decisions within the first hunt sequence and its immediate aftermath can indicate one dimension of what is involved.

1. Michael is dressed in an orange weatherproof jacket and pinned very noticeably to its back is his hunting license (Fig. 1.1). This is the garb of the modern hunter, not of the nineteenth-century backwoodsman. It can remind us that here hunting is a regulated pastime, not a way of life. This is the mid-twentieth century and these are industrial workers

Fig. 1.1

on a recreational hunt, not frontiersmen whose lives depend on their skills. We can note too the high-powered rifle with its telescopic sights. In relation to the ennobling rhetoric of the music these are small but significant incongruities, decisions which were by no means inevitable but which create local disturbances to a wholly affirmative reading of the sequence.

2. The final shot of the hunt sequence. After Michael fires, we see the deer in me-

Fig. 1.2

dium long shot stagger and fall. There is a cut to a closer framing as it lies on the ground, and a zoom into close-up; the deer struggles to raise its head and its eye – open wide – rolls upwards (Fig. 1.2). Michael's one shot will kill the animal but it has not dispatched it instantly: we are witness to its dying moments, although not to its death. Again, there is nothing inevitable about the presence of this shot and it provides another implicit qualification to the tone of the music (now silent at this point) and to the rhetoric of the clean, one-shot kill.

3. From the dying deer the film cuts directly, with an abrupt change of tone and register, to Michael's car speeding into Clairton and finally coming to a halt outside John's bar. The men tumble out and into the bar, singing discordantly. It is night and the shots are

Fig. 1.3

predominantly very dark but we can note (though it is not difficult to miss) the body of the deer draped across the bonnet of the Cadillac (Fig. 1.3). As the men enter the bar, the camera moves briefly down, looking across the car's bonnet, so that the stag's antlers can be seen clearly for an instant before the next cut. The ritual of the hunt, with the implicit dignity it accords the quarry, gives way to the deer's undignified treatment after death; an evocation of the mythic frontier reaching back to Cooper gives way to the emphatically modern image of the speeding, beat-up Cadillac and to the raucous pleasure of the male group.

What weight to give these details cannot be determined on the basis of the sequences alone. As Wood argues about the hunt, we need the full context of the film – or indeed, we might require the benefit of subsequent viewings. But the details exemplify one of the characteristics of the film's mode of address, the presence of potentially discordant or incongruous elements which we are invited to register and to hold in juxtaposition with other elements – the music, the energy of the speeding car, the camaraderie of the group – that can easily dominate our response and flatten out our sense of the film's tone.

I have noted that the hunt is 'rhymed' musically with one of the other key sequences of the first movement of the film, the Russian Orthodox marriage ceremony, one part of the extensive wedding celebration that dominates the earlier parts of the film. Again we can compare some early responses to Wood's somewhat later analysis. Like the hunt, the marriage scenes were often taken as pivotal images, in this case within the film's supposed celebration of Clairton as an apparently homogeneous ethnic community rooted in traditional values.

He has evoked a stunning image of a warm, working-class community where the flow of communal energy and the texture of ritual transcends any of its private agonies and social limitations ... The apotheosis of Cimino's homage to traditional working-class life ... is the ethnic wedding sequence. In this lovingly detailed but overextended scene, we get a full view of the ornate, mosaic and saint-laden Russian Orthodox Church, and lengthy footage of the film's major characters singing, dancing and brawling. The sequence succeeds in evoking communal joy... (Auster & Quart 1979: 6)

David Axeen does not refer in detail to these sequences but comes to a similar conclusion:

The Russian-American steel town readying its boys for war has most of the virtues sentimentally attributed to organic, pre-modern communities. Its citizens are united by ethnic roots, orthodox religion, and unaffected love for each other. (1979: 17)

In developing his utterly opposed view of the film's presentation of and attitude to Clairton, Wood conducts his argument in critical dialogue with Andrew Britton's dismissive account of the film. Wood draws attention to a pattern of incidents and actions that in various ways threaten the characters' mood of celebration or undercut the idea of a positively presented organic traditional community. The wine dripping like spots of blood onto Angela's (Rutanya Alda) wedding dress and the incident with the Green Beret are among the moments Wood identifies as implying the 'hysteria into which the Clairton wedding celebration is imminently in danger of collapsing: in place of harmony, one finds incipient chaos, tension, disruption' (1986: 282). Rather than a community unified by traditional values, he finds their breakdown, touching, for instance, on Angela's pregnancy by someone other than Steven (John Savage), Stephen's mother's (Shirley Stoler) attempt to find comfort and guidance from the priest who seems unable to offer either, the way that characters (he cites Nick and Linda (Meryl Streep) but it seems true of all the main characters apart from John (George Dzundza), who is in the choir) seem ill at ease during the wedding ceremony.

In fact, there is an extensive network of detail to set against the rhetoric of tradition and community and which seems to imply not the continued vitality of traditional family and community life but its failure. Among the most forceful examples are the two scenes involving Stephen's mother (dragging Stephen from the bar and tearfully seeking solace from the priest) and Linda's drunken father muttering grotesquely about women ('fucking bitches, they're all fucking bitches') before violently assaulting Linda as she tries to bring him his meal. Violence against women erupts again in the wedding reception when Stanley punches and knocks out his girlfriend for allowing another man to fondle her bottom as they dance. No one seems outraged by the violence, least of all the woman involved.

Singled out and juxtaposed in this way these take on considerable interpretative power. Cimino's achievement is partly that in the film, while they are there to be observed, they are held in contrapuntal relationship with other aspects of the film which pull in different directions and may command more immediate attention: the establishment of the male group, the emotional power of the wedding sequences. Given appropriate weight, however, and set within the overall context that Cimino creates, the patterns of detail build a picture of a community in which the conventional structures and values of communal life – the nuclear family, relationships between parents and children, marriage as a Christian sacrament – are breaking down. The traditional frameworks and institutions are still in place and exerting a powerful influence on social forms, but their power to command belief and behaviour has diminished: their magnetic field has weakened.

It is this kind of approach to the film's network of decision-making in its early scenes that enables Wood to claim that 'the film establishes quite clearly the archaism of the ethnic rituals whose lingering trace continues, very tentatively, to hold the community together' (1986: 284). Wood's claim that these things are established 'quite clearly' is belied by the many critics who read the film very differently and I will turn later to questions about the contexts in which reading and response takes place. But I want for now to pursue Wood's claim about the film's presentation of its ethnic rituals as archaic and probe the stages of argument it implies. As with his interpretation of the hunt, the fundamental issue is one of context – the ways in which everything that surrounds a scene can alter how we understand the way it wants to be taken.

This is how we might make the considerable conceptual leap from traditional church ritual to 'archaism', a shift not just in linguistic register but in the manner of understanding the film's relationship to its world, its spectator and the means with which it seeks to communicate. Taken in and for itself, the marriage sequence might seem to balance, in an unusually elaborate but nonetheless familiar way, the solemnity of the ritual and the touching and sometimes humorous human detail given in shots of the characters as the service develops. We have seen numerous film weddings that work variations on these familiar conventions. The solemnity is heightened here by the soaring choral sing-

Fig. 1.4

Fig. 1.5

ing and the series of shots which roam across the rich and ornate iconic images that decorate almost every surface of the cathedral, but it is grounded, given a specific human context, by a series of shots of the main characters: the tentative and self-conscious ways in which Nick, Linda and Stephen play their unaccustomed and central roles; Stanley's act of crossing himself, which provokes Michael's expressions of amusement and apparent incredulity (Fig. 1.4); John, up in the gallery as a member of the choir, smiling and then almost laughing as he looks down on his friends. What distinguishes this wedding sequence from others is the weight given to the ritual through the music and the extended visual treatment of the extraordinary setting, effects intensified for many of us by the unfamiliarity of the Orthodox liturgy and the traditions of Byzantine church decoration (Fig. 1.5). Within the context of all that precedes the wedding, however, rather than the liturgy casting a glow of traditional values and faith over the community, we might see both the splendour of the cathedral and the grandeur of the music as incongruous, even anachronistic, in the Clairton we have previously been shown.

These interpretative manoeuvres depend, of course, on the significance and relative weight we wish to attach to the varied material the film presents within its world, and crucially they depend on what we intuit, as the film develops, about the film's intentions. The frameworks adopted by those critics who take the film to be celebrating the organic community and Wood's opposed understanding represent different ways of grasping what the film's makers want us to think and feel. In the first, we are to take the church ritual 'straight', while in the other we should take it as self-conscious deployment of a rhetoric designed to be both experienced and analytically placed within the wider patterns of the film. In the one, potentially discordant detail is overlooked or downplayed; in the other, patterns of discord, disruption and change form the ground which highlights the strangeness of the wedding's heightened register and evocation of changeless tradition. Context and its interpretation are decisive.

To return to the parallel between the marriage ceremony and the first hunt, in the marriage the choral singing is diegetic, its origins firmly placed within the world of the film. We might wish to argue about the extent to which the film establishes or does not establish degrees of 'distance' from the belief system and spiritual aspiration the music embodies, but its source in the fictional world allows for at least the possibility of such distance. Non-diegetic music tends to be different: we are used to it carrying, as it were, 'editorial' authority, not as comment necessarily (though it can have this function, as it does in the example from *Coming Home* referred to above) but as setter of mood and dramatic register. Without the earlier wedding music, the use of non-diegetic choral singing in the hunt would lack the vital parallel that makes possible Wood's interpretation of the rhetoric of the hunt as in 'quotation marks'. With the parallel in place, understood within the texture of incident and image he traces across the first movements of the film, it is possible for Wood to hear in the hunt the self-conscious adoption of an idiom without an implicit assent by the film to that idiom's underlying value system, and to identify in both sequences a deployment for specific purposes of the 'archaic'.

In such an argument these sequences offer themselves as set-pieces, each of which powerfully evokes traditional values and aspirations that are central in different ways to the characters and the film. But the sequences are, to use a version of Wood's analogy with language, more like quotations than declarations of faith, each representing beliefs that the wider context renders anachronistic. These belief systems retain their imaginative power but have no significant social force. The Church seems to have very limited influence over the society the film presents. Michael holds to the mystique of hunting but he is a Leatherstocking clinging to outdated values in a context that renders them largely meaningless.

It will be clear from this discussion that my sympathy is very much with Wood's position on these matters: he seems to me to offer a framework of ideas and a way of seeing that confers significance on and draws into meaningful relationship far more of the early parts of the film than most other accounts. He 'makes sense' of many of the film's strategies that are otherwise difficult to account for and – an important matter – he gives the filmmakers credit for being in control of and meaning everything they do. At the same time, of course, Wood's account, and my extrapolations from it, can be challenged by alternative interpretations of the evidence. Their efficacy can also be finally assessed only in the context of the whole film, the most controversial and divisive of aspects of which I have not touched on.

At the same time, criticism is always written in particular circumstances and is subject to its moment in all sorts of ways. The early writing on *The Deer Hunter* came out of a period in which the politics of the Vietnam War remained at the centre of much debate aroused by the first wave of Hollywood Vietnam movies. Cimino's film, more than any other, aroused criticism for its apparent lack of concern with politics, the isolation of its characters from the controversies about American involvement in South East Asia and its misrepresentation of the war itself, leading some writers to regard it as irresponsible in its attitudes. Wood's account was published later (1986) and his ability to investigate the achievement of the film in very different terms may reflect a certain distance from the immediate circumstances of the film's reception. The main objective here, however, is to highlight a range of issues within the critical debates about *The Deer Hunter* that can be seen to turn on the unacknowledged concept of tone. What I have called the non-discursive methods of the film link it to a variety of movements within early twentieth-century modernism which broke with earlier poetic, narrative and representational traditions by stressing the juxtaposition of images or voices without a bedrock level of narration, or which privileged in the novel 'showing' over 'telling' and abandoned the apparently authoritative narrative voices of the nineteenth-century novel for more partial, limited and uncertain, or even untrustworthy, views of events.

M. H. Abrams writes about the terms 'Persona, Tone and Voice': 'These terms, increasingly frequent in criticism, reflect the recent tendency to think of a work of literature ... as a mode of speech' (1971: 123). He goes on: 'the way a person speaks subtly reveals his concept of the social level, intelligence and sensitivity of his auditor, his personal relation to him, and the stance he adopts towards him' (1971: 124). Correspondingly, for Richards, tone is defined as 'the perfect recognition of the writer's relation to the reader in view of what is being said and their joint feelings about it' (Russo 1989: 232). Jean Paul Russo explains: 'he in fact saw it as a concept able to denote both the author's attitude to the audience, the subject matter, himself, and the "speaker" or "voice" within the poem. At the same time, tone also denotes the speaker's attitude to the audience, the subject matter, and the speaker's self – and their mutual relations, making for a seven-headed Hydra' (ibid.).

Tone in this account designates the outcome of a complex dynamic, implicit in the literary work, in which three agencies are identified (author, 'speaker' or 'voice', and reader) plus the subject matter. Tone implicitly conveys 'attitude' in various dimensions. Thus:

The author's attitude to the author's self
The author's attitude to the 'speaker' of the poem
The author's attitude to the reader
The author's attitude to the subject matter

The 'speaker' of the poem's attitude to the reader
The 'speaker' of the poem's attitude to the subject matter
The 'speaker' of the poem's attitude to the speaker's self

We might add two additional lines to each of these lists, relating to the conventions of language being used, and the 'utterance', the specific uses of language in the work:

The author's attitude to the conventions of language being used
The author's attitude to the utterance

The 'speaker' of the poem's attitude to the conventions of language being used
The 'speaker' of the poem's attitude to the utterance.

These are dimensions of tone that emerge from thinking about literature, the medium of which is language, and some care is needed in transferring these ideas to narrative film, which uses language as only one of its multiple means of communication. In the novel, the distinction between speaker or narrator and author (or more commonly in the post-Richards literature, 'implied author') is well established. In film, a voice-over narrator may be critically placed or even shown to be unreliable but voice represents only one dimension of a film's narration. A parallel duality of narrative levels in images is normally possible only when certain passages of a film are ascribed specifically to a character or some other source in the film's world. In most narrative films, though, the images present a single level of narration. A pervasive distinction equivalent to that between 'speaker' and 'author' or 'implied author' therefore makes no sense in film. Some writers retain the concept of implied author or filmmaker to designate the sense we sometimes have of an informing sensibility in a film, but it may be less confusing to avoid even the carefully circumscribed idea of an *implied* individual in these discussions and to think of the qualities inherent in the film itself as an act of human agency.[3] This would mean setting to one side several of the dimensions in which 'attitude' can be expressed in the model of tone derived from Richards and thinking of the attitudes *that the film implies*. In using 'the film' here and in what follows I am conscious of George M. Wilson's warning that 'it is principally *speakers* who may imply things by what they say, and it is unclear that *films* can imply anything at all unless some responsible agent has had the relevant communicative intention' (1997: 224). Behind this usage stand the filmmakers, the individuals who took the material decisions that make up the film and are responsible for the attitudes the film dramatises and those with which it is imbued. But we will need to be cautious in mapping these attitudes directly onto the historical individuals who made the film, as if the film was a form of speech and the filmmakers were speaking directly to us. 'The film' is not an entity that can itself imply anything but the decisions that made it create for its viewers both a fictional world and implied ways of viewing it.

The remaining dimensions of tone derived from this initial model will therefore be the attitudes implied to:

the film's subject matter;
the film's audience;
the conventions the film employs or invokes;
the film as a film (the equivalent of 'utterance' in earlier discussion).

None of these terms is without difficulty. 'Attitude' in particular becomes a very slippery concept once we leave the comparative security of declarative prose ('My attitude to the government is...'; 'I hate, despise and abominate money'; 'His attitude to romance was consistently cynical') for the dramatic arts. Attitude is also too broad a concept to use without qualification. It will be necessary to think about ways in which it can be opened up and a number of different axes of attitude identified. Tone in film is rarely a singular matter, any more than point of view is: these are unitary terms for complex narrative effects. In addition we will need to consider the affective dimensions of attitude that are so crucial to our experience of tone.

To return briefly to Robin Wood on *The Deer Hunter*, when he turns his attention to the controversial final sequence in which the friends gather in John's bar after Nick's funeral, he makes the concept of tone central to his argument.

> The tone has been widely misunderstood, a local failure that indicates a wider incapacity for dealing with art of any interesting degree of complexity. How one reads it is invariably presented as a simple choice between clear-cut attitudes: either the ending is affirmative or it is ironic. In fact it is neither. Its total effect depends on the organisation of a number of elements that hint delicately at possibilities rather than add up to a single coherent attitude or statement (let alone 'message'). (1986: 287–8)

Of the characters singing 'God Bless America' he writes that it is

> ...obviously the crux of the affirmation vs. irony question. The tone (and it colours the entire sequence) is in fact one of tentativeness. Dramatically, the singing develops out of John's collapse into tears as he tries to cook the omelettes; it is clear that he is weeping not just for the death of Nick, but from a much more generalised sense of loss. The song is his way of cheering himself up. It is then taken up by Linda and subsequently by the others, but the tone of the singing never becomes confident or affirmative. (1986: 289)

Wood's argument is subtle and detailed and readers are urged to read it in full. I quote these passages to reinforce the idea that fundamental matters of interpretation in narrative film can turn on how tone is understood. Of course, a film like *The Deer Hunter*, which aroused such controversy and provoked such different readings and responses, could be considered a limit case, too unusual to base a wider argument on. But perhaps such a case brings to our attention matters that are too often taken for granted. It points, as Wood's analysis eloquently indicates, to the implications of whole dramatic contexts and the need to resist reducing meaning to simple alternatives (as in 'affirmation' or 'irony'). It is very often the case that, as Wood puts it, 'a number of elements ... hint delicately at possibilities', and how we respond to the various elements, their grading and their interrelationship will determine how we understand the film.

The discussions in the rest of this study try to follow this lead. The process of writing was very much one of exploration, of looking at films in detail with tone in mind and of testing the concept against their material reality, rather than of applying a developed theory to film texts, and I have tried to preserve a sense of that process in the finished study.

2. Unpicking tone

Even before we begin to watch a film we tend to prepare ourselves for the kind of experience we expect to have. One aspect of what is involved is described by Deborah Thomas:

> When I approach films (from a variety of genres) in which it is clear that the main char-
> acters will be dogged by an unforgiving fate and that they will almost certainly be caught
> and punished in some way, I often have to steel myself to watch them. In contrast, my
> body relaxes when I'm about to look at films whose tone is very different. What's involved
> here is an extremely broad anticipation of the kinds of pleasure to be offered or withheld
> and the kinds of narrative worlds I'll be invited to inhabit, not in terms of precise settings
> and events, but in terms of the ways they are experienced by viewers and, to some extent,
> by the central characters: on the one hand, there are narrative worlds that feel repressive
> and full of danger and, on the other, those that feel benevolent and safe. Settling down to
> watch a film is, crucially, a case of getting in the mood for the sort of film one is about to
> watch. (2000: 9)

These affective and bodily dimensions of our film-going experience are particularly difficult to analyse but, as Thomas implies, they always accompany and perhaps even
underpin our more cerebral responses. Movies are designed to engage us in a kind of
extended dialogue with and between different dimensions of response – affective, evaluative, cognitive, and so on – as the film develops. As her use of the word suggests, these
matters bear directly on questions of tone – how it is established and how we respond to
it. Thomas's discussion also alerts us to the role played in our response by our apprehension of the kind of film we are about to watch and our sense of the demands it will place
on us. Such predispositions create conditions for the play of tone as we experience the
film itself. They involve, as Thomas puts it, 'getting in the mood for the sort of film one
is about to watch'. Film openings then orient the spectator to what is to follow, introducing the world of the film and simultaneously entering into implicit dialogue with the
expectations the spectator brings to the viewing and the conventions and traditions that
underpin them. Central to the process of orientation will be initial indications of how the
film will address its audience and how the audience will be invited to respond.

Knowing (or thinking we know) the *kind* of experience we are going to have but hop-
ing for the *frisson* of surprise and variation within the familiar framework is one of the
pleasures of popular cinema-going in particular. My interest in this study is mainly in the
interplay that Hollywood traditions make possible between our anticipation of more or
less predictable kinds of pleasure and the ways in which filmmakers work to engage us
in their specific inflections of story and style. However, I want to take as the first of three
openings discussed in this chapter and the next a film that, while engaging with popular
traditions, is also strikingly 'alternative' in its approach to narrative. It is not that alterna-

tive filmmaking provokes no predispositions but the dialogue with conventional forms and expectations that even the most rigorously experimental film implies can challenge expectations and highlight processes of response and interpretation that we often take for granted. These are experiences that can be discomfiting. Jim Hillier writes: 'I am constantly trying to persuade students that frustration of the "normal" expectations of pleasures associated with cinema can itself be a source of pleasure' (2005: 166). When I first saw *Distant Voices, Still Lives* (Terence Davies, 1988) its formal methods puzzled and irritated rather than intrigued me; juxtaposing it in first-year undergraduate teaching with more conventional narratives then gradually led to the pleasure through perplexity that Hillier evokes (2005: 156), via processes of engagement and interpretation in which tone came to play a central part.

The films discussed later in this study work within the broad and flexible conventions of popular American cinema and their makers could have a considerable degree of confidence in their audience's familiarity with the modes of storytelling and the stylistic vocabulary this tradition tends to imply. The relationships between style and the fictional worlds it reveals and shapes are different in each film, but nothing in either breaks the contract implicit in the conventions about the ways in which a fictional world, characters and action will be introduced and developed. It is conventional in such films that the fictional world will appear to exist as though independent of our view of it. Although at some level we know this to be a kind of illusion, the world of the fiction will behave as if it is much like our own world. Characters will tend to act as though unaware of the camera. In their world, indeed, there is no camera.[4]

Distant Voices, Still Lives works very differently. It creates a fictional world that presents aspects of British social life in a particular period but the relationship between this world and the decisions of the filmmakers that give us access to it seems often to break with the familiar convention of the world's autonomy. The conventional relationships between image and sound are also destabilised in various ways.

The film opens with an austere title card, white words on black, accompanied by silence. The card announces, in a plain font, modestly proportioned in the frame: 'The British Film Institute in association with Film Four International presents'. The image fades to black and we hear a distant rumble of thunder. A second title card fades in with the words 'Distant Voices', also white on a black background. A male voice begins: 'Shipping forecast for today and tonight. Iceland, Faroes, Heligoland: fresh to strong south-west winds…'. The voice and distant thunder continue over a fade to black and the fade in of the film's first shot. The opening thus far is rhetorically restrained, the initial silence inviting attention and preparing for the muted sound register of the start of the film. There is no music to signal genre or establish mood but the initial sound decisions, together with the white on black titles, establish a sober, reflective atmosphere. The first title informs us of the film's British origins and a British setting is strongly implied by the shipping forecast. This is such a radio institution in Britain as to produce immediate recognition in British audiences but it is a cultural phenomenon that does not travel far; the film seems immediately concerned to engage spectators who can bring such cultural reference points to bear. However, the broadcaster's voice, the sound quality and the form of the shipping forecast itself also place this particular broadcast in the past, perhaps in the mid-twentieth century. Sonically, the film reaches back to evoke a continuity of British experience but the style of the accompanying titles seem contemporary with the film's production. The film roots itself in the present while beginning to invoke the past.

Although the shipping forecast is addressed to mariners and those connected with the sea, for most British radio listeners it conjures up domestic contexts, listening to the radio at home. The shipping forecast is broadcast on Radio 4, previously 'the Home Service', in the post-war period one of two major family channels on BBC radio. The first image of the film's world both presents a domestic setting and separates image and sound. We hear the radio as though we were in a room with it but we see the facade of a terraced house, framed to show only the ground floor, from a position seemingly across

Fig. 2.1

Fig. 2.2

the street, so that image and sound offer divergent spatial orientations. The camera is square on to the front of the house and remains static. Colour is very subdued and heavy rain is falling (Fig. 2.1). The temporal setting is therefore consistent with the subdued thunder on the soundtrack and geographically we seem to be in an urban environment of nineteenth-century artisan housing characteristic of many British towns and cities, though in films most commonly associated with the Midlands and north of England. The voice and thunder continue. The front door opens and a woman appears, kneels to pick up the milk bottles from the doorstep, looks up at the weather and turns back into the house, closing the door. We see her at some distance but we can make out that she is middle-aged and note that she is wearing a style of apron that is now associated with the middle rather than the later part of the twentieth century (Fig. 2.2).

In a few moments the film has begun to create an archetypal English setting with images and sounds that resonate from decades of British film and television: a working-class area, probably in the Midlands or the North; familiar, dreary English weather; mum about to prepare breakfast, listening to the radio. The shorthand begins to conjure up – for a British audience – a whole world. It also conjures up a fictional mode, working-class 'realism', that forms a significant tradition of British filmmaking and television drama. There are other modes in such settings, such as comedy, but the atmosphere of the opening suggests a serious rather than comedic approach to the nature and problems of this world. There are already hints that this film will not behave in quite the usual way of such dramas (the opening titles, the absence of non-diegetic music, the static camera in place of a more orthodox scene dissection, perhaps the spatial disjunction of image and sound) but the world being introduced is familiar.

V. F. Perkins has eloquently explored the implications of the ways in which films establish, and we come to comprehend, specific fictional worlds and their possibilities. He argues, in relation to Douglas Sirk's *All I Desire* (1953):

> The movie works for an audience that knows the world always to be larger and larger again than the sector currently in view. This knowledge entails an awareness of selection, hence of concentrations and emphases that help to determine tone and viewpoint. *All I Desire* stays within the spectrum of domestic emotional turmoil. Within that spectrum the worst that will happen is heartbreak that may or may not be healed and the best is some occasionally pleasant, more or less tolerable, negotiation of conflict. (2005: 33)

From the traditions of representation on which the film immediately draws, we can infer that the world introduced in the first moments of *Distant Voices, Still Lives* is likely to share something of the characteristics of domestic drama that Perkins outlines, although its cultural context and class location are very different. Our expectations of this world are likely to include familial and romantic conflict within a class framework constrained by economic circumstances and possibly other forms of social disadvantage. The period being suggested makes the film's world part of a wider British society in which class divisions were still entrenched.

So far, however, the film has denied itself the rhetorical heightening (notably through music with its direct appeal to the emotions) that characterises melodrama in both the American and British inflections of that broad mode. Here the mood being established is quieter, observing and listening to the small daily rituals of this world. The sustained shot of the house front before the door is opened establishes proximity but also a spatial distance that is then maintained even when the first character is introduced. As we enter the fictional world, the point of view defined sets us apart from its inhabitants rather than inviting us into immediate association with them.

In discussing point of view in an earlier article (Pye 2000) I identified five axes that together helped to shape a film's point of view: spatial, temporal, cognitive, evaluative and ideological. Rather evasively I also suggested that there are other issues of pressing relevance to consideration of point of view, and identified specifically 'genre, detailed matters of film form and the vexed question of tone'. Without developing these ideas I proposed that a film's relationship to conventions of genre or film style could be considered as questions of 'distance': *generic distance* and *formal* or *stylistic distance*. This still seems a plausible way of thinking about the kinds of implicit dialogue a film conducts with its conventions but perhaps the concept of 'self-consciousness' offers a way of refining at least some aspects of what may be involved.

David Bordwell proposes self-consciousness as one of three major principles of narration, following Meir Sternberg's categories of self-consciousness, knowledgeability and communicativeness (Bordwell, Staiger & Thompson 1985: 25). He uses self-consciousness to denote the degree to which a narration displays 'a recognition that it is addressing an audience' (ibid.) and outlines a number of varied examples from the multitude of forms this can take. For Bordwell, the self-consciousness of 'classical cinema' tends to recede after a film's opening in which narration is often revealed 'quite boldly', whereas in art cinema and the avant-garde self-consciousness is generally more sustained. While the concept is valuable in discussions of narration, defining self-consciousness solely in terms of 'a *recognition* that it is addressing an audience' (my italics) creates problems, as we will see. Self-consciousness here will tend to be overtly signalled, as indeed it can be, rather than implied, as it often is. We need a way of using the concept that enables us to analyse critical relationships to convention which are internalised within whole dramatic contexts and which do not necessarily offer themselves as overt acknowledgements of the audience.[5] I also want particularly to think of self-consciousness as something that, in terms of a relationship to convention, is likely to be pervasive, whether or not it is overt or internalised, even though it may also be selective in its attention to aspects of convention.

In the passage on tone I wrote:

> It needs separate status even though some elements of tone (perhaps the dominant or systemic aspects as opposed to the more local and variable) tend to be intuited when we make initial apprehensions about a film's world and its genre, apprehensions which bring with them intuitions of how the film is to be viewed and responded to (think, for instance, of the different orientations and expectations that we bring to, say, *Rio Bravo*, *Schindler's List*, *Duck Soup* and *Johann Mouse*). (2000: 12)

This recognises two dimensions of tone (the 'dominant or systemic aspects as opposed to the more local and variable') when perhaps a firmer distinction was needed. As the discussion so far suggests, it might be tidier to propose that the dominant or systemic aspects should be referred to in the first instance in terms of 'mood', rather than tone, leaving tone as a term under which to analyse effects created by the film's shifting texture. Mood in this sense takes us from initial predispositions (Thomas's 'getting in the mood') to the film's ways of signalling the nature of its world and how it intends to treat both it and us. Such a use of the term can be found in some discussions of literature. For instance, *The Dictionary of Literary Terms* by Martin Gray defines mood as 'a term used synonymously with atmosphere to indicate in a literary work the prevailing feeling or frame of mind, especially at the start of a play, poem or novel, creating a sense of expectation about what is to follow' (2004: 185). In his approach to the analysis of emotion and film Greg M. Smith uses the concept in a related way but one more directly linked to his concern with feeling. For Smith mood is a crucial initial apprehension that then 'provides a consistent framework for brief emotional experience' (1999: 113). Mood is 'a preparatory state in which one is seeking an opportunity to express a particular emotion or emotion set. Moods are expectancies that we are about to have a particular emotion, that we will encounter cues that will elicit particular emotions' (ibid.). The film will then,

Smith suggests, 'encourage viewers to establish a consistent emotional orientation towards the text (a mood)' (1999: 117); the viewer 'progresses through the film, tending to pick up cues that are congruent with the established mood' (1999: 125). Conceived in this way, mood provides a kind of guide track through the spectator's experience of the film. For Smith these orientations are essentially emotional, but this may be too narrow a focus; since our responses to films encompass various processes of cognition and emotion it may be better to think of mood as having a number of dimensions. As a complex of pervasive orientations mood is intimately linked to apprehension of a fictional mode and/or genre; individual films work variations on the moods associated with modes and genres and simultaneously develop their specific tonal registers. What this suggests is that 'generic distance' and 'formal or stylistic distance' that I previously posited as distinct from tone are probably best thought of as dimensions of a film's point of view structure that can contribute significantly to mood and tone.

...There is now a cut to inside the house and the woman we have just seen walks away from the static camera. We are in a dimly-lit, narrow hallway, looking towards the stairs and the corridor beyond. The shipping forecast is still audible but now seems more distant, as though its sound is coming from a room inside the house. Sound and image have been brought into more familiar spatial alignment. The woman stops at the foot of the stairs, calls, 'It's seven o'clock, you three', and then leaves the frame to go into a room on the right of the hall. A muted rattling of crockery can be heard. She returns to the hall and calls, 'Eileen, Tony, Maisy – better get your skates on', before leaving the frame again (Fig. 2.3).

Fig. 2.3

Sound and image may now be aligned but the use of the camera is unusual in relation to the predominant tradition of working-class realist films, which tend to work within mainstream conventions of scene dissection and dramatic focus. Our view is being held in one position, and sustained so that visual access to the other space, which we can hear, is withheld. The film has the authority to enter the house but now adopts a spatial and epistemic position of considerable limitation, as though it cannot claim the seemingly unrestricted freedom of conventional film narration. If a mode (working-class realism) has been evoked and a serious, contemplative approach implied, the film seems now to be initiating a play with the mode and its conventions and with any associated expectations the film audience might have. What happens next significantly extends that play.

The radio sound has now become inaudible but we hear footsteps apparently descending a flight of stairs. The sound is loud enough for the stairs in question to be those we can see, but no one appears. We hear an exchange between a man and his mother (the voice is that of the woman we have previously seen and heard): 'Morning, Mum'; 'Tony, are those sisters of yours up?'; 'Yeah, they're just coming down.' We hear another set of footsteps descend and a second exchange, this time between Maisy and Mum.

Overlapping this are more footsteps, followed by a final exchange: 'Morning, Mum'; 'Morning, honey. Nervous, love?'

The sound quality places the action close to us (closer than the radio seemed when this shot began) but nothing happens in the image. We are likely to be involved in a process of rapid hypothesis formulation the first time we see the film. Another set of stairs in a house like this would be unusual. The mother has been tangibly present to us yet the children are not. Are we privy to the mother's memories even though the familiar ways of signalling subjectivity have not been employed? Have time dimensions some-how diverged in the film? If so, it has happened without any change to the image, which up to the first sound of footsteps seemed to give time and space their usual consistency. If our epistemic position was initially restricted in terms of access to the spaces within the house, now sound and image, still linked by location, seem to provide access to dif-ferent dimensions of fictional reality. The presence of the camera in the house no longer guarantees access to a consistent fictional world, located in a specific time.

An unaccompanied female voice now starts singing a slow, doleful song: 'I get the blues when it's raining/The blues I can't lose when it rains/Now each little raindrop falls on my window pane/Reminds me of the tears I shed/The tears were all in vain.' The sound texture does not suggest a source in the house, although the vocal quality (it seems a performance by a non-professional singer) could imply that the singer is one of the characters. (The published script suggests that this is the mother's voice and has it starting before the footsteps are heard but in the finished film we cannot attribute the singing with confidence to any character.) The soundtrack's relationship to the image has changed again, away from sound sourced – however puzzlingly – in the house, to

Fig. 2.4

Fig. 2.5

something with a less immediate connection to set-ting. The camera slowly tracks forward as the song begins and pivots right when it reaches the stairs, as if to look into the room that the mother entered. But, with the song continuing, the camera main-tains its slow movement until it has turned 180° and is facing the front door where it remains static until the song ends. The camera asserts its inde-pendence from any action in the film's world and seems at first as though it might be offering to open the house to our view. Instead its movement down the hall becomes less a spatial exploration than a way of anchoring the film within the house, a way of conveying, perhaps, as time and space, sound and image diverge, that this place is our focus.

There is a dissolve to another view from the same camera set-up. The front door is now open and outside we can see a narrow street and the sun shining on the house opposite (Fig. 2.4 and Fig.

2.5). This is the first of several dissolves that link the next few shots. We remain in the house, anchored to the same view, but the dissolve has shifted us to a different time and season. Our epistemic position relative to the film's world continues to evolve according to a logic that is not immediately available to us, though it has something of the quality of a flow of association, one image or sound linking tonally to the next, one dramatised moment evoking another, separated in time. The first song introduced an atmosphere of romantic melancholy. Now a very different female voice begins another, even slower, song. This is an operatic rendering (the singer is Jessye Norman) of the African-American spiritual 'There's a Man Going Round Taking Names' and marks a further transition in the soundtrack away from sound that can be directly linked (however enigmatically) to the world of the film. A hearse drives slowly across the doorway, stopping so that we can see the coffin inside (Fig. 2.6). This performance of the song, intensely felt and dirge-like in tempo, is a fitting accompaniment to a funeral in terms of feeling but at the same time introduces a cultural disjunction we have no way of explaining at this stage. If the previous elements of the soundtrack can be variously located in the fictional world this seems a direct intervention by the film, a kind of cultural intrusion, appropriate in feeling but signalling a controlling sensibility distinct from the world of the film, though responsive to it.

Fig. 2.6

Another dissolve takes us into a room, the camera perpendicular to a wall and facing four figures in a line, all looking towards the camera (Fig. 2.7).The mother is sitting and three younger people, a man and two women (the son and daughters whose voices we heard earlier?), are standing. They are dressed mainly in black, possibly costumed for the funeral, and their manner and expression are sombre. On the lines 'He has taken my father's name/And has left my heart in pain', the camera begins a slow track in. As it does so, the mother stands and moves out of frame left; the others then also leave, one to the left, two to the right of the frame. The camera moves in to frame a sepia photograph on the wall behind where the family was standing, of a working man in shirt-sleeves, braces and open-neck shirt, with a pony (Fig. 2.8). The shot marks a further departure from conventional relationships between camera and action. The characters in this film can respond directly to the camera, acknowledging its presence, almost

Fig. 2.7

Fig. 2.8

as though they were posing formally. Yet they do not acknowledge the person operating the camera, so that the camera itself remains a disembodied, rather uncanny force, able to command such groupings but not claiming a material presence in the space.

Another dissolve to the hall, and the characters come into frame and walk slowly towards the door and the hearse. A further dissolve takes us out to look back at the door as the mother walks forward, stops, and the son puts his hands protectively on her shoulder and arm. With a dissolve to a view from the other side of the hearse, the family gets in and the hearse starts to move. The image dissolves to the same set-up as before, looking down the hall towards the front door, with the hearse moving left across the doorway. The song continues throughout, the association between 'taken my father's name' and the photograph suggesting that what we are seeing is the father's funeral, but reaches its extended peroration as the hearse drives off.

Fig. 2.9

Fig. 2.10

Another dissolve to the same room. The family again faces the camera but this now seems like a group preparing to attend a wedding (Fig. 2.9). One young woman has her arm linked with her brother's. He again wears a dark suit but now has a flower in his buttonhole. All the women are in lighter-coloured dresses than before. The mother and the young woman to the right of the frame both smile slightly. As the song's final line is sung the camera tracks slowly in to frame the central pair, then stops with the photograph framed between them. The woman seems to attempt a smile and after the end of the song she says: 'I wish me dad was here' (Fig. 2.10). The camera pans right to frame the other young woman, her expression responding to what her sister has said, and we hear in voice-over, 'I don't. He was a bastard and I bleedin' well hated him.' Again the characters seem posed for the film camera without it becoming an object in their world.

Throughout this opening section the film sets questions that we are likely to be wrestling with even as we respond emotionally to the extremely slow tempo and increasingly sombre action and music. There are puzzles about the relationship between what we see and hear (the voices of the children who we do not see, the songs that have no obvious source in the film's world but are not orthodox non-diegetic music) and about the relationship between the fictional world and the film itself (what, for instance, are we to make of the characters forming tableaux groupings as though aware of the film camera?). The initial suggestion of a fictional mode (working-class realism) has been inflected towards something stylistically rather different from the norm, those modes of 'alternative' film practice in which film form often takes on a self-conscious independence from what is being represented. The film is involved in a shifting play with conventions of film narrative and with the spectator that in turn creates a tonal fabric in which the dominant funereal atmosphere is just one thread.

As we attempt to make sense of the opening, the title (or what we have seen of it so far) seems to offer a way of linking at least some aspects of what we have experienced. 'Distant Voices' conjures up ideas of the past and, perhaps, of memory. An old version of the shipping forecast is one distant voice; the disembodied sounds of the three children might be others; the songs, perhaps, two more. Is the film looking for ways of dramatising the processes of memory, without falling back on the conventional forms for attaching subjectivity to a character in the fiction? Perhaps, too, 'Still Lives', the other half of the title that has not yet appeared on the screen, offers a second conceptual framework, complementing 'distant voices' with an emphasis on the visual. A still life is a genre of painting devoted to static arrangements of objects, an idea that is resonant in relation to the family tableaux that in turn evoke photographs from the past, but 'still lives' might also come to refer to the lives of characters within the film.

It is impossible to produce more than hypotheses at this stage. The film invites these kinds of interpretative manoeuvres but deliberately withholds a framework that could enable us to anchor the significance of what we see and hear, encouraging initial processes of association but no certainty. It holds us at a distance in various ways – spatially, temporally, cognitively, evaluatively – so that we are required to interrogate what the film is doing and ask what kind of thing it is even as we experience the intensity of feeling communicated by the songs, and begin to understand something of the family and social context being evoked. Working outside mainstream narrative conventions, Davies can self-consciously employ forms of narration that remain emphatically present to us as we watch, refusing any illusion of direct access to the fictional world. Just as the filmmaker's choices remain present to us so does the act of being a spectator.

This account of the opening of *Distant Voices, Still Lives* has left aside knowledge of context and director. It is well known that, in common with several of Davies' other films, it is based on his own family. He and others refer to it as autobiographical,[6] although it is an unusual form of autobiography in that it is inspired by the memories of members of his family rather than himself, so that the film represents Davies' memories of the memories of others. This kind of knowledge can affect our response to and interpretation of the film in a number of ways. Although Davies does not address us directly in the film, if it is a personal film in which the filmmaker attempts to come to terms with his past, we might ascribe the features we have been looking at to Davies himself and to his shifting processes of memory and recall. This would tend to make Davies the subject of the film both in the sense that it represents his subjectivity and that he is what the film is really about. Thinking of it as autobiography can also have the effect of explaining the puzzling features of the film. For instance, Wendy Everett writes:

> By shifting the focus in this way, it is immediately clear that the various conflicts and contradictions identified above can be unproblematically accommodated as defining features

of autobiographical discourse itself: lack of linear chronology; blending of truth and fiction, of reality and imagination; unstable and shifting temporal and spatial viewpoints; complex combinations of narrow subjectivity and universal understanding; and the self-conscious foregrounding of processes of its own construction, for example, all coexist within the genre. (2004: 64)

This is an attractive argument because it offers to provide an explanatory framework for a very puzzling experience. In effect, it offers us a genre in which to place the film and a generic history that can be consulted to offer comparative perspectives. Yet, as we have seen, the film does not attempt to replicate in any literal way the shifting and fragmentary qualities of subjectivity. In fact Davies does not dramatise himself as controlling or narrating subject and the film's approach to memory is distinctly 'cool' formally. The conceptual framework of 'autobiography' offers a way of accounting at a very general level for the film's methods, but it is of little direct help with the specific material decisions that we have to negotiate as we watch the film. Indeed, if we allow the 'various conflicts and contradictions' to be 'unproblematically accommodated' to the concept of 'autobiography', there is a risk that the specific decisions will seem of limited consequence.

Perhaps we should understand the film's methods as simultaneously dramatising family memory and exploring ways in which the paradoxical processes of memory can be evoked. Even the most intense emotional charge from, say, the memory of a death in the past is inevitably and simultaneously bound into a network of perspectives that hold us apart from the event. The film seems committed to acknowledging and dramatising the emotional turmoil of family relationships while retaining perspectives that are analytical and measured. It also seems to want a spectator prepared to withhold judgement and to suspend conventional expectations.

Within the familiar frameworks of popular narrative film all sorts of tonal variations can be achieved on a bedrock of familiarity with the 'language' being used and our understanding of how, in broad terms, we are expected to respond. The more alternative the film form the more difficult it may be for us to grasp how it is that we are being addressed and therefore to tune into a mood and a tonal register. Davies establishes familiar reference points both in the nature of the film's world and in the events portrayed but at the same time makes our relationship to these strange. It is a process in which he guides us through a series of moves, both visual and aural, that allow us time for reflection and speculation. The extreme slowness of the opening may indeed be in part a way of gradually inducting the spectator into the methods of the film.

Tone is gradually implied by the nature of the film's world, the choice and treatment of narrative events and the various ways these are 'framed' by the film's formal strategies and coloured by the mood initially established. One dimension of this framing can be evoked by suggesting that the human subject matter (daily life, funeral, wedding) is presented rather than represented. We can relate to the emotion of the family funeral but both the images and sound hold us at a distance, even the intensity of 'There's a Man Going Round Taking Names' in Jessye Norman's performance having the quality of a quotation in this context, a musical commentary on the father's death that holds us apart from the family context. Yet these forms of detachment do not define the film's tone any more than the song does. The film begins with a carefully modulated nostalgic invocation of the past via the voice of the shipping forecast announcer and the characters are created, even in this short passage, with warmth and empathy. Its methods also signal that film is being used to show us a reconstructed past, that there will be no pretence of being able to inhabit this world and yet sustained consciousness of the gulf between present and past will not result in the easy ironies that the privilege of hindsight can produce. The value of Davies' film in this context is that in prising apart the familiar conventions of film narrative and separating their elements it not only offers instruction into its own methods of narration but also insight into the multiple decisions and interrelationships that can affect our sense of tone.

There is a problem here that haunts our use of complex critical terms. Like point of view, tone seems intuitively to belong to the 'how' of any discourse, the manner in which a story is told or an experience related, yet in analysis it rapidly becomes evident that the distinction between 'how' and 'what' is unsustainable. The choice of subject matter and all the specific decisions taken in creating every aspect of the fictional world, its characters and events, inevitably have effects on mood and tone. In order to register the consequences of particular decisions it is often helpful (it may even be indispensable to understanding) to posit alternative treatments – to imagine, for instance, different ways of taking us into the world and the events of Davies' film, as though they could exist independently of their presentation in the film. This corresponds to our awareness that a story is capable of being told or dramatised in many ways. But the separation of story and treatment that seems implied by this fundamental fact about storytelling can only be maintained as an analytical distinction. For the purposes of analysis such distinctions offer crucial tools but what can start by seeming sharply defined differences are rapidly blunted as we probe the material texture of sequences.

A version of this dilemma crops up in relation to tone as part of Wayne C. Booth's argument establishing the significance of 'the implied author' as a concept in narrative analysis. For Booth, the implied author refers to the 'core of norms and choices' that pervades a novel and he discusses, in order to set them to one side, a number of other terms that have been used to name this core of a work, one of which is tone:

> Tone is ... used to refer to the implicit evaluation which the author manages
> to convey behind his explicit presentation, but it almost inevitably suggests ...
> something limited to the merely verbal; some aspects of the implied author may
> be inferred through tonal variations, but the major qualities will depend also on
> the hard facts of action and character in the tale that is told. (1961: 74)

The distinction between the 'merely verbal' and the 'hard facts of action and charac-ter' now seems strange, as though action and character had a status somehow more tangible ('hard facts') and significant than that of language ('merely verbal'), when it is language that gives us access to action and character. Tone belongs to a vocabulary of critical distinctions that Booth is keen to distance himself from in pursuit of greater precision but its rejection here is logically unstable. Tone is thoroughly compatible with the concept of the implied author (if one wants to make use of it) and the attempt to limit it to one dimension of narration (the 'merely verbal') perpetuates a how/what distinction that is unsustainable.

The difficulty of holding to hard and fast how/what distinctions, and indeed to narrow definitions of concepts such as narration, point of view and tone, is one of the lessons derived from the practice of detailed criticism and it can lead to a healthy scepticism about the reification of analytical distinctions. At the same time, as long as analytical distinctions remain just that – distinctions made for the purposes of analysis – they are as essential to detailed criticism as to any other critical or theoretical approach to the arts. We need, at the very least, to take our bearings and a framework of concepts and distinctions, however provisional, can help to get us going. I ended chapter one by posing four prospective axes of tone: attitudes implied to the film's subject matter; attitudes implied to the film's audience; attitudes implied to the conventions the film employs or invokes; attitudes implied to the film as a film. In this chapter I have also suggested a distinction between tone and mood. These ideas can now be looked at again in the light of the previous discussion.

Mood is first 'a preparatory state' of expectation as we engage with a work, a 'prevailing feeling or frame of mind', incorporating the apprehension of a mode or genre and of the kind of experience we are about to have. It will involve a sense of the film's overall orientation towards the fictional world and action (serious, comedic, satirical, ironic, and so on), towards its conventions (generic and stylistic 'distance') and the audience. It then carries forward as a pervasive orientation, involving different dimensions of understanding, with feeling and bodily response playing as large a part as more cerebral processes. In most cases mood continues to give a significant degree of stability to our relationship with the film, although as the film proceeds these orientations will be inflected (they may be challenged) and developed.

More specific tonal qualities are implied scene by scene and even moment by moment by the network of decisions that create the fictional world, its characters and events, and present them to the spectator. Close analysis makes clear that these networks of decisions and relationships challenge any attempt either to apply as a template the dimensions of tone I have identified, or to treat 'attitude' in any literal way. A term like 'subject matter' also becomes very difficult to define in the abstract: its application can seem extraordinarily elastic. The important thing is to treat it not as a kind of field boundary that demarcates a space and makes clear inside/outside distinctions possible, but to see it as the indispensable but inevitably imprecise concept that it is. Similarly, 'attitude' seems a blunt instrument, especially if we bear in mind Robin Wood's argument about the end of *The Deer Hunter*, that 'a number of elements ... hint delicately at possibilities'. In any reasonably complex film, attitudes to events, characters and action will be implied in ways that draw on multiple and intermeshed strands of comprehension, response and assessment: aesthetic, intellectual, cultural, ideological, moral and, of course, emotional. (We may wish at times to invoke other categories.) Different aspects of response and different axes of 'attitude' may be set at odds, refusing resolution and fostering ambivalence or uncertainty. Like the axes of point of view to which I have referred, 'attitude' and the different dimensions of tone are indicators of complex relationships implied by any film but they do not correspond to neatly divided aspects either of the film itself or of our experience.

3. Tone and style: the openings of *Desperately Seeking Susan* and *Strangers on a Train*

Desperately Seeking Susan (Susan Seidelman, 1985) and *Strangers on a Train* (Alfred Hitchcock, 1951) make contrasting use of the same symbolic narrative motif, that of 'the double', the pairing of two characters who come to represent in some way opposed sides of the human personality. In one of the founding examples in the modern period, Robert Louis Stevenson's *Dr. Jekyll and Mr. Hyde* (1886), they are literally two aspects of the same man. In cinema, the motif evolved in ways that rarely followed the precise model of *Dr. Jekyll and Mr. Hyde* but on the whole dramatised the double through separate and contrasting characters. With the infiltration of Freud's account of the mind's duality (split between consciousness and the unconscious) into popular cinema, many films came to employ doubled characters in ways that dramatised apparent extremes (as in hero and villain) not simply as opposition but as complementarity, two sides of one coin.

Desperately Seeking Susan opens by juxtaposing two sequences, markedly different in tone, that introduce two settings and the two central female characters – Roberta (Rosanna Arquette) and Susan (Madonna) – as well as carrying the superimposed film credits, spread over the six-minute introductory segment. The soundtrack of each sequence is dominated by a pop number that has an informing effect in orientating us to the action, introducing the sequence and playing through much of what follows.

The opening number, 'One Fine Day' by the Chiffons, begins in the final seconds of the Orion logo, the upbeat, tinkling rhythms of its initial chords in themselves beginning to create a mood appropriate to a world – to use Deborah Thomas's words – more benevolent than repressive (2000: 9). The lyrics express a longing for a crush to be reciprocated, so that the song initiates a theme of unfulfilled desire that the film will develop in various ways, but its opening statement is in a register of adolescent innocence and optimism: 'One fine day/You'll look at me/And you will know/Our love was meant to be.' The setting and action introduce an immediate contrast with the hope for spontaneous romantic recognition. The first seven shots make up a montage that introduces the various processes (leg waxing, pedicure, testing lip-gloss, hairdressing) taking place in an up-market beauty salon. This is a world of older women and of more considered and constructed feminine allure than those implied by the song, although we will find that it is a world within which romantic fantasy can still produce startling effects.

The systems of decision-making, both visual and aural, in this initial sequence are neatly calculated to suggest something of the film's attitude to what is being shown. The colour register (pink features in the décor and the lighting is suffused with a gentle pink glow) conforms, with a hint of self-conscious over-emphasis, to stereotypical connotations of femininity. In the very first shot we are shown a pair of legs being waxed and we hear, as the first distinct sound effect, a rasp as the cloth is ripped from one leg (Fig. 3.1). The sound is carefully graded in relation to the music (clearly audible but not too emphatic), creating a momentary undercurrent of pain to the bouncy mood of the number. The film wants us to wince but also to smile. The leg being waxed does not flinch, so that discomfort is shown as being an accepted and familiar part of the beauty regime but in foregrounding the sound (the only diegetic sound we hear distinctly in these early shots) the film reaches to establish a bond with its spectator, rooted in shared cultural knowledge and specifically female experience – a kind of 'ouch' of amused recognition.

Fig. 3.1

The first four shots show only parts of each woman's body – legs, feet, hands, feet again. The images here initially show the clients of the beauty salon as anonymous body parts being subjected to beautification, a process which Seidelman's decisions create as akin to an assembly line: this is a kind of femininity factory (Figs 3.2 and 3.3). That the women are passive recipients of treatment is clearly inherent in the experiences they are undergoing and both the editing and (later) the camera movement reinforce this sense by dissecting the space and directing our gaze independently of the characters. The women's passivity and the relationships of camera and editing to the action will take on further significance in contrast to the subsequent sequence. These interlocking decisions create a context for the introduction of the first major character. Shots 5 and 6 begin to individualise the women undergoing treatment by introducing head and shoulder shots, then shot 7 tracks along a row of women having their hair attended to, the song recedes, dialogue begins to be audible and we arrive at Roberta and her companion, Leslie (Laurie Metcalf). Roberta is one of the women being expensively processed into an image of conventional femininity, the constraints of her world visualised in the film's presentation of the beauty salon's operations (Fig. 3.4).

Fig. 3.2

Fig. 3.3

Fig. 3.4

In unpicking the network of decisions in these opening shots it is easy to overplay the critical attitudes inherent in the film's presentation of the beauty salon. In spelling out what the film implies we risk making its meanings seem too declarative, over assertive. When we watch the film we experience simultaneously the interaction of elements – colour, framing, action, sound and so on – that analysis inevitably separates. The filmmakers' skill is in balancing decisions to achieve a tone in which analytical perspectives suggested by the filmic treatment offer an implicitly quizzical undercurrent to the innocent bounciness of the number. Decisions that with greater emphasis or accompanied by alternative soundtracks might have conveyed an attitude of abrasive mockery are held within an overall context that suggests benign but clear-sighted good humour.

What follows extends and personalises the sense of social constraint lightly sketched in the opening shots. Roberta is absorbed in the personal ads in her newspaper, dreamily spelling out romantic undercurrents that her companion caustically rubbishes. Leslie wants Roberta to have a new hairstyle as a birthday present; Roberta is uncertain but the hairdresser is reassuring as she pushes Roberta's head forward to begin work: 'Don't worry, your husband will love it.' The final passage of dialogue revolves around the advert 'Desperately Seeking Susan', one of a series that enthralls Roberta, as 'Jim' apparently pursues Susan across the country. She muses on the wording:

Roberta: 'Desperate' – that's so romantic.
Leslie: [mockingly] Everyone I know is desperate, except you.
Roberta: I'm desperate.
Leslie: [guffaw] You?
Roberta: [quietly] Well, sort of.

This is potential material for melodrama (unfulfilled longing, domestic entrapment) but played in a mode that remains comedic. The film may be opening a drama of female entrapment and unfulfilled desire but the mood established and the tonal inflections of the sequence at this stage suggest we are being inducted into a film in which the characters will not come to serious harm.

The beauty salon sequence ends with a close-up of Roberta drawing a circle with lipstick around the 'Desperately Seeking Susan' advert; diegetic sound recedes and, in an abrupt shift of tone, the second number, 'Urgent' by Foreigner, with Junior Walker, kicks in with its initial hard, driving drum beats. There is a cut to an exterior shot of the boardwalk of Atlantic City, over which the film's title appears. The image is still suffused by pink but the hue is deeper and duskier now, and colour generally more saturated than in the beauty salon sequence. Another cut takes us inside a room, the camera looking towards a window with closed curtains in front of which is a table-top piled with the remnants of a meal, untidily heaped serving plates and an ice bucket containing an opened champagne bottle. The camera tilts down to show Susan, lying on her back on the carpet with arms outstretched, chewing gum and taking a photograph of herself with a Polaroid camera, plates and scattered playing cards surrounding her on the floor (Fig. 3.5). She examines the photo, puts it in an inside pocket, blows a bubble with her gum, looks out of frame, then gets up on her knees, the camera following her as she moves, still on her knees, to-

Fig. 3.5

wards a bed on which someone is apparently asleep, partly covered by a sheet. She climbs onto the bed, tickles an exposed foot and, getting no response, takes a photograph of the sleeping man, places it on his torso and turns away (Fig. 3.6). This is accompanied initially by the emphatic rhythms and raunchy saxophone introduction of 'Urgent', with the lyrics beginning as Susan looks out of frame.

Fig. 3.6

The contrast with the previous sequence is marked at almost every level. Instead of the schoolgirl dreams of 'One Fine Day', 'Urgent' evokes an independent woman with strong sexual desires:

You're not shy
You get around
You wanna fly
Don't want your feet on the ground
You stay up
You won't come down
You wanna live
You wanna move to the sound
You got fire
In your veins
Burnin' hot
But you don't feel the pain
Your desire
Is insane
You can't stop
Until you do it again.

In a context that suggests at best a short fling in a hotel, the stereotype of the woman sleeping on while the man leaves is reversed and developed. Here the man sleeps on while the woman is up and about. As opposed to the middle-class married women we have just met, here is a woman apparently free of such social constraints. At the same time, in contrast to the women being beautified, Susan's use of the Polaroid camera neatly conveys a sense that she controls her own image and the making of images around her. The film makes full use here of Madonna's established pop persona in Susan's eclectic and idiosyncratic costume and her manner, both of which convey a rejection of conventional femininity. Equally, if Roberta and the other women are passive, Susan is emphatically active. This is reinforced by the visual treatment. Where the women in the beauty salon were anchored, with the visual narration predominantly independent of them and its strategies dominated by editing, here, once the camera locates Susan it follows her in an extended take, as though she controls the space and our access to it.

What could have become signifiers of an unsavoury sexual encounter are contained and challenged by the energy of the music and, crucially, by Madonna's persona and performance. The connotations of strength, independence and control suggested by the combination of song, gender role reversal and visual treatment are embodied in a performance which conveys someone sufficiently at ease with herself and her situation to be playful and gentle as well as sexual. She tickles her lover but does not persist when he fails to wake up. Her air of restlessness is softened by this sense of pleasure in moment-by-moment play, further developed in her interaction with the room service waiter who delivers tequila and the newspaper in which she finds Jim's advert: taking the waiter's photo as he enters the room, pressing money into his pocket when he has delivered the trolley and telling him not to spend it all in one place. We then seem invited to enjoy the casually amoral way in which she bundles hotel cutlery into her case and goes through her lover's jacket, removing money and an ornate pair of large gold earrings. Her final line, addressed to the still-sleeping man, 'Bye, Bruce, it was fun', actually sounds as though she means just that.

By this point the film has set in place the parallel and contrast between Roberta and Susan that is central to what follows. Extending the titles over both sequences and using contrasting pop numbers to accompany them emphasises their formal links and informing status. Roberta's fascination with the advert intensifies what would anyway be a strong expectation aroused by this opening, that these women will meet. The paralleling and Roberta's romantic identification with Jim's pursuit of Susan offers the two women as potential 'doubles' and suggests the film's intention to explore the significance this doubling might have. What is being offered is also, of course, a variant on the dominant male-centred versions of the double. In line with tradition it is important that Susan can be understood as in some way summoned up by Roberta's only half-articulated discontent and that she should offer a radical alternative to the values of Roberta's middle-class, suburban world. In line, too, with the film's use of a familiar trope, Susan, as the 'freer' side of the Roberta/Susan doubling, is associated with danger. It will be fundamental to the development of the plot that the affair with Bruce (Richard Hell) links Susan to criminality and therefore to forces that will also come to threaten Roberta. Here the large hotel room and the evidence of expensive room service provides a basis for later revelations that Susan's short-term lover was a mobster. These are themes and structures perhaps most familiar from crime and horror narratives and it seems part of the intention of *Desperately Seeking Susan* to evoke for the spectator this common narrative pattern while inflecting it in terms both of genre and of gender.

Creating an appropriate mood and developing it through tonal variations enables the film to touch on what is potentially disturbing about the motif while channelling expectations of an ultimately benign world and positive outcomes for the characters. It is also what guides the film's address to its viewer and implies the kind of spectator it seeks to reach. I noted earlier the self-conscious deployment of pink in the opening sequence, part of a play with conventional signifiers of femininity that develops the carefully mobilised contrasts we have looked at and that enables conventions to be deployed, to use

Robin Wood's analogy, 'in quotation marks' (1986: 285). Susan's playfulness is mirrored by the film's play with conventions and with its audience. Its good-humoured and sympathetic engagement with women's roles makes an appeal to what is conceived as a sympathetic audience. The choice of pop songs to provide soundtracks to the opening implies a level of pop-literacy in the viewer: the spectator is intended to respond pleasurably to the two songs, perhaps to recognise them and to understand something of their significance. The film holds out the pleasures of shared knowledge and experience and invites its audience to smile in recognition and wry acknowledgement. Part of this, as I have suggested, is that the film encourages us to feel more relaxed than tense, by remaining, in Thomas's terms, within a comedic register. Further aspects of its engaging self-consciousness are embedded in the bold juxtaposition of the two sequences with its strong nudge to the spectator to pick up the doubling motif. The filmmakers here seem to be enjoying their skill and to be reaching out to involve the audience in a community of good-humoured mutual acknowledgement.

These orientations of the film to its world and to its audience encompass attitudes informed by the ideological perspectives of feminism on the social lives of women, and a certain evaluative distance on what is presented. In dramatising these the film claims familiar forms of spatial and cognitive independence of its characters, providing the spectators with the juxtaposed scenes and significantly shaped sequences that enable them to begin the process of intuiting the film's point of view.

Strangers on a Train contains one of Hitchcock's most striking openings. Like *Desperately Seeking Susan* it juxtaposes the introduction of its two main characters (the basis for its elaborate treatment of the 'double' motif) but through an initial passage of sustained cross-cutting rather than in two consecutive sequences. Hitchcock's decision-making can be highlighted by comparing the film's opening with that of the work on which it was based. Patricia Highsmith's novel (1950) begins on a train, and we are taken into the consciousness of a character (Guy) already well embarked on his journey. The novel is written in the third person but we are given access to the character's thoughts and, via these, to aspects of his situation. After a couple of pages the character that will turn out to be Bruno (his surname in the novel but first name in the film) sits down immediately opposite Guy. Hitchcock and his collaborators change all this: the film begins at the station entrance, the characters appear in taxis and we see them walking into the station building, across the concourse and towards the train; the character who will be revealed as Bruno (Robert Walker) is seen first; Guy (Farley Granger), the novel's protagonist and central consciousness, is introduced second.

The title sequence unfolds over a single static shot looking out towards the station entrance. We are waiting, already in position, for the story to begin. This is a minor but significant indication of what will be a pervasive aspect of the film's narration, that it can anticipate events. In Hitchcock's films this tends to go beyond the widespread convention of what is often referred to as 'omniscient' narration, the kind of freedom taken for granted by many films, and becomes fundamental to the film's epistemic relationship to its material and to its audience. As it develops, it will have a role to play in the film's emerging tone as will its complement, the various kinds of restriction the film places on the spectator's knowledge. More immediately apparent, however, are the music and other signifiers of the kind of movie we are watching. Few audiences, from 1951 to the present, will have watched the film without some pre-knowledge of Hitchcock's reputation and the accompanying pleasurable anticipation of what is to come. The music helps to confirm and channel these expectations. Dimitri Tiomkin's overture, scored for orchestra, establishes a mood for serious drama. It contains brief phrases of a romantic theme for violin but these seem threatened – almost overwhelmed – by passages that evoke stormy, unpredictable emotion and foreboding.

These are initial indications of mode and mood that set a context for the articulation of tone. The kinds of pleasure we anticipate may include passages of suspenseful anxiety and experiences of shock and fright. The events of the story are likely to involve crime – probably including violence and death. Our previous experience, along with the presence of female as well as male actors in the main credits, will lead us also to expect heterosexual romance.

As the titles end a taxi appears in the distance and drives towards us. The camera, placed low to the ground, adjusts left as the car moves through the frame from left to

Fig. 3.7

Fig. 3.8

right and pulls up at the curb so that our view is angled towards the rear of the taxi and we are restricted to the lower part of the rear door. The door is opened promptly from outside. We have a brief view of the cab interior as a porter reaches in to remove a suitcase and we see the legs and feet of the passenger who steps out (Figs 3.7 and 3.8). He pivots towards the front of the cab, as though he might be handing the driver the fare, then turns left and, with the porter following closely behind, walks away from the camera. The camera pans left to follow him, then, after he has taken five paces, stops and lets him walk out of frame.

The music changes to accompany this shot. With the brass taking the lead it anticipates the cab's arrival in rising flourishes, the music lighter in character than that of the title sequence and precisely timed to the arrival of the taxi and emergence of the first character. As he descends from the cab and turns, there is a kind of jazzy fanfare which feels almost like a wolf-whistle – an editorial musical touch that seems to respond to what we can see of the man's appearance. He wears well-cut and carefully creased pinstripe trousers and two-toned brogues, an ensemble that implies a certain level of disposable income and the desire to indulge it showily. As he walks away we can see that he is wearing a suit. This seems someone who likes to make an impression, an extrovert perhaps, with emphatic if dubious tastes. His movements are also poised and stylish – the pointed toe as he descends from the taxi and his gait are almost dance-like in their self-assured elegance. Pizzicato pulses accompany the man's steps.

There is a cut to a second taxi (another 'Diamond Cab' with the same markings); a porter opens the door and removes luggage (this time a case and two tennis rackets) and another man, again framed from the waist down, steps out. The action is accompanied by music of almost identical structure and rhythm but with phrasing and instrumentation that works slight variations as the second man leaves the cab and pays the driver. This man also walks off into the station. This time, however, we do not follow the taxi into the station: it slides into the static frame from the left and stops with the camera again low down and framing the rear door, but angled this time slightly towards the front of the taxi. The figure that emerges after a porter opens the door is dressed in sober, not very well-pressed trousers, with plain, dark shoes, and as he walks away we see that rather than a suit he is wearing a jacket and flannels. His appearance is more conventional than the first man's and although the tennis rackets that the porter pulls from the cab along with a suitcase imply that he might be an athlete, his movements are rather more plodding. He pauses, as if paying the driver, the camera pans right with him as he walks away and, again, after five steps allows him to leave the frame (Figs. 3.9 and 3.10).

There follows a series of four shots, inter-cutting the progress of the two characters across the concourse, maintaining the order in which they arrived at the station and continuing to show only their legs and feet. The camera tracks with each, keeping slightly in front of the characters but looking at them from opposite sides so that it moves left with the first man, who correspondingly walks in a right-to-left diagonal across the screen, and moving

Fig. 3.9

Fig. 3.10

Fig. 3.11

Fig. 3.12

right with the second man whose movement is a left-to-right diagonal (Figs 3.11 and 3.12). In the fifth shot of this series in the concourse the camera is static, looking up from a low angle towards the ticket barrier, and we can identify the two men among other people hurrying to join the train. We see them at full length as they move deeper into the shot but from the rear, so that their faces still remain hidden from us.

From the arrival of the first taxi to the meeting on the train the music is as insistently anticipatory as the editing, building to the arrival of each taxi and greeting the men's appearances in closely paralleled style, then rhythmically matching their inter-cut progress towards the train in rising phrases that strongly reach towards, but keep postponing, a point of resolution.

What Hitchcock has done is to embed the obvious contrasts between the two men in images which are precisely paralleled but visually reversed: although the cabs draw up in left-to-right movements in order to maintain screen direction and sense of location, when they stop we look towards the rear of one and the front of the other; the two men walk in carefully matched but opposed screen directions; to follow the first man the camera pans left, and to follow the second man it pans right. The care of Hitchcock's patterning and the extent to which it mattered to him to achieve precise reversals is highlighted by a decision which we are only likely to notice after repeated viewings, but which is crucial to the whole design – the use of taxis with doors that open in opposite directions. The overall effect, intensified in the shots that follow, is of mirroring, the second shot in each pair reflecting and therefore reversing its predecessor.

The very striking formal decisions have equally strong effects. The two men are simultaneously paralleled by the editing and contrasted by their costume and movement. The restricted framing limits our access and produces a strong enigma: who are these men? The cross-cutting with opposed screen direction creates a sense of their spatial convergence and the inevitability of their meeting, a sense enhanced by the use of music. Even at this abstract level of description and analysis some key aspects of Hitchcock's striking narration are clear: an insistence on the formal pattern that links two men who are, the film's title implies, 'strangers'; the strong privileging of the spectator's access and understanding provided by the cross-cutting; yet a correspondingly striking restriction of view, denying us the most important signifiers of identity and character. These are very emphatic patterns of narration, strikingly shaping the story material and the spectator's relationship to it.

All these decisions have a bearing on tone. The mood established during the credit sequence sets up expectations of a crime melodrama, Hitchcock variety, and is intended, in the conventional manner of studio-period Hollywood movies, to prepare us for experiences of a particular kind. The music after the credits becomes immediately lighter, its structure playfully matched to the developing action. The editing patterns and framing are equally playful, the emphatic nature of the decisions balanced by the buoyant rhythms and sense of enjoyment in the bravura display of filmmaking prowess. Hitchcock is having fun conducting his own homage to Lev Kuleshov's experiments in artificial geography, creating meanings and effects that are the product of what Hitchcock called 'pure film' (see Truffaut 1969: 349). This is a highly self-conscious deployment of film techniques that wants to declare itself as such, while carrying the spectator along in pleasurable anticipation of narrative developments.

The sense of playfulness extends to other aspects of the spectator's relationship to the film. Hitchcock uses our spatial access to the film's world both to enable us to perceive the links he is so emphatically making and yet to limit our visual access to the men. His spatial decisions have cognitive effects, playing on what we are allowed to know and what we must wait to find out. To use David Bordwell's terms (Bordwell, Staiger & Thompson 1985: 25), the film displays its *knowledgeability* but limits its *communicativeness*; in fact it flaunts its ability to restrict what we see and know. Hitchcock teases us and makes it clear by the striking nature of his stylistic and narrative choices that that is what he is doing. The playful spatial and cognitive dynamics of the sequence – producing a brief but focused form of the anticipation that is integral to suspense – are central to its tone.

Susan Smith, one of very few writers to engage in a sustained way with the concept of tone, identifies suspense and humour as the tonalities that seem most deeply embedded in Hitchcock's work (2000: viii). Even in this small example it is clear how the two can intertwine. Suspense can exist in many different registers and here the small-scale build-up to the meeting of the two main characters is created within a context pervaded by playful good humour rather than the anxiety that characterises anticipation in many cases of Hitchcockian suspense. However, like all suspense, the effect is dependent on the audience's subjection to directorial control – what we see, how we see it, when we know and how we come to know it, are out of our hands. Hitchcock makes this basic fact of narrative a blatant feature of this opening and over the course of the film works many variations on it. The lightheartedness which runs through the opening encourages a willing – because pleasurable – participation, while creating conditions of spectatorship that makes us victims as much as collaborators. Part of what is wonderful about Hitchcock's work, here as elsewhere, is that there is no attempt to disguise this or to insinuate himself with us only to pull the rug from under our feet. This opening declares its director's power and control and requires our acknowledgement of this as part of the contract for our participation.

The next shot, dissolving from Guy's retreating body, further demonstrates that power by cutting to a view of the rails from the front of the engine as the train leaves the station. Simultaneously, it channels the energy of the men's movement towards inevitable meeting into the forward momentum of the train that now contains them both, and creates an ironic metaphor that implicitly comments on the limited control of the characters over what is to follow. They are now on the train, their paths controlled by the predetermined trajectory of its journey, an idea that can easily take on connotations of fate or destiny. Hitchcock plays on that idea, showing a single set of tracks that quickly meets a set of points at which two tracks diverge. We bear off to the right, and cross more track intersections. The motif of 'criss-cross' which will play a major part in the film has been initiated by the cross-cutting, with its implication of inevitable meeting, and is given another early articulation here in the crossing of tracks, the image offering the visual representation of 'criss-cross' while at the same time a sense of inevitability is reinforced by the train's pre-determined progress. Even before they have met, the film implies, these characters are locked together. The forces that give meaning to this idea are yet to be defined and they will turn out to be quite other than destiny, but braided in this image of the rails and railway journey is surely also the implication that it is the film-maker who has predetermined the narrative, just as he controls our access to it.

Via another dissolve we are on the train, the camera tracking Bruno's legs from right to left along the carriage's central aisle until he sits, facing across the carriage, stretches out his left leg and crosses the right over it. There is a cut to a matching tracking shot – left to right – of Guy's legs. He sits on the opposite side of the carriage. Another cut takes us to a shot along the aisle at floor level, with Bruno's legs sprawled across the frame from the right, and Guy's to the left. Guy crosses his right leg over his left and in doing so kicks Bruno's foot (Fig. 3.13).

Fig. 3.13

Hitchcock's reworking of the novel's opening requires Bruno to enter first and to be consistently in front of Guy as they approach the train and find seats. Since Bruno is soon going to recognise Guy from having seen him play tennis and from newspaper coverage of his career and his life, Hitchcock, as Robin Wood writes, 'makes it clear that Bruno has not engineered the meeting' (1989: 86). The film's design requires that there must be no possibility that Bruno has followed Guy. Bruno sits first, Guy sits opposite him and it is Guy who, unintentionally, makes the first contact. In order to develop the meanings inherent in the initial patterns of narration – linking and con-trasting the two men – Bruno needs to be unaware of Guy's presence on the train and to be already there when Guy sits down.

We are therefore presented with a meeting that is apparently the merest accident but which the narration makes, simultaneously and paradoxically, inevitable. Two principles of causality are made evident: what seems like chance in the film's world is transmuted into necessity by the narration. The characters have been 'doubled' in ways beyond their consciousness but forcefully present to ours, so that Bruno being 'already there', avail-able to be kicked accidentally by Guy, can begin to take on a weight and significance beyond the literal – bordering, indeed, on the uncanny. Although the analogy is too crude to do justice to the way Hitchcock develops his film, it is almost as if Bruno is the genie waiting to be summoned from the bottle or lamp, Guy's accidental kick being all that is required to make him emerge.

In *Desperately Seeking Susan* the double is called up in response to the explicit discontent of a character who chafes at the mundane reality of her life and desires something more exciting, more romantic. In *Strangers on a Train* Hitchcock's cross-cutting, beginning with Bruno, prepares the ground not just for a meeting but for the implication that Bruno is *already there* because he is a part of Guy, available to be called up in response to a need that Guy cannot consciously acknowledge, for something to cut through the stalemate of his personal life and open his route to political advancement.

Spelling this out so baldly risks giving this dimension of the film's meaning undue prominence. The film's way of showing how chance and necessity can co-exist rather opens a channel of suggestiveness that invites us to consider more than literal significance in this pairing of contrasting characters. These ideas are initiated by emphatic narration but are developed by a variety of means – dialogue, action, performance, the various aspects of *mise-en-scène* – as the story gets going. The suggestions of uncanny links between Bruno and Guy also remain no more – or less – than that: they are overtones of the fully realised fictional world in which characters are not simply symbolic functions but are endowed with their own individual complexity and life. We now engage with the characters and action but Hitchcock encourages us, even as his patterns of narration become less emphatic, to remain alert to what his stylistic decisions in the opening imply.

Also implied by the reflections on causality in these two films are dimensions of their orientation towards their worlds that we could not have apprehended with certainty as we sat down to watch (though previous experience might have created expectations). In both films events respond to the desires of the characters, although in ways that the characters cannot perceive and which are not explicitly pointed out to us. These are familiar narrative mechanisms that can be inflected in many ways but they provide an important tonal dimension rooted in the knowingness of the act of storytelling and the manner in which this is embedded in the film's methods.

Fig. 3.14

We can see how Hitchcock modifies the film's narrational method (and simultaneously one aspect of its tone) in what now follows. Up to this point the film's narration has been foregrounded, its rhetoric and the play with the audience it involves overtly self-conscious. A story is being introduced but the film wants us to be aware of the process of storytelling. As the characters meet and begin to talk, the manifest rhetoric diminishes and narration's overt self-consciousness recedes, although the patterns already established remain (less obviously) present in the next phases of decision-making. This involves a further play on film convention and on audience attention. As we become involved in the interaction of the characters, Hitchcock introduces angle/reverse-angle editing with eye-line match as the dominant method of presenting the subsequent

Fig. 3.15

dialogue (Figs 3.14 and 3.15). In fact, he works a set of variations on these familiar conventions over the next two sequences, in the carriage and in Bruno's compartment. The familiarity of the technique, the most common form of scene dissection in Hollywood dialogue sequences between two characters, enables Hitchcock to maintain cross-cutting and mirroring, both of which are central aspects of angle/reverse-angle cutting, without continuing to flaunt them. The conventions of continuity editing seamlessly articulate the emerging drama and absorb without neutralising the self-conscious patterning of narration.

This is also an example both of why self-consciousness cannot be defined solely in terms of an overt recognition of the spectator and of the way in which the status of formal decisions can never be determined solely on the basis of their presence in the text: the significance of their use (here as in *The Deer Hunter*) is always a matter of context. Angle/reverse-angle editing can be a more or less mechanical solution to the problems of filming dialogue but it can also be much more, its specific status and significance inherently bound up with the film's address to its spectator and therefore with its tone. Here the mirroring of Guy and Bruno in terms of scale of shot, placement in the frame and eye-line, sometimes very precise as in the first few shots and sometimes more flexibly deployed, extends the doubling motif of the opening but now as a less forceful accompaniment to the introduction of the characters and situation. The spatial and cognitive superiority demonstrated exuberantly by the opening is embodied here no less visibly but much less noticeably in the mirroring of the two men by Hitchcock's framing. Part of the tonal colour of these sequences derives from the ironic edge provided by the angle/reverse-angle patterns: the film knows, but Guy and Bruno do not, that they are already linked.

Understanding the reverse field editing in this way has something in common with registering in conversation that someone is employing conventional phrases with a certain ironic distance. Perhaps knowing the speaker and/or responding to the context, we understand that their use of a phrase carries implied 'quotation marks'. Sometimes of course we hear the quotation marks in their voice, but at other times, although there is no change of vocal manner, we intuit that the register is not being used 'straight'. The difference in the use of film conventions is that we do not hear a voice. We have to make a judgement about the film's relationship to its methods, based on our assessment of how particular decisions function in their context. In both these openings an interpretation of tone has developed from response to systematic stylistic choices that accumulate significance as the sequences go on. The sense of playfulness that I have identified in each is an extrapolation, governed in part by an apprehension of each film's mood, from the interaction of several areas of patterned decision-making.

4. Tone and interpretation: *Some Came Running*

The previous chapters have indicated some of the many ways in which filmmakers may attempt to modulate tone, using the opportunities available across the range of material decisions any sequence will involve. As in orchestral music, different strands of decision-making may carry distinct but interwoven tonal qualities, some more dominant than others, held in significant relationship within the patterning of the whole. Because the process is often complex there is inherent instability in the relationship between film and spectator, with problems of communication and failures of understanding a constant risk. We can sometimes impose an overall tonal quality on stretches of a film which, looked at again, imply shifts of tone. In many cases we cannot hope to grasp at first viewing the full significance of how a film is attempting to address us. The dynamism of this situation provides opportunities and challenges for the filmmaker in establishing and developing a relationship with the spectator, and also for the spectator in responding to the interrelationship of elements in the film, all of which potentially contribute to the various axes and dimensions of tone.

In the great Hollywood melodramas of the 1940s and 1950s the protagonists are caught in conflicts of desire from which society offers no escape.[7] The intractable situations defined for the characters are paralleled by systems of point of view that allow the spectator no stable relationship to the characters and action. The melodramatic mode tends to be characterised by high stylisation and emotional extreme, and by pulling the spectator between simultaneous responses of sympathy and distance, recognition and repudiation. Audiences of television soap opera, the most widespread contemporary version of these forms of melodrama, will be familiar with the intensity of emotional response the mode can generate and also the rapid oscillations of feeling and attitude a spectator can experience, from tears of fellow feeling to acute embarrassment, from cries of sympathetic engagement to hoots of derision. It is not uncommon to find, in students beginning to think about Hollywood melodrama, that these strong and conflicting responses raise questions about the adequacy of performance and its control or about apparent obviousness of effect. This is to imply that melodrama is a genre that can pose questions about control and significance of tone, and particularly about how different dimensions of tone and axes of attitude are interwoven.

Traditionally, the emotional terrain of family and personal relationships in the domestic and small-town settings that characterise many of these films is associated more with women than men. Male-centred Hollywood genres (the western is, as so often, the paradigm) tended to focus on worlds to which domesticity was tangential and in which men could express themselves and resolve conflict through external action. In the post-war period, however, the fantasies of male independence and potency negotiated in varying ways in action genres came under increasing pressure. In the western the divisions in the hero between the values of wilderness life and of settlement are inflected increasingly towards a psychic conflict that tears him apart. Caught between contradictory impulses and driven towards psychological and emotional instability, the hero becomes 'melodramatic'. In the period in which Anthony Mann pushed these tendencies to extremes in the western, Hollywood also produced its cycle of male-centred melodramas that articulate parallel dilemmas within contemporary, often family-centred, settings.[8] These are films that dramatise acute issues in the social definition of masculinity, presenting their central male characters not as strong, independent men of action (though such fantasies haunt the protagonists), but as struggling with conflicting desires within networks of responsibility and obligation.[9]

Some Came Running (Vincente Minnelli, 1958) begins with an inflection of a familiar trope: the return of a long-absent character to his home or hometown. In this respect it can be compared to two female-centred 1950s melodramas, Clash By Night (Fritz Lang, 1952) and All I Desire (Douglas Sirk, 1953), each of which begins with the return of the female protagonist to her hometown after many years of absence. Although their circumstances are rather different, the two women (both played by Barbara Stanwyck) have failed to prosper in their years away and for both, as for Dave Hirsh (Frank Sinatra) in Some Came Running, the return is emotionally fraught (the line from Clash By Night, 'Home is where you go when you run out of places', could almost be an epigraph for all three films). As in other female-centred melodramas, the women's emotional and ideological dilemmas are dramatised as a choice between two paths, one involving a life of safety, security and social conformity, and the other more unconventional, possibly more exciting but riskier.[10] Her dilemma is also dramatised in terms of two contrasting men, one conventional, sexually unexciting and dull to whom she is or was married, and the other unconventional and sexier, a threat to her marriage and the security it represents (this is an oversimplification but the tendencies are marked). The strong sense ('happy endings' notwithstanding) is that there is no route through to fulfillment – each path excludes vital needs. Some Came Running employs the same kind of structure, though with a man at the centre and the two paths represented by utterly opposed female character types, a structure also found in some westerns and films noir.

As we have seen, our grasp of tonal modulations depends on our apprehension of the pervasive orientations of mode and mood that a film seems to imply. This generally provides a significant degree of stability, anchoring our understanding of how the film wishes to be taken and guiding our responses. But the stability is always provisional: as a film unfolds we can come to understand that its address is in certain respects other than we intuited and that we have to adjust our understanding of mood and tone. This may involve, for instance, sharp contrasts of tone and dramatic register such as those in Jean Renoir's Partie de campagne (A Day in the Country, 1936), for example, which invite an unaccustomed and challenging synthesis. Some films that make use of suppressive narrative, such as Beyond a Reasonable Doubt (Fritz Lang, 1956), Vertigo (Alfred Hitchcock, 1958) and Psycho (Alfred Hitchcock, 1960) build to moments of revelation that radically undermine our epistemic security and require us to reassess what we have previously been shown and the mode of address it implies. Sometimes, as in Beyond a Reasonable Doubt and Vertigo, this changes our understanding of what kind of film we have been watching and, when we see the film again, permanently transforms our understanding of its relationship to its conventions, its material and to us: our apprehension of the film's tone can never be the same again. These are extreme examples but many films work in less spectacular ways to develop our understanding of how we are being addressed as narrative and/or other structural patterns unfold. That is to say that our sense of a film's tone may shift significantly as we come to perceive broad narrative and symbolic structures that govern the unfolding action and that narrow or even define likely outcomes, as well as shaping fields of meaning.

In *Some Came Running* two structural features seem particularly significant. One is the way in which Dave's return is causally connected to the violence of the film's climax and I will return to this in the discussion of the film's opening. The second informing feature is that the film's world is patterned, even more schematically than in *Clash By Night* and *All I Desire*, in ways that hyperbolically reflect conflicts within Dave. The world of *Some Came Running*, focusing on the small town of Parkman, is to a large extent structured by oppositions (though, as we will see, this dualism is inflected and complicated on both sides). In this respect it also evokes the western, with its conflicts between the claims of domesticity and male freedom. Joe McElhaney in fact proposes that the film can be seen as 'a kind of Midwestern western' (2003: 5), and there are enough allusions to the West and to the genre in *Some Came Running* to suggest that the filmmakers wanted to animate these associations. The name Parkman echoes Francis Parkman, author of *The Oregon Trail* (1857); the town's centennial celebrations are advertised using the imagery of the old West; and not least, as McElhaney points out, there is the cowboy hat worn constantly by Bama (Dean Martin). Dave's two paths are also represented by generic archetypes familiar from the western: the bargirl and the schoolteacher. But in the mid-twentieth-century world of smalltown America the unsettled West is no longer available to offer a fantasy of male escape from social restriction.

The main oppositions can be expressed in diagrammatic form:

	Dave	
	Ginny	Gwen
	Bama	Frank
	(Rosalie)	(Agnes)
	Raymond	Professor French
	Smitty's	Country Club
	Bama's house	The French house
		The Hirsh house

This gives us a cast of major supporting characters constructed in schematic opposition and representing extreme versions of gender roles. Raymond (Stephen Peck) and Bama embody the film's two versions of assertive machismo. In Raymond the need to assert control over the woman and the fear of diminishment if control is challenged is compulsive and finally psychotic. Bama, it transpires in the hospital scene after he has been stabbed, is literally killing himself with drink – a slow suicide caused by living out a fantasy of male toughness. On the other side, Frank (Arthur Kennedy) and the Professor (Larry Gates) are embodiments of enfeebled, respectable masculinity, the price that seems to be paid by socialised men in Parkman. The Professor is amiable and apparently at ease with himself, even at times ruefully aware of how circumscribed his life is but apparently reconciled to it. He may be a widower; certainly he lives with his adult daughter who keeps house for him as well as following in his professional footsteps. He seems wholly desexualised. Frank and Agnes (Leora Dana) are the film's chilling example of an established married couple, a relationship in which they have become 'Mommy' and 'Daddy' to each other when other members of the family are present, while in private their mutual hostility is barely contained. Beneath the social veneer they both seem intensely unhappy in social roles that they have struggled to achieve yet which offer no fulfilment.

Agnes, defined wholly by her role as wife and mother, is the structural opposite of Rosalie (Carmen Phillips), Bama's girl, one of the women from the brassiere factory that Bama refers to as 'pigs' and whose essential role is to be at the beck and call of men. They are by implication sexually available and disposable, though it is a striking fact that there is hardly a hint of sex in what we are shown of the relationships between Bama and Rosalie and Dave and Ginny (Shirley MacLaine). In this part of the film's world it is as though what matters is not the satisfaction of sexual desire but the playing out of a given role, the woman a necessary presence to confirm male heterosexual identity but little more. Ginny and Gwen (Martha Hyer) are the more developed but equally extreme female archetypes, versions of the bargirl and schoolteacher/respectable girl figures familiar from the western: Gwen intellectual, conventionally moral and sexually inhibited; Ginny uneducated, morally unconstrained and sexually uninhibited. At least, this would be the expected antithesis but the film inflects the pairing so that Ginny's childlikeness and vulnerability almost entirely cancel out the sexual connotations of the bargirl archetype. What she retains from certain versions of the type is emotional warmth, the ability to love unconditionally.

These terms by no means define the film but they chart its ideological force field. It is also a world split largely on class lines and, apart from Dave who moves repeatedly across the divide, characters make very few forays away from their class territory. The world reflects Dave and Dave is defined by the possibilities the world allows, which exclude a fulfilling middle way or an alternative mode of life. Escape finally seems as illusory a possibility for Edith (Nancy Gates) and Dawn (Betty Lou Keim), the two young women who are poised to leave Parkman before the violence erupts, as it proved for Dave. Our developing awareness of this dualism and its consequences provides a framework that intensifies our ironic distance from the characters and evokes a deepening mood of fatalism.

At the same time, some characters are contextualised in ways that hint at why they might have become what they are. Frank seemingly had to take over the family from his feckless, drunken father (the mother is not mentioned). As a result Dave was put in a home. Bama's attempt to live out his image of what it means to be a man is located (in a conversation with Dave) in the attempt not to be like his father, an unsuccessful farmer. Gwen has become, again in the absence of a mother, her father's housekeeper and has followed his professional path. In each case family circumstances seem to have determined defining aspects of the characters' lives, a perspective that intensifies the sense of their entrapment but can also qualify our ironic awareness with various forms of pathos.

The first shots of the film are from inside a travelling bus, the driver's back visible to the right of the CinemaScope frame and the only other character in shot a man, apparently asleep, his head visible to the left (Fig. 4.1). The same static framing is held for most of the credit sequence, through two or three barely noticeable dissolves, as the bus approaches a river and finally crosses a bridge. Although what we see is mundane and

Fig. 4.1

peaceful the accompanying music is urgent and dramatic with insistent, sombre bass chords. This is a score already seemingly powered by testosterone, asserting against the uneventful images an underlying energy and threat.

One effect is to establish a mood suitable for a narrative world, in Deborah Thomas's words, 'repressive and full of danger' (2000: 9). Simultaneously the apparent discrepancy between image and sound sets up narrative expectations that at some point violence will erupt, and introduces a privileged informing viewpoint for the film as a whole by exposing the emotional turbulence concealed and apparently denied by appearances. The same music will recur at intervals throughout the film until its final extended treatment in the climactic sequence that culminates in the shooting of Dave and Ginny. While the images here are relatively bland and convey limited narrative information the music is highly rhetorical and informative. This is a familiar enough strategy in Hollywood movies, but it forms here a significant basis for later systems of point of view that bear strongly on tone.

As the credits end there is a cut to a slightly wider shot, and the camera moves slowly forward towards the driver, who then turns to call out 'Parkman'. A reverse field cut shows the sleeping man and, just visible in the seat behind, another figure, apparently a woman, also asleep. The man (this is Frank Sinatra, in army uniform) wakes up, apparently disorientated and hung-over (Fig. 4.2). Dialogue reveals that he had told companions in Chicago that Parkman was his hometown and that they had put him on the bus,

Fig. 4.2

charging the driver to get him there. The bus stops, the driver pulls a kitbag and a suitcase from the rack and both men get off. The sleeping young woman (Ginny) wakes up and pursues the Sinatra character (we will discover that his name is Dave Hirsh) off the bus.

In their unobtrusive way, Minnelli's initial decisions about how to get the story started also create an informing image cluster for the film as a whole, although we are likely to perceive its various levels of significance only in retrospect. *Some Came Running*'s take on the familiar motif of the return home is to make it the result of unconscious motivation rather than conscious choice, a mention of his hometown when he was drunk that led to a journey he would not have chosen to make had he been sober. In films that feature this motif, although the circumstances and motivations vary widely, to return is normally a decision consciously taken (as in *Clash By Night*, *All I Desire*, *Human Desire* (Fritz Lang, 1953) and *The Searchers* (John Ford, 1956)). Here the film begins with a protagonist who does not even exert this degree of control over his actions and who is driven by unacknowledged but powerful wishes that surface when he is drunk. This brings into play a version of the pattern that we have already encountered in *Desperately Seeking Susan* and *Strangers on a Train*, in which desire that is in some way blocked or repressed initiates the major action. We cannot yet know what underlies Dave's repressed wish to return, only that the need is strong enough to reveal itself when his guard is down. That he is asleep when he arrives and oblivious to what has brought him can also be taken as a metaphor for his state throughout the film. Like Jeff (James Stewart) in *Rear Window* (Alfred Hitchcock, 1954), what follows his waking can be seen as acting out his anxieties and compulsions.

The other structural pattern referred to earlier (the link between Dave's return and the climactic violence) follows from this. Adhering to the familiar logic in Hollywood movies by which desires denied or repressed call up forces that prove difficult or impossible to control, Dave brings with him from Chicago the agents of disruption. This means on the one hand Ginny (who came at his drunken invitation and who is the unwitting agent of what comes after as well as the victim) but also Raymond, uninvited and unwanted, who later follows Ginny to Parkman and will finally kill her as she attempts to save Dave. Dave and Raymond are as linked as, say, Ethan and Scar in *The Searchers* in which, as many commentators have argued, the apparent coincidence of the Comanche attack following Ethan's return home can be understood as having a much darker significance in terms of the logic of Ethan's unconscious. Correspondingly, the forces underlying Dave's return explode in the film's action climax.[11]

We begin the film on the bus in spatial alignment with Dave and we will continue to follow him for most of the film. But even at this early stage Minnelli establishes the spatial and cognitive independence that will characterise the film's narration, the camera remaining on the bus as Ginny wakes rather than following Dave by immediately cut-

Fig. 4.3

ting to the exterior. When she gets out the camera frames them together, giving them equal weight in the composition. It is already implied that Dave has a limited grip on his life and the scene with Ginny (shot in a single take that remains static after an initial pull in) dramatises some of the consequences of this, the camera enabling us to observe and evaluate the exchange with minimal rhetorical emphasis from Minnelli's staging decisions (Fig. 4.3).

Dave's response to the driver's account of the night before suggests that getting drunk is far from a new experience; after his initial disorientation there is a tired acceptance of what has happened and Sinatra's performance conveys an impression of world-weary and hard-bitten masculinity. This carries over into Dave's initially dismissive response to Ginny: he fails to recognise her and treats her as though she is trying to pick him up ('Baby, it's a little early for...'). When she remonstrates ('Well, I like that, you ask a person to come on a trip with you and...'), the intonation in his response ('*I* asked *you*?') eloquently implies the way he now sees her. The stereotype Dave sees is also manifested for the spectator in the way Ginny is created through costume, make-up and voice. Simultaneously, though – for us – Shirley MacLaine's performance animates and challenges the familiar type with a child-like impulsiveness and a guileless, vulnerable manner that makes her immediately a focus of sympathy. She also has a directness of emotional expression that will become one of the few positive forces of the film.

The scene is structured to provide initial evaluations of character. In the phases of dialogue as Dave resists or questions what Ginny says, her indignation ('What am I, a tramp?') is momentary and her equanimity and good humour reassert themselves. Even in the face of Dave's blankness about the night before she remains touchingly grateful to him for being 'real nice' to her. When he makes it clear that he does not want her she is hurt and disappointed but not deflated, accepting it without resistance or cynicism. Her initial response to his offer of money ('You don't have to do that') is neither dignity affronted nor a token move before acceptance. She unfolds the bill he presses on her and responds almost like a child receiving an unexpected present: 'Gee, $50.' It is a performance of considerable delicacy when the character, situation and dialogue make delicacy unexpected.

Dave is unexpected in a different way. He has no memory of what happened the night before; he resists both the idea that he wished to come to Parkman and that he invited Ginny to travel with him. In effect he tries to deny the desire or need that underlay both actions. In contrast to Ginny's transparency and generosity of feeling he is initially brusque and then, tempering his response, takes refuge in an appeal to her understanding of male drunken irresponsibility ('A guy gets loaded and ... you know'). His tone modulates throughout the exchange as what has happened becomes clear. He feebly offers, 'This is no town for a girl like you', then in the face of Ginny's obvious hurt rapidly denies that he does not want her here and embarrassedly reaches for money while suggesting that she takes the next bus. Dave's embarrassment qualifies his initial hard-bitten persona but his evasiveness and evident eagerness to shake Ginny off remain. He leaves her with 'You're a nice kid', 'I really like you' and a muttered 'Take care'. Sinatra's performance of these lines does not make Dave obviously phony (indeed Dave seems to want to sound – and he might feel – sincere, even as he makes his escape) but we can also understand this as a ploy, an assertion of feeling to placate Ginny and avoid further unpleasantness. At the same time, Dave is imbued with the powerful connotations of

Sinatra's star image so that the analytical perspectives Minnelli's treatment encourages us to develop are accompanied and to an extent challenged by the positive charge Sinatra's brand of charismatic, nonconformist masculinity brings.

A further element in the dialogue, and one that touches enigmatically on Dave's motivation for returning, is reference to his family. From what Ginny says, it seems that Dave has invited her to Parkman to meet them ('just about the highest compliment a fellow can pay his girl'). We will discover what Dave's remaining family is like but already a sense of his estrangement from 'home' is coming across. Sober, he tells Ginny, 'this is no town for a girl like you', but drunk he invited her along, as though unconsciously he was driven by a fantasy of homecoming and family welcome, or possibly by a desire to scandalise by presenting Ginny to his social-climbing brother and sister-in-law, or indeed by both. The film includes these details, allowing us to speculate on what they might imply about Dave's actions, but (as with later episodes) remains reticent about how his motivation should be understood.

In his formative 1972 essay, 'Tales of Sound and Fury', Thomas Elsaesser uses the terms 'irony' and 'pathos' to focus his discussion of the different levels of awareness between characters themselves and between characters and spectator that contribute so intensely to structures of point of view in family melodrama.

> Irony privileges the spectator, vis-à-vis the protagonists, for he registers the difference from a superior position. Pathos results from non-communication or silence made eloquent – people talking at cross-purposes (Robert Stack and Lauren Bacall when she tells him she's pregnant in *Written on the Wind*), a mother watching her daughter's wedding from afar (Barbara Stanwyck in *Stella Dallas*) or a woman returning unnoticed to her family, watching them through the window (again Barbara Stanwyck in *All I Desire*) – where highly emotional situations are underplayed to present an ironic discontinuity of feeling or a qualitative difference in intensity, usually visualised in terms of spatial distance or separation … In the more sophisticated melodramas this pathos is most acutely produced through a 'liberal' *mise-en-scène* which balances different points of view, so that the spectator is in a position of seeing and evaluating contrasting attitudes within a given thematic framework – a framework which is the result of the total configuration and therefore inaccessible to protagonists themselves. (1987: 66–7)

Irony is the product of the spectator's spatial and cognitive privilege, seeing and knowing more than the characters. Although such privilege is the common currency of narrative construction it is, as Elsaesser indicates, particularly central to the mood of melodrama.

But as Elsaesser's emphasis on pathos indicates, structural and local irony can also be used to elicit emotional responses from the spectator and these complicate our overall orientation to the film's characters and events. In their reformulation of approaches to irony in Sirk, Bruce Babington and Peter Evans refer to this passage in Elsaesser's essay in support of their view that 'empathy and detachment exist in a mutually qualifying relationship' in audience responses to melodrama, and they coin the useful term 'critical pathos' to evoke 'empathy qualified but not destroyed by critical understanding' (1990: 50). In resisting a crude opposition between intellect and feeling, however, there is a danger, even in Babington and Evans' carefully nuanced argument, of converting the emotional side of 'critical pathos' too readily into 'empathy'. How we respond emotionally depends on the total range of decisions that go into the creation of a particular moment within an evolving dramatic whole but one of the features of melodrama is that, while often offering us privileged access, it wants to pull us between extremes of feeling. In these contexts emotion can provide a broad register of tonal colouring, from compassion and fellow feeling to intense emotional affinity, from pity and sorrow, through embarrassment to contempt. What the most complex melodramas often seem to work for is an uncomfortable mix of responses, simultaneously qualified, as Babington and Evans suggest, by other perspectives less tied to feeling.

This kind of dynamic is evident in the opening scenes of *Some Came Running*. The communicative dimension of narration represented by the opening music recedes and although the dialogue provides some exposition and explanation, a process of epistemic restriction begins that will characterise a good deal of the film, especially in relation to Dave's actions and motivation. Minnelli's staging for the camera also provides a sustained viewpoint that enables us to scrutinise the characters and their actions: there is no overt intervention to guide our response. This method of filming with long, relatively static takes and compositions that present the characters with considerable space around them in the CinemaScope frame characterises many sequences in the film. Both Joe McElhaney (2003) and Dana Polan (2002) contrast Minnelli's account of basing the colour palette of the film on the inside of a juke box ('garishly lit in primary colours') with the muted style of many sequences. Sustained observation of performance, unobtrusively sustained by long takes, is crucial to the tonal quality of much of the film (its orientation to its material, to the formal conventions of continuity filmmaking, and to its spectator), defining a way of seeing that presents without overt emphasis and requires the spectator's active interpretation. We are held at an observational distance and encouraged carefully to assess and evaluate what we are shown. McElhaney observes: 'It may be best to see Minnelli as a filmmaker who presupposes a spectator capable of looking at images that are rich, detailed and often theatrical in terms of composition and staging' (2003: 7).[12] Simultaneously, though, the scene makes Ginny the focus of pathos and presents Dave's limited self-knowledge and uneasy modulations of attitude in ways that make him an uncomfortable protagonist. It is symptomatic of the emotional balance of the scene that as Dave leaves the frame we stay with Ginny until the shot ends.

The next movements of the film introduce the major characters and locations within Parkman and the patterns that link them. In broad terms the first day is dominated by the 'respectable' settings and inhabitants, but these scenes are interrupted by the initial – relatively brief – scene in Smitty's bar and followed by long night-time sequences there that conclude with Raymond's first attack on Dave as he leaves the bar with Ginny and the arrest of all three of them. Smitty's embodies all the disorderly impulses and appetites that the respectable side of Parkman attempts to deny. It is a world of assertive traditional masculinity in which women are tolerated strictly on male terms, whereas in respectable Parkman masculinity is domesticated and disempowered. The dynamic of the narrative enacts the way in which Dave rebounds between the extremes: from his first encounter with his brother Frank he goes directly to Smitty's, where he meets Bama, Frank's structural pair (a surrogate 'brother' for Dave); from Gwen's first refusal of his advances he returns to Smitty's where Ginny re-enters the story and Raymond makes his first appearance. This is a particularly clear example of the structure Deborah Thomas sees as a defining feature of what she calls 'the melodramatic':

> Melodramatic films typically contrast a social space of some sort (a domestic setting, a small town, a community, or some other, more general representation of civilisation) with an alternative space (the city's criminal underworld, a battlefield, the wilderness, for example) where social values and expectations to some extent break down. Both sorts of space give rise to their own characteristic fantasies. Thus, inherent in the normal social space, where men and women settle down in marriage and domesticity, are corresponding male and female versions of fantasies which emphasise the struggles for dominance between men and women in what is a rigidly hierarchical world ... In contrast, the space of adventure away from the everyday social world embodies a fantasy of masculine escape where male toughness replaces augmentation: that is, fantasies of violent self-assertion replace those which offer a mere appearance of domination ... within the marital and familial home. (2000: 14)

In *Some Came Running* the two spaces are both within the small town. The only spaces we see outside Parkman are the club and gambling rooms in neighbouring towns that function essentially as extensions of the world represented by Smitty's, and a bus depot in which Dave sets Dawn on the journey back home. Meaningful escape to a space elsewhere, even as a fantasy, seems closed off by the film. However, if Smitty's and the male fantasies with which it is associated can be described pretty accurately in Thomas's terms, Dave's relationship to the social space of family and home is less clear-cut. In *film noir* the protagonist is sometimes drawn to a 'nice girl' with whom a normative family future beckons, but the *femme fatale* draws him away. A melodrama that links the return of a soldier to his hometown and this *noir* inflection is Fritz Lang's *Human Desire*,[13] a film in which the image of family carries at least some positive force and the 'nice' girl is the daughter of a contented married couple. *Some Came Running*, in contrast, contains a 'nice girl' but she is Dave's niece and the film offers, through Frank and Agnes, a view of married life that is wholly negative. If Dave is drawn back to Parkman by some deep-rooted desire for home, there seems little in his past that could directly feed such a desire and nothing in the present that could satisfy it. What animates Dave's fantasies may be his early trauma of banishment from the only home he knew but they express themselves as forms of neediness, especially in his relationships with women, that do not wholly conform to the binary structures of his world. This is to say that neither Ginny nor Gwen are defined straightforwardly by their contexts and as a result, at different moments in the film, they seem to hold out the fantasy that Dave can make a life in one half of the film's world.

Although to a large extent *Some Came Running* follows Dave, throughout the film we are given privileged access to scenes and views Dave cannot witness. So we see Frank covering up the fact that others know before he does that Dave is in town. When the bank manager calls Frank to tell him that Dave has deposited money in the 'wrong' bank, we cut between Frank and the manager. After Frank has invited Dave to dinner the film cuts between Frank and Agnes as they argue over the invitation and Agnes refuses to have Dave in the house. This separation from Dave offers a potential for ironic detachment produced by our cognitive privilege but here, if anything, the film seems to encourage an evaluative closeness to Dave. Although there is a certain pathos in Frank's ignorance of Dave's arrival, and Dave's deliberate provocation of putting money into the rival bank, this does not seem intended to elicit much sympathy. These scenes are designed and played in ways that present the world of the small town as repressive, stultified and hypocritical, dominated by a desperate need to keep up appearances. When Frank visits Dave in the hotel Dave deliberately refuses to indulge his brother's performance of welcome, reminding him (and informing us) that Frank had placed Dave in a home when he and Agnes married.

The implied attitudes here seem unambiguously critical of Frank and his world. Arthur Kennedy brilliantly creates Frank as someone whose aspirations to social standing are shadowed by anxiety (preparing us for the later exposure of the emptiness of Frank's life) but at this stage we are encouraged to see him much as Dave does. The film later complicates, though it certainly does not overturn, these implied judgements. But it opens something of a trap for us if we identify our view too readily with Dave's. He has good reason to despise his brother and the world of respectable smalltown society, but the film creates Dave in ways that also suggest a childlike impulsiveness and an attitude of unearned superiority. The childlikeness is in part quite endearing – requesting the best room in the hotel because he promised himself that if he ever returned that is where he would stay (the best room, it turns out, is nothing to write home about). We are also encouraged to enjoy Frank's discomfiture when Dave puts money in a rival bank, though the pettiness of this gesture also registers. More significantly, although he appears relaxed his action and his manner in the hotel scenes carry the sense of someone performing the role of returning prodigal, reaching for the telling gestures that will embody what he hopes to convey rather than acting out of a secure sense of self. This reading is partly informed by what we know already about his arrival but it seems confirmed by the gestures themselves – the early morning drinking that asserts his toughness, the disdain he exudes as he looks down from his hotel room, the cheque he has ready for Frank to repay the costs of his childhood care. The account in his conversation with Frank of how Dave was placed in a home allows us to understand the experience of disempowerment and loss that underlies his fantasies of toughness and power, while Frank's very obvious performance of exaggerated brotherly affection can by contrast seem to construct Dave as straightforward and even authentic in his responses. But the trail Minnelli and Sinatra are laying depends on our being able to register that the brothers are to differing degrees acting out roles underlain by insecurity and self-doubt.

The specific way in which the dualistic world of Parkman is then developed hinges on the fact that Dave is a writer. This is revealed in the hotel room when he unpacks and takes out of his kitbag several anthologies of twentieth-century American male nov-

elists, and then a battered manuscript (Fig. 4.4). It is a moment that parallels Dave's links to Ginny and Raymond, a characteristically bold melodramatic statement in which the bulky volumes and typescript are literally part of his luggage, but also the embodiment of a less literal 'baggage' that he carries around with him and that the film will later identify with his 'sensitive' side. The moment is underlined by actions that dramatise further aspects of Dave's confusion – throwing the manuscript into the bin in a gesture of repudiation, only to take it out again and place it in a drawer. Throughout the scene, with the exception of three inserts – a close-up of the books, a close-up of the manuscript's title page, and a point-of-view shot out of the window of Frank's shop – the camera follows Dave round the room, inviting us to observe and to assess what we see.

Fig. 4.4

I want to focus the rest of the discussion mainly on selected sequences involving Dave's relationships with Gwen and Ginny, parts of the film that raise some of the most acute issues about tone and point of view both in terms of the analytical perspectives the film encourages and the often uncomfortable feelings it generates.

It is as a writer that Dave attracts Gwen French and her father. It becomes clear from Frank's surprise when Agnes says they are expected that they are not habitual guests in the Hirsh household – indeed they apparently rang Agnes after hearing that Dave was in town. They represent the cultured end of Parkman society (both teach in the local college) and a secure class position (the Frenches are 'an old family') that contrasts with Frank and Agnes's newly-acquired social status based on success in business, but they are firmly aligned with Frank and Agnes in their association with the 'respectable' side of Parkman. They (and particularly Gwen) provide the necessary counterbalance to the attraction for Dave of all that is represented by Smitty's and their introduction completes the structural pattern that focuses Dave's ambivalence.

The major narrative incident of the scene in which they are introduced is the meeting of Dave and Gwen but this is embedded in the most complex sequence of the film so far in terms of the number of characters involved (Agnes, Frank, Dave, Dawn, Wally, Gwen and her father) and this sets their meeting within a number of different articulations of gender and of gender dynamics (Dave's drunken attraction to and later rejection of Ginny is already in play and available for contrast). It is also a scene which turns on different versions of social unease and embarrassment and so begins to animate a tonal register that is central to a number of episodes that follow. The sequence begins with the juxtaposition of Frank and Agnes's performance of hearty hospitality and family unity and their bitter recriminations with each other as they retire to the next room to fix cocktails. That we see both the exaggerated social performance and the private recrimination creates one level of ironic awareness for the spectator, making the shifts Agnes and Frank have to negotiate painfully comic but deeply uncomfortable to watch. Privileged viewpoint here inflects pathos into embarrassment. Meanwhile, Dave has been introduced to his niece Dawn and they are left alone while Agnes and Frank leave the sitting room. Given her parents, Dawn seems remarkably mature and normal (a 'nice girl', in fact). Urged by her parents to kiss her uncle she offers her hand in a self-confident assertion of being grown-up. When she is alone with Dave she engages him in earnest conversation:

Dawn: I envy you, Dave.
Dave: You do, why?
Dawn: Well, you left home when you were my age. Lived your own life. Had experiences. A girl couldn't do that.

In retrospect it is striking how much Dawn's manner, turn of phrase and tone antici-pate Gwen's. There is a slightly declamatory edge to the way in which she addresses Dave, and a hint of self-consciousness in the dic-tion, syntax and delivery as there is in the poise of her position – apparently casual, in fact carefully considered, with her legs tucked up and arm ex-tended along the sofa – when she sits (Fig. 4.5). It is an eloquent performance by Betty Lou Klein of a young woman who has been well trained in how to

Fig. 4.5

conduct herself socially and also educated to think and express herself independently. Dawn's words and the undercurrent of self-consciousness in her performance introduce what will become a major concern of the film, developed mainly though Gwen: the condi-tions under which a woman's independence can be expressed in this society.

Prefacing Gwen's entrance with Dawn's first appearance establishes the basis for a link between the two women which in turn implies that these are social, not merely individual dilemmas. It also provides a small-scale but significant introduction to a style of performance and accompanying questions about how it should be read – questions essentially about control of tone – that will become central when Gwen appears. Her entrance changes the dynamics of the film. We do not know in advance the narrative role that Gwen will play as Ginny's structural opposite, but this rapidly becomes clear when Dave's vehemently expressed dislike of 'the literary crowd' in advance of Bob and Gwen's entrance gives way first to polite greeting and then to his evident attraction to Gwen. Bob French is unselfconsciously at ease in greeting and establishing a joking rap-port with Dave. He then pulls back in order to introduce his daughter and Minnelli cuts from the wide framing that contains all the characters to a shot of Dave alone, looking out of frame at Gwen. There is a significant pause before he says 'Hello' and shakes her hand so that, as wider framings resume, Gwen has to negotiate the weight and signifi-cance of the pause and of his look, while maintaining the apparent ease of the social occasion and relaxed tone her father has struck. She does this almost immediately by sitting down, avoiding face-to-face contact. 'I'm an admirer of yours, Mr Hirsh', the line she delivers on sitting, takes the initiative by moving the conversation from the initial references to a shared past in school to a carefully-phrased compliment that also inserts a note of formality ('Mr Hirsh'), as though to counter Dave's pointed look.

It is the line that most clearly echoes Dawn's 'I envy you, Dave' in its manner of delivery, overtly bright in tone but slightly self-consciously so, the confident conversational gambit shadowed by a hint of stiltedness. When Dave rejects her reference to him as a writer ('I'm not a writer. I haven't been for years') Gwen counters with; 'I'm not sure I agree with you. Just because an author is inactive doesn't necessarily mean he isn't an author.' While Dave remains standing, looking down at her, Gwen avoids sustained eye contact, her manner outwardly poised and even mildly combative but her choice of words and delivery slightly pedantic, the generalisation ('Just because an author is inactive…') deflecting Dave's muted aggression by means of a teacherly abstraction that implicitly claims superior insight. When Dave presses her ('What exactly does it mean?') Gwen turns away from him towards her father, Frank and Agnes, and makes her reply into a joke to be shared by the company: 'I suppose it could mean he should get back to work' (Fig. 4.6). However, Dave refuses the release offered by laughter and the joke against

Fig. 4.6

Fig. 4.7

him that Gwen has contrived, cutting across the laughter with 'I'm told you teach creative writing', as he sits close to Gwen on the sofa, encroaching on her and denying her the disengagement her joke had aimed for. 'Will you teach me?' brings uneasy laughter, mainly from Frank, and good-humoured encouragement from Bob, whose line 'She needs that – give her more' acknowledges the sparring that is taking place but looks to defuse the slight tension that Dave has produced (Fig. 4.7). Gwen finally deflects the implied challenge of Dave's question by taking it literally: 'I'm afraid my classes are full this semester. Perhaps next year.'

Throughout, the predominant wide framing of the room has been intercut with closer shots of Dave and Gwen and the sequence ends with three such shots, the first and third frontal views of Gwen alone and the second of Dave staring down at Gwen, whose back is in the right of the frame. She drinks a little awkwardly in the first shot and in the last she is in obvious embarrassment under Dave's gaze, looking down, then up towards him and down again, away from his eyes, as the image dissolves to the country club (Figs 4.8 and 4.9). These shots emphasise what has been at issue from Dave's first look at Gwen: her awareness of his directly sexual gaze, her attempt not to acknowledge it and her corresponding need to claim and even assert her autonomy and equality.

This is to imply that we should read what can seem stiff and stilted in Martha Hyer's performance – the qualities that in later scenes provoke, in this viewer at least, responses of considerable emotional discomfort and even alienation – as strategies carefully managed by the film to dramatise in heightened melodramatic form the acute social and sexual dilemmas of the character. The film is consistently aware of the ways in which all the characters (Ginny is a partial exception) are held within various forms of social performance, their identities asserted through poses held and images aspired to. This is central to the ideological entrapment that preoccupies both the film and the genre.

Fig. 4.8

Fig. 4.9

In this initial exchange Dave's verbal responses to Gwen, from the point at which she expresses admiration for him as a writer, have an aggressive edge that has to be defused in laughter and finally by Frank's toast to 'the return of the conquering hero'. It is consistent with Dave's dislike of this social situation that he should refuse a performance more in accord with social propriety, but it is also as though his immediate attraction to Gwen is accompanied by a need to negate the challenge she makes to his sense of himself, a need in effect to embarrass her into silence. The sexual aggression inherent in his look, his actions and dialogue in this scene is even more emphatic in the next, which opens with Dave's attempt – smiling but insistent – to pull Gwen into a close embrace as they dance, and her embarrassed attempts to keep him at a distance. It is a moment which we might see as rhymed with the much later sequence in the night club in which Dave dances with Ginny and Bama with the catatonically drunk Rosalie, and where the distressing comedy turns on the reduction of Rosalie to little more than a marionette, her gestures and movements manipulated by Bama – the film's most extreme dramatisation of gender inequality (Figs 4.10 and 4.11). That Sinatra is playing Dave is of course crucial to how the

Fig. 4.10

Fig. 4.11

character is developed. Here actions that could in other contexts be presented as simply unpleasant are more poised, allowing us to enjoy Sinatra's performance of Dave discomfiting the uptight Gwen by trying to smooch with her on the dance floor of the country club, while also perceiving the boorishness of Dave's behaviour and the control over Gwen it attempts to assert.

This tension in point of view is sustained when they go to the bar. Dave maintains the sexual pressure, giving Gwen no space and scrutinising her intently. Gwen tries to deflect Dave's sexual attention into discussion of his writing but he refuses to engage on her terms, making witty and cynical rejoinders as she tries to talk about his work. Again, his attempt seems to be to silence and reduce her to sexual compliance while Gwen resolutely continues to try to engage him in a serious conversation about his writing. She will not let him off the hook or conduct a dialogue on his terms, pointedly turning to him to reinforce her replies but at the same time revealing the pressure of the exchange by becoming increasingly pedantic ('It might have lacked something in craftsmanship but it was a really powerful study of rejection'; 'You underrate yourself. Your second novel was undoubtedly the best book of its kind I ever read'). Minnelli frames the scene in another long take, enabling us to observe and evaluate the characters' interaction, and therefore the performances, in real time.

Dave's behaviour is characteristically both assertive and contradictory. He is attracted to Gwen but his social unease at their first meeting and the challenge of meeting an articulate woman, determined to engage him in conversation, provoke him to discomfit her socially, behaviour hardly likely to win her over. His sexual advances here and in the next sequence become increasingly blatant and correspondingly less likely to succeed (from the invitation to his hotel room, to clichéd compliments on her hair and eyes, to a suggestion that they go and park somewhere), as though he was running through a repertoire of seduction manoeuvres he has never had cause to question or amend. If the attempt to smooch was a self-conscious provocation (Dave's exaggerated smirk of bliss as he pulls her close) his later moves carry no sense of irony: indeed, as they talk he shifts from humorous attempts to undercut her seriousness to tones clearly intended to communicate the sincerity of his feelings (the tone of voice that we heard first in the opening scene with Ginny and that becomes a major part of Dave's register). It is the performance of an unsophisticated adolescent with a crush on teacher and its consequence is that Gwen constructs herself increasingly in that way, in the car offering Dave analysis of his problems ('I have an idea you're running away from something'; 'I have a theory that writers compensate for some lack in their personal lives') as a way of holding him at bay. But at issue between them in these exchanges is not an age discrepancy but a class difference. Dave is out of his class and the film develops a strong sense here and in what follows that his desire for Gwen is intensified by pursuit of the unattainable, though in this matter as in others Dave has no significant insight into his own motives. What is at stake surfaces recurrently when she rejects him and – in tones that begin with irony but end in bitterness – he calls her 'teacher'.

Much of the unease in these scenes arises from the contrast between seemingly relaxed and tense bodies. Sinatra's performance conveys a character, whatever his complexities and confusions, who is physically at ease. Martha Hyer's expresses someone socially adept in certain ways but deeply uncomfortable with her body and with herself as the focus of sexual feeling. While Dave moves fluidly and seems to act spontaneously (which is not to say 'authentically'), Gwen is physically stiff and inhibited. This contrast is intensified by the script which provides Dave with a good deal of colloquial dialogue but allocates Gwen formally-structured sentences that sound stilted and unnatural as conversation. Gwen is being created as a character who in principle could become the focus of pathos and empathy but who seems calculated by the performance decisions to distance us emotionally. Dave's behaviour is boorish and sexually aggressive but he carries the powerful associations of Sinatra's sexual charisma and his embodiment of one kind of 1950s ideal male.[14] Martha Hyer's unselfish performance makes Gwen combative but humourless and emotionally withdrawn. That the emotional balance of these sequences, focusing on the performances, seems weighted against Gwen, while the filmic presentation and overall context encourages a more nuanced understanding of the characters and situation, makes the tone distinctly uncomfortable. One way of putting this might be to say that emotional allegiance and both moral and intellectual awareness are set at odds.

The crux for these matters is the extended sequence in which Dave first visits the French house, bringing his manuscript, and which culminates in the lovemaking in the garden cabin where Gwen reads Dave's story. He had offered the night before to take Gwen to his hotel room to read the story but she had refused the obvious sexual invitation and told him to bring his story to the house if he wants her to read it, as though she took that to be a refusal of sexual intimacy. He now brings it to her after a night that ended with his arrest. What seems implied is the pendulum swing of desire and repudiation mentioned earlier, but we are given no insight into Dave's more specific motives in bringing the story to Gwen at this point. Does her attitude and her social position challenge his ego and intensify his desire? Has her interest in his writing flattered him? Is bringing the story to her a ruse to feed the only interest in him she has expressed, and to weaken her sexual resistance? Refusing to allow Dave to articulate or betray motive leaves us in the dark about what is in his mind and may indeed suggest that Dave is no clearer about why he acts than we are. This reading would be consistent with what is implied by the opening sequences, that Dave acts on impulses he does little to understand or control.

The staging of the sequence in the French house again preserves spatial and temporal continuity while maintaining physical distance. Almost the whole of the scene between Dave and Gwen, once Bob has excused himself with what may be an engagement invented to leave them alone, is shot in a single take of over three minutes, the camera following as they move around the room and adjusting its distance without ever framing them tightly, so that we have every opportunity once again to observe their extended interaction. What Minnelli creates is a scene of painful unease, masked at first by Gwen's social manoeuvres. She tells Dave 'We're glad you're here', avoiding a first-person welcome, and then invites him into the kitchen, 'our nicest room', in a tone self-consciously bright, covering the unexpectedness of Dave's arrival (we see her initial surprise in a shot of her alone when Bob calls out 'It's Dave Hirsh!') with a performance of social assurance.

It is certainly an extraordinary room – a combination of sitting room, study and kitchen, much of it lined with bookshelves. Gwen explains its eccentricity in terms of her father's impracticality: 'Dad insists on keeping books in here. I keep telling him the grease from the cooking will ruin them but he's an obstinate man.' Dave's response – 'It's beautiful' – could be a spontaneous exclamation of pleasure and approval but

Sinatra conveys a sense of Dave reaching for an unaccustomed register and an appropriately respectful tone. Dave is out of uniform for the first time; his sweater, open-neck shirt and slacks conveying a sense of casual smartness that enhances the bodily ease of Sinatra's performance. But whereas Dave's behaviour with Gwen the previous night had been crudely direct and socially inept, he is now more 'civilised'. Minnelli's treatment of the scene and Sinatra's performance make no suggestion that Dave is cynically performing a role but, for all the apparent ease of his manner, he is treading carefully.

This underlying tension emerges in this scene and the next in notes of falsity in Dave's dialogue, a sense of emotion and thought willed into expression but not convincingly expressed. It is at its most explicit here in his declarations of love, the second of which provokes Gwen into a direct response to his delivery: 'You said that with the ease of a man who's said it rather often and to a variety of women.' What Gwen thinks that what she detects is insincerity, a move by a practised womaniser; what Sinatra conveys is something less obvious and more confused – Dave thinks he means what he says. His discomfort – social, physical, emotional – is captured eloquently in the awkwardness of his words and actions after Gwen's attempted disengagement: 'I'd much rather discuss your story – what's it about?' Dave has turned away towards the window just beyond

Fig. 4.12

Gwen. The gaucheness of his reply, 'It's about love – and I think I've learned a great deal more about it now', is heightened by the clumsiness of his attempt, as he negotiates the inelegant final clause, to perch on the narrow arm of Gwen's desk chair and pull her face towards him (Fig. 4.12).

Martha Hyer communicates a more evident feeling of unease beneath the overtly confident manner and verbal dexterity, maintaining the physical stiffness and formality of speech that characterised Gwen in her previous scenes. Gwen works to maintain literal and emotional distance between her and Dave, using the coffee tray and the desk as physical barriers, refusing to be shocked by the news of his brawl and arrest, and attempting to treat him almost as though he was a talented but wayward student. The timbre of her voice and the slightly stilted rising inflections enact personal interest but deny emotional engagement. The anxiety that underlies Gwen's treatment of Dave surfaces in two moments that acknowledge in different ways the strain of maintaining her poise. In the first, after Dave has quizzically tried on her glasses that were lying on the desk and then polished them with his handkerchief, she hurriedly puts them away when his back is turned. In the second, though she has earlier calmly deflected his suggestion that she might be shocked, her less than sanguine attitude to Dave's sexual history breaks through her studied calm in the sharp and emotionally charged 'Shall we read your press notices?'

The scene that follows is perhaps the most tonally problematic of the whole film. It intensifies the tonal complexity that Minnelli has so skilfully developed around Gwen and Dave but pushes a number of elements – of action, dialogue, performance and *mise-en-scène* – to extremes. As they leave the house to walk in the grounds, a new musical theme, for piano and orchestra, is introduced, in contrast to the assertive jazzy accompaniment to the title sequence. Its more 'classical' form picks up on the civilised bourgeois setting of the house and grounds and its tone is redolent of romance. There

is a dissolve. Dave is alone in the grounds and we see Gwen reading inside a cabin-cum-summer-house. In the build up to Gwen's reaction to Dave's story and the love scene that follows Minnelli introduces a strange interlude involving two rabbits. Dave leans on a fence, takes out a cigarette and looks out of frame. There is a cut to a rabbit that then hops away. Dave's business with the cigarette continues and he looks out of frame again. There is a cut to another rabbit. Dave looks towards it and says, 'Your girl went that way'. The second rabbit hops off (Figs 4.13 and 4.14).

Fig. 4.13

Fig. 4.14

Dave's anthropomorphism is a joke (though it speaks of what is on his mind) but how should we take the film's tone here? It invokes a register of imagery and feeling so at odds with the film up to this point that it can feel like an extraordinary lapse into sentimental romanticism, as though nature might be in tune with Dave falling in love.

What follows Gwen calling Dave into the summerhouse is tonally even more difficult. We have been led to expect a romantic encounter and indeed this is as close as the film gets to a conventional love scene. But the film has to find ways of producing, from the tensions between Dave and Gwen, an expression of mutual passion. One option might have been to use Gwen's reading of the story to ease tension and to suggest the emergence of reciprocal authentic feeling. If we take it that this is the effect aimed for then the scene fails spectacularly – many of the decisions taken tend to distance and detach us (this is a scene that often produces laughter in spectators) rather than encourage sympathetic involvement. Most strikingly, the scene ends with an extraordinary manipulation of lighting – unique in the film – so that a brightly-lit room is plunged into dark-

ness as Gwen and Dave move closer to the camera and kiss. Dave unpinning Gwen's hair as they first embrace is also, in this context, a strikingly literal image to associate with the release of repressed passion (Fig. 4.15). The dialogue and performances leading up to this moment intensify rather than minimise the awkwardness we have been identifying

Fig. 4.15

in the characters. Both are given lines that hinder rather than help convincing expressions of feeling. Gwen's opening line ('Dave, you have a very exciting talent') is horribly prim, but some of Dave's dialogue matches it in maintaining deeply uneasy registers of language ('So help me, I didn't know there were women like you'; 'Gwen, I truly love you, don't you know that?') and a tone of exaggerated humility and sincerity that seems to strive for conviction. Minnelli's editing further heightens the rhetoric of the scene. He cuts from the long take in which the scene is mainly filmed, first into a medium close-up of Gwen as she breaks from Dave, showing her conflicting feelings and the breakdown of her inhibition, and then to a matching reverse-shot of Dave, before returning to the wider framing as Gwen kisses Dave. Holding the wider framing would have been a plausible option here, especially since the axis of the characters' movement towards the camera had been established and the scene ends with the original framing. The editing engages a familiar convention of inter-cut close-ups in love scenes but here the break with the continuity of the long take feels rhythmically and emotionally clumsy. Closer framing also makes considerable demands of Martha Hyer, requiring her to enact intense feelings in close-up. Both these effects are jarring in the context.

How should we understand this section of the film? Our answer will turn on how we read the tone and the underlying attitudes it carries: do we take the film to be embracing the whimsy of the rabbits and trying for a convincing and involving love scene, or is it possible to suggest alternative explanations that can account for the decisions taken and the disturbing emotional dynamics of the episodes? What if the film intends a play on, rather than an adoption of, romantic convention? For instance, the business with the rabbits can be connected to dialogue in the previous scene. When Dave tells Gwen, 'I'm glad you're not a teacher of biology', she replies, 'If I was, I wouldn't confuse biology and love', a comment on what she takes to be Dave's confusion. Dave's anthropomorphic joke makes the rabbits into girlfriend and boyfriend – turning, one might say, biology into love. In that reading, consistent with the film's perspectives on Dave up to this point, the rabbits comment on the human action not cosily but critically. If this is a plausible connection then the break in tone that might seem to signal an unprepared shift into whimsy can be thought of as deliberately grating – not a miscalculated invitation to think 'how sweet' but a jolt of dissonance in preparation for a love scene that will be far from 'romantic'. What follows might then be read not as an unconvincing dramatisation of authentic reciprocal passion but as a sexual encounter that is intended to feel very uncomfortable, with the emotions of both characters strongly determined by the contexts of their meeting and the immediate circumstances of the moment. Dave's unpinning of Gwen's hair picks up on their dialogue of the previous evening when Dave complimented her on it, only for Gwen to rebuff him with 'I wear my hair this way to please the school board'. Unpinning it can be taken for a cliché but it can also be understood as Dave's self-conscious response to what Gwen said the night before and his attempt to dismantle her teacherly persona.

The lighting change is particularly striking and strange. Whether we think of it as an aesthetic miscalculation, a considered distancing device, or take some intermediate position, the jolt of its obvious artifice pulls us away. In a treatment more integrated into the lighting design of the space, a movement into darkness could both provide an appropriately discrete exit from the love scene and intensify the atmosphere of romantic passion. The sudden darkness here has the force of a comment on the deathliness of this coupling. What underlies this may be that both characters are dominated by fantasies of the other; Gwen seduced by her vision of Dave as the great writer who can be saved,

Dave by a view of Gwen ('So help me, I didn't know there were women like you') that all but describes her as fantastical. Her class location and profession seem to dissociate her from Frank's tawdry materialism, though she belongs emphatically to the respectable world. She is sexually attractive, admires his work and unlocks the secret of the unfinished story. Dave can convince himself that he is in love with this impossible figure and that marriage would offer a plausible future.

As a matter of critical practice it seems to be best (though it is not always easy) to give films the benefit of any doubt and to look for ways of making sense of decisions within the overall patterns and approaches of the film. The most powerful critical readings are invariably those that account persuasively for many or most of the major choices the filmmakers have made. In these terms I prefer the analytical reading of this section that looks for ways of linking these choices to the film's broader patterns of decision-making to a view that it represents a failure of control. Part of me wants to celebrate what Minnelli is doing here as an extremely bold solution to an acute problem of how to manage point of view in this episode. In these terms his decisions can be thought of as producing critical distance or even 'distanciation'. But it would be unwise to seek entirely analytical perspectives or to fall into a version of the 'affirmation vs. irony' opposition challenged by Robin Wood's reading of the *The Deer Hunter*'s final sequence. A focus on tone brings with it a need to wrestle with the various dimensions of 'attitude' – affective as well as, say, moral and intellectual – and to allow for complexities that resist articulation in neat binary terms. Each time I return to arguments about this sequence, uncertainties return. Analysis of pattern and possibility is persuasive up to a point but the circle never closes – my experience of the tonal dynamics will not entirely synthesise with my preferred analytical account.

On the other hand, there seems no doubt that here, as elsewhere in the film, sequences and characters are patterned to echo, contrast with and implicitly comment on each other. So we move from Dave and Gwen's kiss to a scene in which Frank tries to tempt the totally resistant Agnes into going upstairs to 'relax'. Her refusal ('Don't be silly Frank, I've got a headache') leads Frank to ease his restlessness by going into town and this in turn leads him to Edith. The parallel with Dave's movements from Gwen's rejection of him to Ginny is unforced but telling. Less immediately, we can see in retrospect that the sequence of Gwen reading the story and what follows is paired with the much later sequence in which Dave reads it to Ginny. In each case reading the story leads, though very differently, to a short-lived union of the couple, but if there is a suggestion of deathliness in the darkness that enfolds Gwen and Dave, Dave's offer of marriage to Ginny has deadlier consequences.

The relationship between Ginny and Dave is played out in terms established in the film's opening scenes, that Dave is 'real nice' to Ginny when he has been drinking and treats her badly in various ways when sober (the crucial, and ultimately disastrous, exception to this being his proposal of marriage). This is one aspect of the unmanageable contradiction between 'worlds' and aspects of the self that the film dramatises in Dave and that animates the structural pattern of Dave's repeated movement from rejection by Gwen to another encounter with Ginny. The first example of this is when Gwen drops Dave outside Smitty's and he immediately encounters Ginny in the bar and encourages her to hang around. When Gwen tells him at their next meeting that she 'doesn't want this kind of relationship' and rejects his proposal with 'I'm not one of your bar-room tarts', he returns to Bama's and agrees to take Ginny and Rosalie on their gambling trip. Finally, after the scene in Gwen's bedroom in which, following her meeting with Ginny, she retreats from Dave again ('I don't like your life, I don't like the people you like'), we have the scenes with Ginny that lead up to Dave's proposal.

However, this sense of the women as, at one level, equivalent but opposed terms in a generic equation is inflected by contrasting ways in which they are presented and by correspondingly different tonal registers. The film's emotional detachment from Gwen is paralleled by its emotional engagement with Ginny, a contrast that is crystalised in Ginny's visit to Gwen's school room, the only scene in which the women meet. As Ginny approaches the school we see Gwen in class, responding to a question from Wally (John Brennan) about whether Zola was 'immoral' and whether different standards apply to literary men. She denies this, but her answer that they have 'greater appetite for life' and that though she might disapprove of their conduct she would try to understand it comes over as pat and abstract, an intellectual acceptance of such appetites that is in sharp contrast to her inability to deal with the more personal and emotional challenge represented by Dave. It is symptomatic in this respect that in a scene slightly earlier in the film her declaration to him that 'I've missed you … and I'm not confused anymore', the only unequivocal statement of commitment she utters, is made not in person but on the telephone.

The scene between the two women is tonally very rich but painful to watch. Embarrassment, pathos, pity, emotional engagement and critical detachment mingle with extraordinary intensity. The sequence can be linked with scenes in other melodramas, such as Stella (Barbara Stanwyck) at the hotel resort in *Stella Dallas* (King Vidor, 1937) or Annie (Juanita Moore) in the schoolroom in *Imitation of Life* (Douglas Sirk, 1959), where her daughter is attempting to pass for white. These episodes depend for their effects on a dual response in which we squirm with embarrassment but simultaneously want to repudiate the basis of the emotion. In these two cases our feelings are engaged at least partly on behalf of Stella and Annie but their actions are concurrently the cause of the negative emotion. In the schoolroom scene part of the effect comes from what we know of the two women and from the cognitive and evaluative perspectives we bring from the preceding action: it is impossible to anticipate anything but a deeply difficult and embarrassing meeting. The film also encourages closeness to Ginny in a way denied to Gwen: Ginny's emotional openness and trust are consistently more sympathetic than Gwen's primness and mistrust of feeling. Gwen, too, is on home ground and Ginny is taking all the risk (of rebuff, of humiliation) in coming to the school. We are also placed

Fig. 4.16

with Ginny on her approach to Gwen's room, even seeing and hearing the final part of Gwen's homily from outside the classroom, with Ginny in the foreground (Fig. 4.16). So the meeting is prepared in ways that ensure that our anxieties will be more on Ginny's behalf than Gwen's. And yet the film does not encourage our greater engagement with Ginny to elide into a corresponding commitment to Dave and Ginny as a couple; as we have been seeing, a central part of its strategy is to deny the possibility of a choice for Dave that could point to a 'happy ending'. Our awareness of the hopelessness of Ginny's cause contributes significantly to the pathos of the sequence.

Minnelli shoots the scene largely in an angle/re-verse-angle pattern that is relatively unusual in the film. He initially cuts between two-shots in which the women face each other and we are placed be-hind each in turn (Fig. 4.17). He then cuts between close-ups of varying scales after Ginny sits so that, unlike the long take sequences that hold us at a

Fig. 4.17

distance, observing characters within the single space of the frame, here the editing separates the women and makes our view pivot between them. The scene is also staged to intensify the differences in status. Gwen makes no attempt to move towards Ginny – she stays behind her desk, in the authoritative position it provides. Ginny sits in a student chair, her physical placing and the deference she shows to Gwen constructing her as child to Gwen's grown-up. Gwen remains largely composed but defensive. She is unable or unwilling to engage with Ginny and, although she is mainly polite, Ginny's expressions of feeling and her attempt to elicit how Gwen feels clearly make her very uncomfortable, so much so that she finally asserts that 'there is nothing between Mr Hirsh and myself', a denial of her own feelings which seems driven by a need to dis-sociate herself completely from the imputation that she might have anything in common with Ginny ('…consequently, I'm not your rival'). Ginny, on the other hand, makes herself vulnerable and open to potential humiliation by expressing her love for Dave so nakedly to Gwen. The intensity of feeling with which Shirley MacLaine imbues Ginny here is very moving, as is the remarkable unselfishness of her appeal – 'I want him to have what he wants, even if it's you instead of me.' If there is a certain pathos in Gwen's inability to deal with strong emotion, there is much more in Ginny's confession of how scared she had been to come to the school, and her acute sense of inferiority: 'I know you could take him away from me if you want. I'm not smart like you. I ain't got nothing. Not even a reputation.' Coming at this moment in particular, Gwen's momentary breakdown in politeness, the barbed comment, 'I'm sure you have a reputation, Miss Moorhead', feels especially unpleasant.

Ginny is certainly the most likeable of the film's characters, her generosity of feeling, openness and lack of guile contrasting in one way or another with everyone else in the movie. Shirley MacLaine gives her a life and a subtlety of feeling that challenges both the traditional stereotype her character relates to and the attitudes towards her of other characters in the film, including Dave. When he is sober Dave seems to see Ginny largely as a type. When he is drunk and 'real nice', what is implied is not that he finds her sexually attractive (the lack of an overtly sexual dimension to the relationship is surprising and significant – the only kiss is entirely one way, when Ginny kisses Dave as she leaves Bama's house to prepare for the wedding) but that he responds to other qualities, or that they speak to needs in him. What these qualities are is associated with Ginny's construction as like a child. The film follows convention in linking the lower classes with the free play of impulse and desire, an absence of restraint and direct expression of feeling that carries positive connotations in comparison to the much more buttoned-up and inhibited middle classes. Retaining a certain child-like spontaneity in these contexts is often to be more open to life and to be able to live more fully and authentically than the socially wary and controlled bourgeoisie. Aspects of this coding are present in *Some Came Running* but the free play of impulse in Bama and Raymond is presented as respectively self-destructive and psychotic, while in Ginny the positive associations of child-likeness are present but she is created less as a character who has retained in adulthood the spontaneity of childhood and more as someone who is in many respects still a child, almost a case of arrested development.

Dave's ambivalence is central to almost all their scenes together. When he gives up on Gwen after the country club evening and asks to be dropped off, the car stops under the red neon of the 'Smitty's' sign. Ginny is sitting at the bar with Raymond (his first appearance in the film) and we witness the deeply unpleasant harassment to which he subjects her. Raymond's violently assertive claim to Ginny is one extreme in the film's presentation of male/female relationships but we are encouraged to see a continuum of behaviour linking Raymond, Bama and Dave. Bama is a much more appealing character than Raymond but his repeated reference to the women he meets in bars as 'pigs' is disturbingly misogynistic. Dave seems in comparison much less objectionable, his attitude to Ginny often indulgent and at times even caring. But his oscillation between being 'nice' to and rejecting Ginny represents a negotiation and not a repudiation of the attitudes to women in Bama's world. He holds himself apart from Bama's overt misogyny but not from Bama; he treats Ginny well compared to Raymond, although his offer to her to 'stick around' while he plays poker gives her the status of appendage rather than companion. That Dave attaches himself to Ginny immediately after leaving Gwen

Fig. 4.18

(even though he had told her to go back to Chicago only that morning) suggests a need to confirm his sense of himself following Gwen's rebuff. His neediness here amplifies our sense of the need implied by his drunken invitation to Ginny to travel with him to Parkman. Minnelli's framing places Dave and Raymond on each side of Ginny at the beginning of the scene, constructing them as rivals but implying parallels as well contrasts in their conduct (Fig. 4.18).

It is in the bar later that night, after the poker game, that Ginny observes with some feeling, 'the only time you talk nice to me is when you're loaded'. This comes after Dave had responded to her declaration that she could fall for him with, 'Me? A cute-looking kid like you? With such class. Such a fine mind? You're pulling my leg.' He later punctures Ginny's description of her previous job as a hostess with further sarcasm: 'I bet that's a fine, intelligent and interesting job.' Dave's bantering tone slightly softens the unkindness of the words, but the attack on the defenceless Ginny and the impulse to hurt her remain distasteful. It is as though, sober, Dave has to distance himself from any serious engagement with Ginny. Some of the words he uses – 'class', 'fine mind', 'intelligent' – are also eloquent of an underlying comparison with Gwen and of a distinctly snobbish tendency that it takes a good deal of alcohol to anaesthetise.

Dave's most prolonged and intense attack on Ginny, a sequence in which what he says is not softened in any way, is when he finds her waiting for him on Bama's porch after the final break up with Gwen. Ginny is basking in the reflected glory of Dave's new story. She has bought up all the copies of the magazine in town and has been signing them as presents for her friends and colleagues. Dave takes out on Ginny, in deeply unpleasant terms, all the bitterness of his parting from Gwen: 'Can't you get it through your thick skull?'; 'You haven't got the brains or the will power to sit down and read the story'; 'You haven't got enough sense to come in out of the rain unless somebody leads you by the hand – and that's only because you'll go anywhere with anybody.' The scene is shot in another of the film's long takes, the frame holding us outside the porch and creating a sustained and stable viewpoint on the action (Fig 4.19). Dave's anger and hostility and

Fig. 4.19

Ginny's pain and confusion are simultaneously present to us throughout, but the stylistic restraint, as so often in the film, creates a spatial disengagement even as we respond to the intense feelings generated by the characters. The violence of Dave's attack is all the more shocking for being so disproportionate and misdirected; Ginny becomes the hapless target of a rage generated elsewhere.

The implication of the scene with Bama that follows is that in giving up drink in order to prove to Gwen that he is capable of change Dave has cut himself off from the safety valve and the respite from control that drunkenness provides. But Dave drunk and Dave sober are not completely antithetical. We saw in the opening scene that he softened his rejection of Ginny with apologies and tones of regret when he saw her hurt, and a similar pattern is followed here. When Bama goes upstairs, Dave takes a drink of whiskey, mutters 'Dames!' and calls Ginny in. There is considerable pathos in Ginny's attempt to remonstrate with Dave ('You got no right to talk to me like that – I'm a human being with the same rights and feelings as anybody else') and acute engagement with her pain in what follows. At first Dave is impatient with Ginny's attempts to challenge him and to assert her dignity; he walks away from her, into the right foreground of the frame, and sits down with his back to her. He does not look at her again until she runs forward, throws herself onto him and cries in despair, 'Dave, be in love with me. I love you so much. I've never met anyone like you before in my whole life.' She then compels a response by pulling his arm around her and now he holds her tightly and apologises, although his lines ('I'm sorry if I hurt you. Forgive me. I didn't mean it. I'm terribly sorry') are delivered with no hint of genuine feeling, almost as though by rote.

Emotionally, the weight of these scenes seems very much with Ginny but it is an engagement with someone who is more child than adult. She has no resources except her feelings with which to counter Dave's assault and, although his attack on her is inexcusable, the actions Dave reacts to are so naïve as to seem almost dim-witted. Our response is given particular intensity by the discrepancy in power and understanding between the two characters, but although Ginny's simplicity and emotional honesty can in itself seem a rebuke to Dave's confusions and aggression, the film does not allow us to forget that hers is a response to the world bordering on the simple-minded.

These perspectives are further played out in the following scene, which we enter as Dave finishes reading his story to Ginny. The film gives us no sense of how this came about – whether Dave offered or Ginny asked – but it comes over initially as another stage in making peace between them, a gesture by Dave to offer Ginny the link with him and the story that he had so emphatically refused her before. But here she is construct-

Fig. 4.20

ed, even more obviously than in Gwen's classroom, as a child – sitting on the floor listening, with a look of intent but perplexed concentration, to an adult reading to her (Fig. 4.20). Again, Dave attacks her, this time for a lack of understanding which, in the context of a scene that parallels the earlier reading of Dave's story in the summerhouse, means for not being Gwen. He bullies her with questions as she tries to articulate her responses to the story, like an overbearing teacher losing patience with a dim but willing student. Minnelli begins with a wide shot that establishes Dave and Ginny at opposite sides of the frame, the viewpoint slightly elevated and looking down on them. Unlike the scene on the porch, however, he then cuts into angle/reverse-angle, a method that parallels Ginny's meeting with Gwen, the editing emphasising the characters' separation as Dave badgers Ginny, until he cuts back to the original framing for the climax of their exchange:

Dave: You don't understand the story at all.

Ginny: No, I don't, but that don't mean I don't like it. I don't understand you either but that don't mean I don't like you. I love you. But I don't understand you. What's the matter with that?

We cut back to the frontal view of Dave, then to Ginny, and back to Dave who eventually gets up and is followed in a panning shot across the intervening space to Ginny, where he proposes to her. The emotional dynamics of the scene are mirrored here in the editing, framing and camera movement, the significance of Dave's movement to Ginny underlined by the camera which follows him from his space to hers. But Minnelli also retains the more detached view that places the characters in space and defines for us the adult/child axis of the scene.

Why does Dave propose? Nothing in the film so far has indicated that, drunk or sober, he thinks of Ginny as a possible wife. In the scene that immediately follows Bama puts the objections brutally: 'All due respect to Ginny, you ain't going to marry this broad'; even Ginny knows she's a 'pig'; she is a 'dumb pushover'. Bama's misogyny is at its starkest here but these are attitudes very similar to those Dave himself had articulated on the porch not that long before. Bama is also clear-sighted enough to recognise that behind this must be 'what went on between you and that schoolteacher'. What seems to happen here is the collapse of Dave's ambivalence, previously defined by his drunk/ sober oscillations of attitude to Ginny, in the face of her declaration of love unconditioned and unconstrained by understanding. The film's attitudes are carefully shaded. Any ro- mantic satisfaction we could be tempted to feel is cut off by Bama's entrance and his caustic response to the news. At the same time, the construction of Dave and Ginny as adult and child remains strongly in play from the previous action. Even in the proposal and Ginny's response the film makes no attempt to create the image of a plausible romantic couple.

Dave explains himself to Bama after Ginny leaves in terms that feel almost despair- ing: 'I'm just tired of being lonely, that's all. And the way she feels about me, well nobody ever felt that way about me before. Besides, maybe I can help her. I sure can't help myself.' Dave's confession that he 'can't help' himself is one of his few moments of self- awareness in the film, but here it involves a capitulation to self-pity rather than imply- ing clear-sightedness about his situation. Bizarrely, he becomes as childlike as Ginny, looking for something like the unconditional love of a mother for her child from the most helpless character in the film.

After the stylistic restraint and muted colour of most of the film, what follows feels, in style and tone, almost like a sequence from another film. The centre of Parkman has been turned into a fairground, with some rides and sideshows already in action while oth- ers are still being constructed as excited crowds pack the space. Parkman has become a night-town, 'garishly lit in primary colours' (Minnelli 1974: 325) and the brash energy of the fair is intensified by editing which accelerates as the sequence goes on, cutting both between different views and different strands of narrative with a rapidity unlike any other section of the film. Literally, this is the celebration of the town's Centennial that has been promised throughout the film, although the stylised lighting and choreography create a sequence that exceeds any plausible representation of a smalltown fair. Less literally, it is the explosion of energy (and eventually of violence) that is threatened in the combination of uneventful images and turbulent music associated at the beginning of the film with Dave's return and, correspondingly, as the action builds towards its climax the driving chords of that music return. It feels as though 'everything this culture seeks to repress comes bubbling to the surface' (Polan 2002: 2). More specifically, however, there is a strong poetic logic in the conjunction of the fair and the wedding. The first images of the fair immediately precede and introduce the marriage scene and Dave and Ginny emerge onto the street into the excited activity and raucous noise of the fairground. It is as if these pent-up forces have been finally released by the marriage itself.

The film has allowed us to forget Raymond since his arrest with Dave and Ginny. His reappearance is prefaced here when Bama, drinking in Smitty's, receives a message that

Fig. 4.21

Raymond has heard of the wedding and is on the loose with a gun, looking for Dave. But he returns in an extraordinary image, bursting into the frame as a silhouetted figure swigging from a bottle against a wall vividly lit in red (Fig. 4.21). The extreme stylisation of this image and of a number of similarly-lit shots that trace Raymond's frenetic pursuit of Dave give Raymond's return an overtly symbolic force, as though he is a creature released from the underworld. The change of register and the corresponding assertiveness in the film's tone now point up the significance of Dave having unwittingly brought Raymond with him from Chicago when he invited Ginny. In terms of narrative causality, Raymond is Ginny's obsessive suitor, enraged by the marriage; in terms of the film's poetic logic, he is Dave's double, 'called up' by what the marriage represents – Dave's attempt to resolve his contradictions by finally accepting the need in him that his attachment to Ginny implies but that he has previously been unable to acknowledge.

The morality-play dimensions of melodrama come very close to the surface here. According to this logic, Raymond's murderous attack in which Ginny is killed and Dave wounded represents Dave's revenge on himself for his capitulation to feminised weakness (the admission of loneliness and the craving for unconditional love), and also on Ginny who is the embodiment of that weakness. In fact, in a way that parallels the intensely violent struggles between the hero and his double in some of Anthony Mann's westerns, there is something suicidal about the violence here: Ginny is a distinct character in the fiction but also, like Raymond, a part of Dave, something he brings with him because he has no alternative. As in Mann's greatest films, the question that the end of the film poses about the hero is 'what's left?'

The final sequence, of Ginny's funeral, offers no positive answer. The tone is solemn but the action enigmatic. I certainly find it difficult to perceive even the qualified hope (Dave and Bama as 'men who grow and seem to learn') that Dana Polan identi-

Fig. 4.22

fies (2002: 2). After the first shot of the clergyman intoning the funeral service, the film cuts to Gwen and her father driving up, getting out of the car and standing at some distance, looking towards the gathering around the grave. A close-up isolates Gwen, her expression set in concern (Fig. 4.22). Does the film allow here for the potential of reconciliation with Dave? Or does it imply that, with Ginny's death, Gwen might now feel that all she hated about Dave's life has been exorcised? We cannot be certain, but Gwen is not shown again and the whole weight of the film seems set against her. The final shot pans from Bama, alone, past the few other mourners, including Rosalie, to Dave, also standing alone, his arm in a sling, then back to Bama who slowly removes his hat as the camera moves past him to frame the distant view of the river, beyond the cemetery (Figs 4.23 and 4.24). The acknowledgement Bama's gesture represents is moving but is too little, too late, while the telling last image of Dave is of a figure injured, motionless and apparently drained.

Fig. 4.23

Fig. 4.24

5. Afterword

This study began from a feeling that tone, for all its problems as a term, deserved to be rehabilitated. After all, it pointed towards significant aspects of our movie-going experience and yet it was largely absent from debates about point of view and narrative meaning in film. In our experience of the dramatic arts we often need to speak not just of the story, the characters, or what a work signifies, but about the attitudes, feelings and values with which it is imbued. Part of the problem for criticism is that such things are difficult to pin down. What we are trying to describe or evoke can feel almost intangible, more like a gravitational field the work generates than an aspect of the work itself. Language tends to reflect this difficulty: the words we use most commonly to evoke these phenomena (atmosphere, mood, tone itself) in themselves suggest how elusive they seem. Correspondingly, responses to tone can feel subjective, as though its intangibility left us floundering in personal response in comparison to discussion of other, somehow more substantive, dimensions of meaning. Yet experiences of tone, in film as in language, are real enough to shape our understanding profoundly, while the inherently social nature of language and of movies means that, however difficult we may find it to articulate them, these are not experiences that confine us in our own subjectivity: more often than not our grasp of tone is shared to a significant extent by others.

In retrospect, perhaps, the question posed in chapter one – whether tone could become a *functional critical concept* – gave a misleading impression. As a concept it remains inherently baggy and indeterminate. I defined it at the outset (following I. A. Richards) as a way of designating various dimensions of 'attitude' implied by a work but we have seen that in practice 'attitude' itself becomes a tricky term, almost dissolving into its many potential axes. We have seen, too, that the expression of attitude in movies, as in language, invariably has a pervasive affective dimension. Susan Smith, in fact, initially defines 'issues of tone' as 'the kinds of attitudes and feelings we deem to be embodied in a film's stance towards its narrative subject matter' (2000: vii), treating 'feeling' and 'attitude' as separate dimensions of response. For Deborah Thomas, too, feeling is one half of a binary: tone is 'the emotional and moral colouring of the experience that the film offers us' (2005: 167). These differences of emphasis provide opportunities for enjoyable debate but, whether we see attitude as incorporating feeling or feeling as somehow a distinct realm of response, tone remains an unwieldy concept.

The extended analyses in this study took a different direction – less concerned with the concept as a concept than with how what might count as tonal qualities could be identified in specific cases. Critical controversy over *The Deer Hunter* provided an initial context in which consideration of tone seemed inescapable, although the term itself cropped up infrequently in the critical writing on the film. At the heart of the debates were often assumptions – rarely argued at length – about the film's attitudes to its material and its audience. In some of the early writing these assumptions were inherent in readings of particular sequences that took the film's attitudes to be signalled by dominant signifiers such as the choral music in the first hunt. The importance of Robin Wood's analysis of *The Deer Hunter* for my purposes was twofold: he made clear that debates about the film's achievements needed to focus explicitly on its orientation to its material, traditions and spectators; he also showed that such matters could not be asserted or assumed but had to be argued by reference to relationships within and between patterns of detailed decision-making in the context of the movie as a whole.

In following something like that process I wanted to explore the extent to which the attitudes and relationships signalled by the term 'tone' could provide a consistent focus in detailed analysis, and how far a discussion of such matters could escape the vagueness of evocation by grounding itself in the choices that made up the film. While the analysis was guided by the preliminary framework provided by the dimensions of implied attitude I outlined early on, I wanted as far as possible to work 'bottom-up', allowing the detail of the sequences under discussion to shape the course of the discussion. The detailed analysis confirmed what I had felt at the outset, that mood and tone (a duality that became essential without ever becoming entirely clear cut) were as much part of the total 'meaning' of a film as matters that could be more readily formulated. Working through the specific detail of films also suggested that, although it was intuitive to think of tone as intangible, the relationships (for example to subject matter, conventions, spectator) implied by the term were embedded in the material fabric of the film. As George M. Wilson argues, 'meaning' in film is rarely a matter of decoding an underlying semantic schema; it is more often a question of finding 'a pattern of explanatory connections' (1997: 229–30). Causal connections (as in the two forms of causality identified in *Strangers on a Train*) are to that extent *articulated*, not in the sense of being expressed by the film in language but in the sense that the links between different parts of the film imply and can support such ways of accounting for and understanding them. Tone and mood need to be thought of in similar ways – as rooted in decisions that can be specified and the consequences of which can be argued.

At the beginning of chapter four I suggested that, like orchestral music, different strands of decision-making in films can imply distinct but interwoven tonal qualities, held in significant tension, and this analogy suggests both the skillful patterning that can underpin our experience of tone and that tone and mood are pervasive, potentially affected by every aspect of decision-making. That it is impossible to predict in any detail how choices and interrelationships will contribute to mood and tone also indicates why they can never be an exclusive focus of analysis: the attitudes and relationships they designate are key dimensions of response and interpretation but are inseparable from our wider understandings of the film.

I have written elsewhere in almost exactly the same terms about point of view and something more needs to be said about the relationship between point of view and tone. I still tend to think that point of view is a concept most effectively used to designate the total network of 'a film's relationships to its material and its attempts to position the spectator' (Pye 2000: 8) and that tone should be thought of as part of this broad field, although perfectly cogent arguments could be mounted both for narrower approaches to point of view and for maintaining its conceptual distance from tone. I am not sure, however, that such differences matter hugely, provided that we recognise this totality of relationships and attitudes as crucial aspects of our engagement with any film. Thinking about point of view directs our attention to how multi-dimensional our relationships to narrative film invariably are. As a vital dimension of point of view, tone alerts us more specifically to the pervasive evaluative and affective orientations implied by the film. It reminds us that, at every level of their design, film narratives are inherently and often complexly value-laden, and that they address us in ways that require correspondingly multi-faceted responses and understanding.

NOTES

1   In film criticism there are some welcome signs of a revival of interest: Susan Smith and Deborah Thomas, for instance, have both made significant use of the concept (see Smith 2000 and Thomas 2005).

2   John Paul Russo, the author of *I. A. Richards: His Life and Work*, writes: 'Richards took the word *tone* from Edwardian etiquette, as when one speaks of raising the tone of a conversation. Manners imply adjustment and control of social relationships across the social spectrum: the French word *moeurs* includes manners and morals and better indicates Richards' intentions' (1989: 232).

3   For a fuller discussion of narrative agencies see Pye (2000).

4   See Perkins (2005) for one of the most developed accounts of the 'worldhood' of fictional worlds and its implications.

5   I take issue with aspects of Bordwell's account of 'classical Hollywood' in 'Bordwell and Hollywood' (Pye 1989).

6   See, for instance, the introduction to *A Modest Pageant* (Davies 1992), the collected scripts of Davies' early films.

7   The term 'melodrama' has been at the centre of much debate since the early 1970s. The main focus has been on films that Michael Walker has called 'melodramas of passion' (1982: 16) to distinguish them from the 'action melodrama' (broadly the predominantly male-centred action genres) and I follow current usage in using 'melodrama' to designate the former grouping.

8   It is a striking fact that central to the achievements of Hollywood melodrama in the 1940s and 1950s is the work of several directors (Max Ophuls, Nicholas Ray, Douglas Sirk, Vincente Minnelli, Otto Preminger) celebrated by authorship criticism in the 1950s and 1960s for the detailed significance of their visual styles. Ray, Sirk and Minnelli are all, in varying degrees, directors of melodrama and notable contributors to the cycle of male-centred movies. There is a strong case to be made for also associating Hitchcock, whose generic base is outwardly very different but whose concerns are equally with masculinity and its discontents, with this group.

9   Michael Walker's four generic groups within the melodrama of passion are: (i) melodramas in which the narrative focus is on a woman; (ii) romantic melodramas; (iii) family and/or small-town melodramas; (iv) melodramas in the Gothic horror tradition. The third category could be used to contain a number of what I have called male-centred melodramas but I think there is a case for singling out films in which the main narrative focus is a man.

10 For example, *Ruby Gentry* (King Vidor, 1952) and *All That Heaven Allows* (Douglas Sirk, 1956).

11 There is a further link with *The Searchers* in that Dave returns, three years after the war, in army uniform. *Some Came Running* makes much less of the recent World War than Ford's film does of the Civil War but the implication may be that, like Ethan, the uniform represents an escape from a troubled peacetime identity. In both cases the uniform is shed during the film and the psychic divisions in the characters become increasingly extreme. In these respects the 1948 setting is relevant, though in other ways, as Michael Walker has pointed out to me,

the film feels as though it should be set in the 1950s (teenagers, for instance, figure significantly).

12 Dana Polan makes a similar point about the effect of Minnelli's CinemaScope staging: ' ... the learning process is extended ... by the Cinemascope composition to we the spectators who have to discover how to read the frame and learn to modify what we think we're seeing' (Polan 2002: 2).

13 I am indebted to Michael Walker for this observation.

14 See Ian Garwood (2006) 'The Pop Song in Film' for a discussion of these qualities in *Pal Joey* (1957).

BIBLIOGRAPHY

Abrams, M. H. (1971) *A Glossary of Literary Terms* (third edition). New York: Holt, Rinehart and Winston.

Auster, Arnold and Leonard Quart (1979) 'Hollywood and Vietnam: the triumph of the will', *Cineaste*, ix, 4–9.

Axeen, David (1979) 'Four Shots at *The Deer Hunter*', *Film Quarterly*, 32, 4, 10–22.

Babington, Bruce and Peter Evans (1990) 'All that Heaven Allowed: Another Look at Sirkian Irony', *Movie*, 34/35, 48–58.

Booth, Wayne C. (1961) *The Rhetoric of Fiction*. Chicago: Chicago University Press.

Bordwell, David (1985) *Narration in the Fiction Film*. London: Methuen.

Bordwell, David, Janet Staiger and Kristin Thompson (1985) *The Classical Hollywood Cinema*. London: Routledge.

Callenbach, Ernest (1979) 'Four Shots at *The Deer Hunter*', *Film Quarterly*, 32, 4, 10–22.

Davies, Terence (1992) *A Modest Pageant*. London: Faber and Faber.

Dempsey, Michael (1979) 'Four Shots at *The Deer Hunter*', *Film Quarterly*, 32, 4, 10–22.

Elsaesser, Thomas (1987 [1972]) 'Tales of Sound and Fury: observation on the family melodrama', reprinted, with revisions, in Christine Gledhill (ed.) *Home is Where the Heart Is*. London: British Film Institute, 43–69.

Everett, Wendy (2004) *Terence Davies*. Manchester: Manchester University Press.

Garwood, Ian (2006) 'The Pop Song in Film', in John Gibbs and Douglas Pye (eds) *Close-Up 01*. London: Wallflower Press, 89–166.

Gray, Martin (2004) *The Dictionary of Literary Terms*. London: Longman/York Press.

Hillier, Jim (2005) 'Swimming and sinking: form and meaning in an avant-garde film', in John Gibbs and Douglas Pye (eds) *Style and Meaning: Studies in the Detailed Analysis of Film*. Manchester: Manchester University Press, 155–66.

Kinder, Marsha (1979) 'Four Shots at *The Deer Hunter*', *Film Quarterly*, 32, 4, 10–22.

Lang, Robert (1989) *American film melodrama : Griffith, Vidor, Minnelli*. Cambridge, MA: Princeton University Press.

McElhaney, Joe (2003) 'Medium Shot Gestures: Vincente Minnelli and *Some Came Running*', http://www.16-9.dk/2003-06/side11_minnelli.htm.

Minnelli, Vincente (1974) *I Remember It Well*. New York: Doubleday.

Perez, Gilberto (1998) *The Material Ghost*. Baltimore: Johns Hopkins University Press.

Perkins, V. F. (2005) 'Where is the world: the horizon of events in movie fiction', in John Gibbs and Douglas Pye (eds) *Style and Meaning: Studies in the Detailed Analysis of Film*. Manchester: Manchester University Press, 16–41.

Polan, Dana (2002) '*Some Came Running*', http://www.sensesofcinema.com/contents/cteq/01/19/some_came.html.

Pye, Douglas (1989) 'Bordwell and Hollywood', *Movie*, 33, 46–52.

___ (2000) 'Movies and Point of View', *Movie*, 36, 2–34.

Russo, John Paul (1989) *I. A. Richards: His Life and Work*. Baltimore: Johns Hopkins University

Press.

Richards, I. A. (1961) *Principles of Literary Criticism*. London: Routledge & Kegan Paul.

Smith, Greg M. (1999) 'Local Emotions, Global Moods and Film Structure', in Carl Plantinga and Greg M. Smith (eds) *Passionate Views: Film, Cognition and Emotion*. Baltimore: Johns Hopkins University Press, 103–26.

Smith, Susan (2000) *Hitchcock: Suspense, Humour and Tone*. London: British Film Institute.

Thomas, Deborah (2000) *Beyond Genre*. Moffat: Cameron and Hollis.

___ (2005) '"Knowing one's place": frame-breaking, embarrassment and irony in *La Cérémonie* (Claude Chabrol, 1955)', in John Gibbs and Douglas Pye (eds) *Style and Meaning: Studies in the Detailed Analysis of Film*. Manchester: Manchester University Press, 167–78.

Truffaut, François (1969) *Hitchcock by François Truffaut*. London: Panther Books.

Walker, Michael (1982) 'Melodrama and the American Cinema', *Movie*, 29/30, 2–38.

Wilson, George M. (1985) *Narration in Light*. Baltimore: The Johns Hopkins University Press.

___ (1997) 'On Film Narrative and Narrative Meaning', in Richard Allen and Murray Smith (eds) *Film Theory and Philosophy*. Oxford: Oxford University Press, 221–38.

Wood, Robin (1986) 'Two films by Michael Cimino', in *Hollywood from Vietnam to Reagan*. New York: Columbia University Press, 270–317.

___ (1989) *Hitchcock's Films Revisited*. London: Faber and Faber.

Woolf, Virginia (1938) *The Common Reader*. London: Pelican Books.

2.2 READING ROHMER
Jacob Leigh

ACKNOWLEDGEMENTS

I am grateful to Royal Holloway, University of London, who allowed me a term's research leave in the autumn of 2004. This enabled me to do most of my initial research. Students and staff in the Media Arts department there have been enthusiastic supporters of my interest in Eric Rohmer, but I especially want to single out for thanks Loreta Gandolfi and the group of third-year students who comprised my first Film Aesthetics class, in 2003–04. Classroom discussion of *Conte d'automne* was the first stage in sensitising me to the complexity and richness of Rohmer's work.

John Gibbs and Douglas Pye, series editors of *Close-Up*, have been consistently helpful and encouraging. During the long process of writing and editing, their feedback immeasurably improved my work. Many thanks to both.

All the translations from French are my own in that I claim responsibility for any errors or mistakes in them. In most cases, I was able only to translate the meaning broadly and literally. Thankfully, several people assisted me greatly by performing the invaluable task of turning my bald and clumsy translations into comprehensible English. These people are: John Ellis, Steven Marchant, Andrew Leigh and Sarah Guest. I am extremely thankful to all of them, but in particular to Sarah, who helped on the majority and was always ready at a moment's notice to provide expert guidance. With love and thanks, this study is dedicated to her.

INTRODUCTION

There is little written in English about the French director Eric Rohmer. Two recent pieces discuss two of Rohmer's third series of films, *Contes des quatre saisons* (*Tales of Four Seasons*, 1990–98): William Rothman (2004) writes about the philosophical dimensions of *Conte d'hiver* (*A Winter's Tale*, 1992) and Andrew Klevan (2000) writes about Rohmer's interest in the everyday in *Conte de printemps* (*Tale of Springtime*, 1990), but so far the only book on Rohmer in English is Colin Crisp's *Eric Rohmer: Realist and Moralist* (1988), which covers Rohmer's first series, *Six contes moraux* (*Six Moral Tales*, 1962–72), and the first four films of his second series, *Comédies et proverbes* (*Comedies and Proverbs*, 1981–87). Crisp's study concentrates on relating choice and knowledge in *Six contes moraux* to Catholicism; it also devotes lengthy chapters to a discussion of Rohmer's criticism of the late 1950s and early 1960s, arguing that, as editor of *Cahiers du cinéma* between 1956 and 1963, Rohmer inherits André Bazin's ideas. Since Crisp's book, Rohmer has completed the *Comédies et proverbes* and the *Contes des quatre saisons*. These ten films represent Rohmer's finest accomplishment as a film artist and it is unfortunate that, along with Claude Chabrol, he is such an under-valued director in the English-speaking film world. In contrast, in France during the past few years six single-authored scholarly books (Magny 1995, Hertay 1998, Bonitzer 1999, Tortajada 1999, Serceau 2000 and Cléder 2006) have been published on Rohmer, while journals such as *Cahiers du cinéma* and *Positif* have repeatedly dedicated special issues to his work. Additionally, while several critics (including Jonathan Rosenbaum, Adrian Martin and Geoff Andrew) have expressed admiration for Rohmer on-line, in particular for the journal *Senses of Cinema*, printed English-language journals still contain little on his work. My contribution to the *Close-Up* series aims to restore Rohmer's reputation as a major filmmaker, worthy of sustained critical attention.

This study focuses on three of Rohmer's films: *Le Beau mariage* (*A Good Marriage*, 1982), *Le Rayon vert* (*The Green Ray*, 1986) and *Conte d'automne* (*An Autumn's Tale*, 1998). Each of the following three chapters deals with a single film and proceeds by offering an analysis of the film's major strategies, isolating sequences as a means of discussing exemplary techniques. The motivating enquiry has been to investigate the artistic impact of decisions made by Rohmer and this method informs all aspects of the study.

Chapter one, on *Le Beau mariage*, begins with a discussion of three elements related to the film's opening, all of which are central to Rohmer's work: firstly, his interest in daydreaming; secondly, his depiction of movement and stasis; thirdly, his use of colours. These three things feature throughout Rohmer's work and therefore recur as subjects for discussion here. The represention of daydreaming comes from his interest in filming the contrast or conflict between our thoughts or desires and our actions; most often the dramatic interest of his films comes from the contrast between what characters say and what they do. His use of movement and stasis takes various forms. In *Le Beau mariage*, Sabine's (Béatrice Romand) commuting by train and car contrasts with another character's walking: while Sabine has to travel between her home and her places of work and study, her friend is able to walk conveniently between these. The chapter discusses both the significance of this and the extensive development of it as a dramatic method within the film.

Chapter two looks at the way in which *Le Rayon vert* alternates between Delphine (Marie Rivière) walking alone and sitting down at mealtimes; it also discusses her travelling across France in search of a holiday and romance. While *Le Beau mariage* is concerned with the repetitive nature of commuting, *Le Rayon vert*'s interest is in the variation from everyday experiences that holiday travel can provide.

Chapter three looks at *Conte d'automne*'s use of both mealtimes and driving as dramatic methods for exploring the characters' lives. This film's characters live in the countryside and as their lives become more entangled so their criss-crossing of the region becomes more entwined.

Finally, all three chapters discuss Rohmer's use of colour. Few writers have examined this but Rohmer is a superb colourist, one who handles the expressive dimensions of colour in a way more familiar from the great 1950s melodramas of Nicholas Ray, Douglas Sirk and Vincente Minnelli. Like these directors, he coordinates the colours of costumes, sets and lighting. In some films Rohmer links the colours to characters as expressive motifs or to the seasonal setting of the story. In *Le Beau mariage* and *Conte d'automne*, the dominant colours are autumnal. Late autumn's light browns and pale pinks dominate in *Le Beau mariage*; early autumn's dark greens and reds stand out in *Conte d'automne*. *Le Rayon vert* uses the colour green as its main motif and it elaborates this by repeating green and red on costumes, settings and props. Patterns formed from Rohmer's colours provide a notable unity for the film; most noticeably, the repetition of the colour green connects to and expands upon the film's central metaphor, the green ray itself, a rare and ephemeral atmospheric light effect, but also the title of a romantic novel by Jules Verne, from which Rohmer took inspiration for his film.

Rohmer's approach to filming *Le Rayon vert* was, for him, unusual. When making his previous films, he tried to control all parts of the work; for *Le Rayon vert*, though, Rohmer set out to make an improvised film. He filmed it almost as a documentary, without either script or schedule; and yet, despite this, it is one his most self-reflexive films. The subject of the film grows from his exploration of chance and control; Delphine's story centres on the relationship between leaving things to luck and planning. During filming, Rohmer tried to abandon his control and maintain a flexible openness to chance, spontaneity and improvisation; the result was an unusual roughness. Nonetheless, though it might seem to lack the stylistic coherence of his earlier films, *Le Rayon vert* is one his most sophisticated works.

Commenting on Rembrandt's *Aristotle with the Bust of Homer* (1653), G. L. Hagberg notes of critical interpretation that 'we cannot know, in advance of our active processes of the interpretations, contextualisations and understandings of words and of deeds, which parts of the picture, or even which categories or groups of parts, "go together"'

(1994: 128). The guiding aim of this study has been to work out which parts of Rohmer's films 'go together'. As I have discovered, this has involved most often the detailed study of the relational properties between an actor's words and gestures because, as already mentioned, the dramatic interest of Rohmer's films often derives from the contrast between what characters say and what they do: 'All my films', says Rohmer, 'play on the contradictions between what is said, what is done, what is seen and known' (quoted in Goudet 2004: 25). It is because of this that studying Rohmer's films closely is especially revealing.

Certain topics recur in Rohmer's films throughout the six decades in which he has been making them. Rohmer is, for example, deeply concerned with thought and thinking. As Tamara Tracz notes: 'The films do not make moral judgements, neither on the characters nor on the issues that face them. Their concern is the exploration of the dilemma, and what it reveals of the human' (2003). That may sound far-fetched, but if Rohmer has one central concern in all his films it is to represent thoughts and feelings; most often his intrigues are, as Raymond Durgnat (1988) argues, dramas of consciousness.[1] Rohmer repeatedly acknowledges Balzac as his model for a socially analytical fiction, one which scrutinises and probes the morals and manners of contemporary society. His *nouvelle vague* colleague Chabrol uses the thriller form to examine contemporary French society's attitudes and morals, and Rohmer uses the romantic or social comedy to examine similar things: whereas Chabrol often focuses on murderers as a way of analysing deep structures of society, such as those of class, Rohmer, like an anthropologist, patiently reveals people's ordinary way of living, of behaving and of feeling.

The first film that drew me to study Rohmer in detail was *Conte d'automne* and one of the first things that I read was Rohmer's interview about this film in a *Cahiers du cinéma* special issue (de Baecque & Lalanne 1998). In this, he talks about the 'germ' of *Conte d'automne* being a scene in *Le Rayon vert*, during which Béatrice Romand and Marie Rivière argue about the best way to find a man. This intrigued me and spurred me on to study *Le Rayon vert*; *Le Beau mariage* seemed the logical choice for a third film because it was Béatrice Romand's other major film with Rohmer, after *Le Genou de Claire* (*Claire's Knee*, 1970). I have tried to write about Rohmer's work with the two actresses as if I was writing about Hitchcock's work with Cary Grant and James Stewart or Hawks's work with John Wayne.

Rohmer draws on the personalities of his actors, composing two scripts – first an overall sketch, second after tape-recording conversations with his actors. He describes the process as follows: 'I always write my films twice. The first time, my story is written in outline, but it has no body and stays very slight. Not abstract, but a bit basic. To give it shape, I need to know the actors and the places (quoted in Anger, Burdeau & Toubiana 1996: 45). Although Rohmer finishes his scripts after getting to know the actors he has cast for the film, he refutes the inference that the characters are the same as the actors, saying of *Le Genou de Claire*: 'I didn't want to make a psychodrama but a work of pure fiction, with the conscious collaboration of the cast' (quoted in Nogueira 1971: 120). The process involves writing his characters' dialogue to suit the actors' ways of talking, just as Hawks and his collaborators did, although Rohmer insists that 'hesitations, parentheses, repeats, etc – all are written out';[2] the actors have to learn their lines exactly as they are written and rehearse extensively with the camera; there is no improvisation. The exception to this is *Le Rayon vert*.

Decisions about casting connect, therefore, to decisions about story and structure. Rohmer's primary source for material during the development of his films is his actors and actresses; he takes his subjects from their lives, as much as he incorporates their characteristic ways of talking. Thus Béatrice Romand, like her characters in *Le Beau mariage* and *Conte d'automne*, was born in Algeria in 1952 and came to France in 1960. In Paris Romand studied dance, art and photography; in 1970 Rohmer cast her as Laura in *Le Genou de Claire* after seeing her modelling as a teenager. She was 18, and although Claire (Laurence de Monagham) forms the object of Jérôme's (Jean-Claude Brialy) obsession in the film, Romand's Laura is a strong presence. In 1971, an interviewer notes the quality of her performance in *Le Genou de Claire*; Rohmer replies:

> There is something about her … you don't meet girls like her every day, maybe once every five or ten years. I don't know how the character [Laura] would have worked out if I hadn't found her: I know Laura would have been less interesting. I developed the character for her. And I'm sure she can play very different types of role from the one I gave her here: she is more conventionally beautiful in real life than she looks in the film, because I had to make her seem a little younger. I see her perhaps as a Dostoevsky or a Chekhov heroine – very touching. But she can play anything, and whatever she does she will bring an extraordinary power to it. (Quoted in Nogueira 1971: 121)

Since *Le Genou de Claire*, Romand has acted in five more of Rohmer's films, taking the lead in two, *Le Beau mariage* and *Conte d'automne*; her role in *Le Rayon vert* is short but important, and she has brief appearances in *L'Amour l'après-midi* (*Love in the Afternoon*, 1972) and *Quatre aventures de Reinette et Mirabelle* (*Four Adventures of Reinette et Mirabelle*, 1987). Rohmer uses both her personality and her appearance meaningfully; and in her films with Rohmer, Romand plays characters that are intelligent, stubborn and provocative.

Marie Rivière's first film with Rohmer was *Perceval le Gallois*, 1978); besides her leading roles in *La Femme de l'aviateur* (*The Aviator's Wife*, 1980), *Le Rayon vert* and *Conte d'automne*, she has also featured in Rohmer's *Quatre aventures de Reinette et Mirabelle*, *Conte d'hiver* and *L'Anglaise et le Duc* (*The Lady and the Duke*, 2000). In *La Femme de l'aviateur*, she might be having an affair with a married man; in *Le Rayon vert*, she passes a summer searching for contentment and a happy relationship: as both Anne in *La Femme de l'aviateur* and Delphine in *Le Rayon vert*, Rivière is tearful and unhappy. *Le Rayon vert* contrasts Rivière's weepy vulnerability as Delphine with Béatrice Romand's confidence. For Rohmer, their interaction was a point of departure for *Conte d'automne*: 'The dynamic between the two characters is quite similar to the dynamic between them in a short scene at the beginning of *Le Rayon vert*. So, I amused myself by reversing their roles' (quoted in de Baecque & Lalanne 1998: 32).[3] Aware of the links and connections that Romand and Rivière bring to *Conte d'automne*, the director remarks:

> Each time that I have used Béatrice Romand and Marie Rivière, I've really tried not to use them in the same way. In *Le Beau mariage*, Béatrice Romand played a character that wanted a man at any cost. Here, she maybe also wants a man, but she doesn't want him 'at any cost'. Therefore, the situation seems similar, but in some ways the character is constructed the other way round. As for Marie Rivière, her role is more comic than in my previous films. (Quoted in de Baecque & Lalanne 1998: 33)

The reversal of roles for *Conte d'automne* means that while the behaviour of Romand and Rivière's characters recalls their characters in earlier Rohmer films – Sabine in *Le Beau mariage* and Delphine in *Le Rayon vert* – Rivière's confidence has now increased whereas Romand's has all but disappeared. Because of this way in which Rohmer finds inspiration in his actors and their performances, the discussion of Romand and Rivière's work is central to this study and I have devoted a long section of chapter two, on *Le Rayon vert*, to analysing the 'germ' of *Conte d'automne*.

Rohmer's films of the 1980s, the six *Comédies et proverbes*, are about young women living after the major social changes brought about by the influence of feminism and the introduction of easily available contraception. Rohmer's actresses were of the age and experience where these things were relevant to their everyday lives: Béatrice Romand, the oldest of the leads in Rohmer's six *Comédies et proverbes*, was born in 1952; Marie Rivière was born in 1956; Pascale Ogier of *Les Nuits de la pleine lune* (*Full Moon in Paris*, 1984) was born in 1958; Arielle Dombasle of *Le Beau mariage* and *Pauline à la plage* (*Pauline at the Beach*, 1983) was born in 1958; Emmanuelle Chaulet of *L'Ami de mon amie* (*My Girlfriend's Boyfriend*, 1987) was born in 1961. Rohmer's heroines may have been too young to participate in the social protest movements of the late 1960s and the early 1970s, but they grew into maturity during this period and they lived with the consequences of these social changes in the 1980s. One result of his method of drawing inspiration from his actresses is that Rohmer's films respond, however obliquely, to the impact of these changes on the young women at their centre. Consequently, my work on Romand in *Le Beau mariage* and Rivière in *Le Rayon vert* culminates in an analysis of both of their work in *Conte d'automne*, which examines maturity and the apparent stability of married life. The appeal to the reader will hopefully be twofold: an interest in Rohmer's subjects and styles, but also an interest in watching these three films together.

1. *Le Beau mariage*

The credits of Eric Rohmer's 1982 film *Le Beau mariage* are written in dark orange on a light brown background. The title music, credited to Ronan Girre and Simon des Innocents, is a simple upbeat melody played on an electronic keyboard, backed with a drum machine and synthesised sound effects which emulate the sound of a train. It is typical of early 1980s electronic popular music of the kind that teenagers might play at a party. The credits end with a proverb:

> Quel esprit ne bat la campagne?
> Qui ne fait châteaux en Espagne?

Le Beau mariage's proverb comes from Jean de la Fontaine's fable, 'La Laitière et le Pot au lait' (1678) or 'The Milkmaid and the Pail of Milk'. The fable describes how a young woman named Perrette goes to market one day with a pail of milk balanced on her head. As she walks, she daydreams about what future riches her pail of milk may bring: the sale of the milk will enable her to buy a hundred eggs; selling the chickens will enable her to buy a pig, which she can fatten and sell for a cow and a calf. Unfortunately, her daydreaming leads her to stumble and spill the milk. The proverb used in *Le Beau mariage*, which begins the concluding verse, can be translated as 'Can any of us refrain from building castles in Spain?'; the whole verse has been translated by James Michie as:

> Who doesn't build castles in Spain?
> Which of us isn't mildly insane?
> Picrochole, Pyrrhus, the dairymaid,
> Wise men and fools alike, we all daydream
> (No pleasure in life is so sweet)
> And each of us is betrayed
> By flattering self-deceit –
> The world's riches and honours seem
> Ours then, and all its lovely women at our feet. (La Fontaine 1982: 88)

The proverb introduces the subject of daydreaming and from it *Le Beau mariage* fades in on a medium shot of a dark-haired young woman sitting on a train. This is Sabine, played by Béatrice Romand, whom *Le Beau mariage* follows almost exclusively, all but two moments featuring her. She is holding a book about Gothic art, but not reading it – she is daydreaming, gazing off into space (Fig. 1.1).

Le Beau mariage's reference to La Fontaine's fable of the milkmaid daydreaming of 'castles in Spain' whilst she carries her milk to market introduces the film's interest in the relationship between what we think of when we drift off into thought and what we do. In *Le Beau mariage*, a young woman imagines that marriage to a young man is possible, though he does little to indicate his attraction to her; like the milkmaid, Sabine daydreams of wealth, honours and beauty being hers and the film enacts what happens when she tries to bring her daydreams into reality. An important rhetorical figure in *Le Beau mariage* is Sabine gazing absentmindedly or looking intently at views through other people's windows; it recurs at three significant times in the film and it is one of the ways that the film dramatises the connection between Sabine and her milieux. Daydreaming always has a social

Fig. 1.1

context and, although the opening focuses on Sabine's daydreaming, *Le Beau mariage* carefully explores the contrast between Sabine's daydreaming and her actions within sharply-drawn social settings. *Le Beau mariage* follows Sabine and scrutinises her actions, but by placing her in wider contexts it allows us to note her reasons for behaving the way she does.

Rohmer spends a lot of time selecting his locations and, just as he does with casting, once he has made a decision about a location he incorporates much of that setting into his film. Marie Binet-Bouteloup, production assistant on *Le Beau mariage* and *Pauline à la plage*, recalls that during the development of *Le Beau mariage* Rohmer asked if he could talk to her about her life. She told him about Sarthe, the region where Le Mans is, and about how she spent several days each week there. Her commuting intrigued Rohmer and it became the main topic of their conversations (1982: 35). The director began his research by taking the train between Paris and Le Mans several times, studying the timetables, thinking about how a student would travel, how much it would cost, what kind of luggage they would carry, who they would meet, what kind of people took the train, and so on. In Le Mans, Binet-Bouteloup explains, Rohmer walked the streets and studied the views and the integration of the new buildings with the old town, the authenticity of which especially attracted him as a setting. Perched on a hill overlooking the River Sarthe, Le Mans' old town is famous for its medieval streets, Renaissance architecture and the Roman walls that surround it – Sabine comments on these to Edmond (André Dussolier) at Nicholas's (Pascal Greggory) wedding party. At the town's centre is the large Gothic cathedral of Saint-Julien, towards which Sabine drives from the station and in which she bumps into Claude (Vincent Gauthier), her ex-boyfriend. Binet-Bouteloup recalls when Rohmer found the two shops to use in the film:

> Rohmer did the journey between those two places, maybe twenty or thirty times, explaining what would be best in terms of framing and the way of life that it implied. When he is developing his film, Rohmer is an architect, a geographer, a sociologist. He tries to get as close as possible to reality, to the life of an area, yesterday unknown to him, today its identity known and respected. However, Rohmer was not coming to make a film on Le Mans, he was coming to set the second film of the *Comédies et proverbes* there. (1982: 36)

For Rohmer, this was normal, doing all the research himself, much of which he then incorporated into the script, enabling him to use Le Mans to reveal the acute social differences between Sabine and her friend Clarisse (Arielle Dombasle).

In the discussion below, I examine Sabine's interaction with a series of locations and characters. These include Simon (Féodor Atkine), her lover in Paris, Clarisse in her home and shop in the chic old town of Le Mans, Sabine's mother (Thamila Mezbar) in the family home, her ex-boyfriend Claude in his council flat, and finally Edmond, the man whom she pursues in his Parisian chambers. Just as Rohmer organises the locations in *Le Beau mariage*, he also organises several other elements into strict patterns, a number of which the opening introduces. One of these is his use of colours; the opening shot takes up the key colour scheme of the credits: Sabine wears a pale pink blouse and sits in the light brown leather chairs of a train carriage; behind her, orange curtains block out the sunlight. The film's first shot also introduces the pattern of Sabine commuting by train. The film includes seven of Sabine's train journeys between Paris and Le Mans. In two of these, those that begin and end the film, she sits in a carriage. For the other five she stands in the corridor, although we do not always see her; point-of-view shots of fields taken from moving trains represent three of her journeys between Paris and Le Mans. Two of these shots move from left to right, or west to east, that is, from Le Mans to Paris; one moves from right to left, from Paris to Le Mans. The other two journeys show her standing by a corridor window looking out as the countryside passes from right to left, from Paris to Le Mans. Sabine's commuting between Le Mans and Paris illustrates her restlessness; but *Le Beau mariage*'s inclusion of seven train journeys connects with its repetition of other elements; the film also includes ten telephone calls and it shows Sabine making ten drives, although in two cases we do not see the journey, just the driving into or out of a parking space.

The unifying of colours produces visual harmony but the repetition of colours, train journeys, telephone calls and drives also establishes an ironic perspective: repetitions, rhymes and parallels create links of which the characters remain unaware. The ironic mode is central to Rohmer's art, and the creation of rhymes and parallels is one of the primary means by which he develops dramatic irony, focused around the contrast between what his characters say and what they do. Furthermore, *Le Beau mariage* begins and ends with a scene of Sabine daydreaming on a train journey; in both instances, she sits opposite the same young man (Patrick Lambert) (Fig. 1.2). He has long, floppy hair and wears a tweed jacket, a blue cravat topping off his shirt. He resembles a student or young intellectual; in the opening scene, some papers lie in front of him on the table, though he, too, is daydreaming, frequently looking up and absentmindedly holding the end of his pen against his lower lip. A shot/reverse-shot couplet and the daydreaming of

Fig. 1.2

both characters link them as a pair about whom we may start to ask questions. Already we know that she is finding it hard to concentrate; she may be unhappy or just distracted by the attractive man opposite. At the film's end, she has apparently returned to a situation identical to where she began; although her awareness of her self and her situation may have deepened, it is characteristic of Rohmer to leave us with doubts about the story's conclusion.

Sabine is a postgraduate student at the University of Paris, doing an MA in the history of art – the film shows her entering the Bibliothèque d'art et d'archéologie, Fondation Jacques Doucet, the University of Paris art and archaeology library on Rue Michelet, a short walk from Gare Montparnasse, where the Le Mans train terminates. She spends part of each week in Paris in a small apartment typical of student accommodation, with only a bedroom/study and a bathroom. She has a lover in Paris, Simon Leghen, a painter, played by Féodor Atkine. He is slim and muscular, in his late thirties; his hair is cropped short and he has tattoos on his arm, as if he used to be in the army. He has a strong masculine presence, which Rohmer again exploits in *Pauline à la plage*, in which Atkine takes a central role as a duplicitous seducer. As Simon, Atkine is almost a caricature of the virile male artist, handsome and attractive to women. One night, the third scene in the film, when Sabine and Simon are making love in his studio, a telephone call from his wife and son interrupts them. Sabine responds to the interruption by storming out of his studio. As she is leaving, she tells him: 'I'm going to get married.' Romand stands with her hands on her hips as she says this, the pinks, red, browns and yellows of her jumper contrasting with the grey light of the stairs and hallway: 'You're married – why not me?' Simon stands bare chested in front of her: who is she going to marry? Sabine replies: 'I don't know, the man I decide on, who appeals to me.' He strokes her head affection-

Fig. 1.3

ately, but patronisingly: 'Good luck' (Fig. 1.3). He tries to persuade her to come for dinner the following night, but she refuses. Finally, he lets her go, but he calls after her: 'You're completely crazy.'

In an interview with Claude-Jean Philippe and Caroline Champetier from 1982, Rohmer remarks of Sabine that 'it was important to show that she was a girl who loves art – she studies art history – but who can't express herself creatively or artistically'. Both Sabine's lover and her friend are painters, although the latter makes lampshades rather than paintings. Alain Hertay notes that Sabine's apparently triumphant declaration, 'Je vais me marier', said first to Simon, then to her friend, her employer, her ex-boyfriend and finally her mother comes from her frustration with her situation (1998: 38). It originates in her defiance of Simon, her desire to thumb her nose at him, and, as Serge Daney points out, it is mimetic in that it copies him (1982: 56). Sabine's response to Simon rebels against her personal situation, but it also reacts against her social situation.

Sabine's best friend, Clarisse, is married, wealthy and professionally satisfied. Their different social status complicates their friendship and by focusing on the relationship between Sabine's daydreaming and her reality, *Le Beau mariage* develops a strong strand of social critique, elaborated through settings and performances.

The main example to illustrate this comes from the long sequence during which Sabine talks to Clarisse in Le Mans, after returning from Paris. The sequence begins with Sabine driving her dark green Renault 4 from Le Mans station to the old town; in this transition, there is a sense of her approaching a wealthy area as she passes old timber-framed houses and the cathedral. As she walks along narrow streets, her heels clattering on the cobblestones, the camera frames her surrounded by impressively old and picturesque buildings. We see where Sabine works, inside an antique shop in this exclusive part of town; glass, china and ceramic ornaments decorate the room. The owner (played by Huguette Faget), an elegant middle-aged woman, puts a brown coat on top of a dark green dress; she exudes wealth and sophistication. Just as she leaves, Sabine remembers that 'Madame de Saint-Biez called about her Jersey porcelain'. The owner is not interested, yet: 'She wants too much. She'll come down.' Physically, they exchange places: the owner leaves and Sabine takes her place in the shop; later Sabine also takes her place in the negotiation with Madame de Saint-Biez (Denise Bailly).

If Sabine's employer presents one tempting model of an upper-class life, her friend, Clarisse, presents another; like Sabine's boss, she owns her shop, rather than just works in it. Clarisse's establishment is similarly tasteful, with nothing jarring or modern in the décor: the walls are yellowing, with bits of plaster missing and the shop is filled with old dark woodwork. Rohmer has dressed Arielle Dombasle in a pale pink t-shirt and a brown apron as she paints a light brown colour onto a yellow stretched silk that will become a lampshade: these correspondences in colour comfortably fix Clarisse within this setting, one which values permanence and tradition. When Sabine comes to visit her in the shop, they talk briefly about Clarisse's work in progress. Clarisse questions whether Sabine 'really' likes it; her friend reassures her: 'You know I say what I think.' As if to prove this, she adds: 'I liked the last one less.' Clarisse continues to paint the stretched silk while Sabine stands behind her watching. Then, in response to Sabine's comment, she moves behind Sabine, touching her shoulder as she passes and saying: 'It takes all kinds.' Sabine snaps argumentatively, leaning in to confront Clarisse: 'I disagree. You don't care if you sell them or not.' On this, Clarisse turns to resume her work.

Arielle Dombasle is taller than Béatrice Romand; and while Romand has dark brown, almost black hair, Dombasle has blonde hair. Furthermore, while Romand moves quickly and bluntly, Dombasle moves her long limbs with a slow grace that looks measured. Dombasle is the same height as another Rohmer actress – Marie Rivière from *La Femme de l'aviateur*, *Le Rayon vert* and *Conte d'automne*. However, whereas Rivière's movements are often awkwardly angled, with knees and elbows protruding, Dombasle's are gracious; she holds herself erect, as if she has spent years doing ballet. With strong cheekbones and nose, she is handsome rather than pretty. In her costume, movements and general demeanour, she evokes a life untroubled by material constraints. Dombasle's Clarisse (and her Marion in *Pauline à la plage*) never hesitates and, in contrast to Rivière's characters, is never dreamy or distracted; she conveys a class-based confidence. Everything is always in its right place, including her as she punctuates her dialogue with precise gestures. Yet, for all their elegance, Dombasle's characters rarely invite sympathy; Rohmer uses her confidence as a foil for other characters' uncertainty, either that of Romand's Sabine in *Le Beau mariage* or of Amanda Langlet's Pauline in *Pauline à la plage*.

Ignoring Sabine's ill-temper, Clarisse continues to paint while Sabine stands looking glum, her hands crossed behind her back and her head leaning down (Fig. 1.4).

Sabine often appears ungracious; her mother calls her 'impetuous'. With Simon, frustration leads her to declare stubbornly that she is getting married; with her employer, impulsiveness, and perhaps a buried resentment, lead her to go behind her back to negotiate the sale of the Jersey porcelain for Edmond. When her employer confronts her about this, Sabine reacts childishly, walking out of her job. Béatrice Romand, in contrast to Arielle Dombasle, has a petite and muscular physique and she moves vigorously. In *Le Beau mariage*, there is a sense of barely-contained energy in her, which occasionally

Fig. 1.4

leaps out either physically or verbally, as in the tart comment and scowl at Clarisse during their lunchtime conversation or the violent pushing of Edmond's client (Catherine Réthi) as she leaves his office. It is appropriate to this suggestion of contained impetuousness that throughout *Le Beau mariage*, Romand's hair is tied or plaited against her head, sometimes in a compact bun; in only two scenes – with Simon and at the end with Clarisse – is her hair loose (by contrast, in *Conte d'automne*, Romand's bushy long hair is unrestrained).

Clarisse appears used to Sabine's outbursts, though, and she continues painting. Rohmer's dialogue can frequently be understood in more than one way. In this scene, when Sabine says miserably 'You know I really envy you?' she means that she envies Clarisse's ability to create things, but, although they talk about creativity, Sabine's envy also focuses on Clarisse's married life and her social status. 'Do what I do' Clarisse proposes, blind to the circumstances that have led her to this position. When Sabine expresses her frustration with her work, Clarisse offers her a job as her assistant, painting the lampshade bases. Despite this charitable offer, Sabine rejects it in a way that explains much about her character: 'I hate taking orders.' Clarisse points out that Sabine takes orders where she works now; but for Sabine, 'It's just a boring job. I'll quit one day.' What emerges during this long scene between Sabine and Clarisse is that Sabine's daydreaming derives from three kinds of frustration: not only dissatisfied with her relationship with a married man, she is also frustrated with her job and, implicitly, with her social position.

Sabine's relationship with Clarisse only exacerbates her frustration. Clarisse offering to become Sabine's employer does not help; although Clarisse insists 'you'd be my partner', Sabine replies, 'I'm too independent'. After declaring her independent nature, she then repeats her declaration: 'I'm going to get married.' Clarisse asks if Simon is getting a divorce, but Sabine explains that she is planning to get married to 'nobody in particular'. Sabine's abstract plan to get married surprises Clarisse as much as it surprised Simon: 'You can't just decide to get married. I got married because I loved Frédéric.' This understandable scepticism provokes further explanation from Sabine: 'The point is that I've changed my attitude. The other night at Simon's, I said to myself "what am I doing here?" This guy has a wife and kids, when so many men are unattached.' Sabine has

Fig. 1.5

walked across the shop and the camera has followed her while Clarisse brushes her hair and puts on her coat. Outside, they walk slowly away from the camera, diminishing in size as they proceed down one of Le Mans' streets (Fig. 1.5). The surrounding road, walls and roofs all look grey under a slight drizzle, but their wealth and age impresses.

In the following two sections, inside Clarisse's house and then back on the street, Rohmer continues to use performance, setting and camera to inflect the dialogue suggestively. Inside her house, Clarisse has removed her pink top and wears a loose black t-shirt to match her skin-tight black leather trousers. A high ponytail pulls her hair back; gold bangles dangle on her wrists as she takes some perfume out of a pink make-up bag. This is a woman whose appearance is as immaculate as her well-appointed house, the walls of which are bright white. Clarisse tells Sabine astutely: 'You amuse me. You sound like you calculate every move, but in fact you're the opposite. You act purely on impulse.' Rohmer cuts to Sabine agreeing as Clarisse finishes her line; however, instead of framing Romand frontally, as he had done with Dombasle, he frames her from the side, at an angle which shows three-quarters of her face. She agrees that she

Fig. 1.6

is impulsive: 'That's why I need principles. I decide what I want in general … Anyway, you're like me.' But Clarisse disagrees: 'Ah no. Not at all. My only principle, if I have one, is to be guided only by love.' As they talk, Sabine walks towards Clarisse and the camera pans to follow her until it frames the two friends together. Clarisse sprays on some perfume, rubbing it in on each side of her neck with an extended finger (Fig. 1.6). Sabine then walks in front of her and puts on her cream cardigan. Clarisse's polished movements reach their zenith as she expands on her principles. She enters the frame to sit on the arm of a large chair, adopting a characteristic posture, thrusting her chin forward and looking down her nose.

To suggest the tension between characters conversing, Rohmer often uses a slightly longer take with characters moving both within the frame and in and out of it. Here, when Clarisse sits on the chair's arm, Sabine, in a precisely choreographed response, exits the frame on the left. Sabine's hostess now fully claims our attention and assumes a self-conscious pose: laying one hand on top of the other, interlacing her fingers, she moves her bottom further back, transferring more weight onto her arms, leaning forward and extending her neck. As she talks, Dombasle moves her right hand sharply in front of her, making visible her manicured nails with their pale pink varnish (Fig. 1.7). Romand and Dombasle's differences, those of physique, poise and manner, evoke the social differences between Sabine and Clarisse even before they discuss their respective milieux: Clarisse is apparently from an old bourgeois Le Mans family; Sabine's parents, as she tells Edmond, are 'from the colonies'. Perhaps they met at school or at college, when their shared experience obscured their different backgrounds. Now, though, Sabine notices them and this extended conversation with Clarisse establishes how she sees them.

Fig. 1.7

When Sabine, off-screen, says, 'You got married', Clarisse insists it was 'for the sake of convenience, and to please my family'. Sabine thinks differently: 'You've thought of nothing else since you were a babe in arms.' As she says this, Sabine walks back into frame and perches on the other arm of the chair, also crossing her hands in front of her (Fig. 1.8). When Clarisse argues that her own marriage is 'simply a concession to society', Sabine insists that 'it makes you feel more secure'. This is one of the film's most significant framings of Clarisse and Sabine. It emphasises their disagreement: on one arm of the chair, Dombasle faces the camera; on the other arm, Romand, in profile, faces Dombasle. Prominent against the white background, their costumes and hair reflect their opposing positions: Clarisse's black leather trousers, black t-shirt and blonde hair contrast with Sabine's creamy white cardigan and black hair. As Sabine says 'love changes', enunciating each syllable slowly, she leans back to face the camera more. Clarisse claims romantic idealism as a defence, leaning forwards, almost lecturing her friend. The scene comprises two shots, initially put together as a shot/reverse-shot sequence – the first shot was of Clarisse alone with her pink make-up bag; but the reverse-shot of Sabine develops into this extended take and panning movement,

Fig. 1.8

which comes to rest on the pair of them on the chair, framing them from thighs to head. Rohmer does not break the scene into close-ups of the two women; he wants us to see the way they position themselves, the way they move their hands and the way in which they relate to the setting and to each other. All these things elaborate the disagreement between the two friends.

The tension develops further outside Clarisse's house: as they walk slowly towards the camera, arm in arm, through the courtyard and gates, Sabine expresses in words what the interior sequence has expressed visually – the 'big difference' between them. The depth of field makes visible the grandness of Clarisse's house; the large stone gateway and the huge brown metal gates look about 500 years old (Fig. 1.9). Crucially, it is at this point that Sabine criticises Clarisse: 'You fit perfectly in your milieu. So you feel free as air, without realising your freedom comes from being accepted.' Rejecting this analysis, Clarisse stops and unlinks her arm from Sabine's; the framing emphasises Clarisse's height as she turns away from Sabine and fiddles with her scarf, stretching it across the back of her neck (Fig. 1.10). As they pause at the gateway between Clarisse's house and Le Mans' old town, Sabine explains: 'For me it's different. I have to leave my milieu.' Whereas Clarisse fits in comfortably to both private and public spaces, neither easily accepts Sabine; furthermore, while Clarisse travels between home and work by walking between two expensive properties in the same part of town, Sabine makes lengthy commutes between home and work, by train and by car.

Fig. 1.9

Fig. 1.10

Fig. 1.11

Rohmer continues to emphasise the tension between Clarisse and Sabine when he cuts to a close medium shot of the two friends as Clarisse, attempting reconciliation, puts her arm around Sabine, the latter holding her friend's hand over her shoulder. The camera pans with them as they walk back up the cobblestone street towards Clarisse's shop. Clarisse naively remarks, 'we're more or less from the same milieu'. This prompts Sabine to remove abruptly her friend's patronising arm, pointing out: 'Your father's a doctor; mine's dead. Your husband will be a doctor, like his father and yours.' As she says this, Sabine, with her hands on her hips, pulls completely away from Clarisse, though they both continue to walk up the street (Fig. 1.11). Clarisse provocatively tempts Sabine with, 'You could marry a doctor, an engineer, a lawyer too. You can seduce any man you want.' On this, Rohmer cuts to a reverse-shot of Sabine and Clarisse walking towards the camera up the street.

This sequence forcefully establishes their social positions and, therefore, a context for Sabine's daydreaming, one which makes understandable Sabine's earlier declaration to 'escape my background by an act of will'. When Clarisse asks if Sabine has someone in mind to marry, Sabine insists that she does not, then laughs and spins on her heel, walking away; but Clarisse's invitation to her brother's wedding party arrests her. After offering as an excuse her 'books from Paris', Sabine replies frankly, leaning against Clarisse's shop window as she does so: 'To tell you the truth, I like seeing you in the daytime when we're alone, but I'm not comfortable with your family.' 'And you want to find a new milieu!', exclaims Clarisse. Sabine steps away from the window: 'Yes, but the milieu of a man I love.' Finally, she agrees to come to the reception, but not the wedding, commenting, with an irony that is lost on her, 'weddings depress me'. She walks off, hands crossed behind her back.

Rohmer uses four locations for this conversation between Clarisse and Sabine: the inside of Clarisse's shop; the street between her shop and her home; the inside of Clarisse's home; the courtyard and street outside Clarisse's house, from where the pair retrace their steps back to Clarisse's shop. The proximity of these locations allows for the appearance of a continuous conversation; it also marks the integrity of Clarisse's social arena. Michel Serceau describes the importance of Clarisse's environment:

> Sabine's friend ... whose husband is a doctor, lives in the medieval part of a provincial town, a place with lots of antique shops and art shops ... The decision to live in very old restored houses in this part of town actually conveys the persistence of a system of values and tastes which are the legacy of the past. (2000: 24)

The film's settings express the social differences between Sabine and Clarisse, but importantly they are meaningful for Sabine as much as for us. When Sabine meets Edmond at the wedding reception, the film develops this system.

Despite her flat in Paris and her Parisian lover, Sabine's postgraduate study extends her dependency on her familial home; as she supports herself with a job in Le Mans, for part of the week she still sleeps in her childhood bedroom. When Sabine drives home, the view through the windscreen is of a flat countryside, grey under a cloudy sky. Sabine's destination is Ballon, twenty kilometres north of Le Mans, where she lives with her mother and sister in a modern house on a small street in a modest suburban area, a great contrast to Le Mans' old town. As she parks, Rohmer shows us a washing line hanging in her garden, two sheets drawn across it – such a thing would be unthinkable in Clarisse's Renaissance courtyard. Inside her house, Sabine invites her mother to come to the wedding reception that evening with her. Her mother declines, saying that she will be uncomfortable there, she will not know anyone: 'It's nice of them to invite me, but they don't care if I come. And since I don't want to…'. Sabine tries to persuade her mother to attend, if only to see the 'fantastic view'. Her mother chuckles like a kindly parent, knowing and sympathetic: 'I know the view. It's the one you see from the road.'

Daydreaming involves gazing off into space; in *Le Beau mariage*, it also involves looking at views through windows, either absentmindedly or curiously. Sabine looks through the windows of Clarisse's shop, of trains, of Clarisse's parents' house, of Claude's tower block and, lastly, of Edmond's Parisian chambers. Rohmer does not place Sabine behind window bars or frames; instead, he shows her looking in and out at views that do not belong to her. In Le Mans at the wedding reception and in Edmond's chambers, the views represent power, money and social status; Sabine daydreams of acquiring such a view for herself. Rohmer uses Sabine's gazing through windows as a rhetorical figure to evoke her perception of other people's lives. The shot of Sabine staring out of the window at Clarisse's parents house, looking at the 'fantastic view', forms a coda to Sabine's initial meeting with Edmond (Fig. 1.12). Furthermore, the event at which Clarisse introduces Sabine to Edmond is also the first of a pair of contrasting parties. The sophisticated wedding reception for Clarisse's brother, Nicholas, is held at Clarisse's parents' house; similarly, the second party, for Sabine's birthday, is held at her mother's house in Ballon, although this one is populated by bopping teenagers. The dramatic focus of both parties revolves around one guest's social uneasiness: Sabine at the wedding reception and Edmond at the birthday party. André Dussolier's Edmond is a stiff lawyer, as unlike Féodor Atkine's Simon as Clarisse is unlike Sabine. The film only ever shows him formally dressed in a suit, even at Sabine's birthday party, at which everyone else is younger and more casually dressed than him.

Fig. 1.12

After Clarisse's arch introduction, Rohmer frames Edmond and Sabine standing together in the garden, their backs towards the camera, looking out from the terrace of Clarisse's family home across the countryside (Fig 1.13). Sabine says: 'I love houses with views like this.' Edmond responds: 'For that you have to live in the country.' At that moment, Edmond is called away by a telephone call, this interruption rhyming with the earlier one that prompted Sabine to leave Simon. We follow Edmond to the telephone, in one of the film's two moments of separation from Sabine; urgent business calls him back to Paris and while on the telephone he asks the Pommiers, the cousins of Nicholas's bride, for a lift into town. He leaves without saying goodbye to Sabine, though he

Fig. 1.13

calls out to Nicholas and asks him to explain to 'everyone'. His sudden departure is justifiable, although it is rude of him not to tell Sabine that he is leaving; his haste indicates his commitment to his work and his lack of interest in Sabine; by initially only revealing this to us and not to her, Rohmer increases the sense of an ironic distance from Sabine. How can she not notice, we might ask, that he is not interested in her? This question automatically leads to a further one: why does she not notice? Presumably it is because her desire to find a husband overrides any rational assessment of the situation.

Alain Hertay suggests that Clarisse creates the 'character Sabine', by throwing her into the arms of Edmond and dictating her attitudes and actions (1998: 38). Michel Serceau also suggests that Clarisse lives vicariously, pushing Sabine to take risks that she would never imagine taking (2000: 111). The married woman gives herself the pleasure of a little adventure by proxy with her cousin, Edmond, whom she may find attractive; she certainly teases him flirtatiously when she introduces him to Sabine. Serge Daney perceptively describes Arielle Dombasle's Clarisse as Sabine's 'evil genie', her 'blonde demon' (1982: 56). The scene between them in the antique shop, following the wedding reception, allows us to see Clarisse's influence on Sabine. It comprises one shot, just over two minutes long; the camera frames them frontally throughout, panning occasionally while Sabine and Clarisse walk in and out of the frame. As Clarisse persuades Sabine to phone Edmond, they both handle valuable objects.

Sabine polishes the antiques and arranges them on a shelf, dressing the shop, ensuring its attractiveness to customers. Clarisse, as she talks, clasps a green vase to her chest, in front of the red cross of her scarf (Fig. 1.14). In a high-spirited, self-dramatising pose, standing with her hip pushed out, her weight resting on one side, her posture produces an exaggerated, model-like version of feminine poise that may irritate some. She looks upwards as she talks, pressing the extended fingers of one hand against her chest, clasping the vase with the other,

Fig. 1.14

then rubbing a long middle finger against it. 'I saw it in his eyes', she tells Sabine, 'and I saw in yours that he interested you. It was the first time I'd ever seen it, love at first sight. It was like a lightning bolt.' Clarisse's handling of the vase is not careless, but, in contrast to Sabine's careful arranging and polishing, she uses it as a prop for her story about 'love at first sight'. She can afford to pay for any breakages and she takes some things for granted. Again the film places Sabine's quest for a husband in a precisely observed economic context. The scene ends as it began, with Sabine centre-frame alone and exposed, her 'blonde demon' pushing her from off-screen.

Rohmer continues to interweave romance with socio-economic difference in the scene in which Sabine takes Edmond to buy some Jersey porcelain at a large country château. When she introduces Edmond to Madame de Saint-Biez, the latter recognises Edmond's name as being that of an established Le Mans family, whose social status she acknowledges. While they chat about his father, Sabine interrupts Edmond's conversation with Madame, as if annoyed by the easy way in which they have quickly established a rapport, one which excludes her. She attempts to close the deal and she does successfully negotiate a cheaper price with Madame de Saint-Biez for the porcelain; yet her apparent irritation with Madame and Edmond's connection manifests itself in unnecessary brusqueness. As a consequence, Madame treats Sabine like a trader. Furthermore, when the deal is done and Madame and Edmond resume their conversation, Rohmer shows us that Sabine has efficiently brought a box, tissue paper and adhesive tape, and her handling of the porcelain as she deftly wraps it up again invites comparison with Clarisse's use of the antiques as props for her fantasies. Outside, Sabine tells Edmond that she does not want to be a businesswoman, but she has been business-like with the woman.

The lift that Sabine gives to Edmond when she takes him to Madame de Saint-Biez's château contrasts strongly with the lift she gives to her ex-boyfriend, Claude, when she takes him to the tower block that houses the small council flat he shares with his wife and children; the destinations starkly symbolise their social status. Two shots show Claude and Sabine approaching his apartment: the first shows them in medium long shot walking along a balcony to a lift shaft; the second is a long shot that films them as tiny figures in the middle of a huge tower block. The camera tilts up after they enter the door, revealing the scale of this ugly modern building (Fig. 1.15). The first thing Sabine does when she enters his flat is walk towards the window and look out at the view of Le Mans' suburbs which Claude's window offers (Fig. 1.16); this seems to encourage her to explain her plans to get married. While she looks at the view, Claude says, 'But you'll depend on him'. After replying sharply, 'And you? Aren't you dependent on your wife, and she on you?', Sabine again looks out at the view, leaning right to extend her panorama, before turning round to approach him and declare: 'This may sound cynical but with a hardworking husband I'll be freer to do what I want, days and even evenings, than if I had a nine-to-five job.' 'Don't worry', she lies to Claude, 'I'm deeply in love.' While he gets her a drink, she sneaks a look at the rest of the flat; point-of-view shots reveal untidy rooms, including a broken light switch, which she fixes neatly. Their meeting ends with her saying, 'with you I couldn't move up'; he retorts scornfully: 'That's not moving up, it's social climbing.'

Fig. 1.15

Fig. 1.16

Claude's quotidian life represents for Sabine everything that she does not want: an unappealing council flat with children's messy bedrooms. As Alain Hertay points out, in the face of this Sabine declares her intentions more strongly (1998: 39); she lies about her love for Edmond and comes across as more self-seeking than the film elsewhere shows her to be. Claude is more concerned with equality with his wife than with a broken light switch, but Sabine perceives only an unattractive view and a messy apartment; she does not see the choice that Claude and his wife have made to strive for personal and professional equality. Significantly, Vincent Gauthier's Claude has a gentle manner, different to both the virile masculinity of Atkine's Simon and the stiff professionalism of Dussolier's Edmond.

Sabine has yet to work out how she can be independent professionally and personally, yet to work out what kind of relationship she wants to have with a man. Her revelation that she has resigned from her job and is going to get married surprises her mother, especially when Sabine says: 'To get a man to marry me, I mustn't sleep with him. I want to be respected, to be idealised by my husband. For that he must respect me.' A close-up of her mother shows her listening attentively to this; she responds: 'That's how people talked a hundred years ago.'

Sabine's confusion manifests itself in her contradictory behaviour: although she says that she wants to be idealised by a man, she takes the traditionally masculine role and pursues Edmond. The contrast between what Sabine says she wants and what she does provides the source for the film's scrutiny of her behaviour, revealing her self-delusion; but Sabine's interaction with various settings and characters simultaneously allows us to perceive the reasons for her behaviour. The result is that we can be both critical of her, yet sympathetic; we can see her as superficially obsessed with finding a man and securing a wealthy lifestyle, yet also see her yearning for independence and freedom as well as a relationship. This shapes the film's depiction of her pursuit of Edmond, which intensifies after her birthday party; the alternation between scenes of Sabine on trains and scenes of her telephoning Edmond quickens. Eventually, she invades Edmond's chambers and the final confrontation takes place. The scene in Edmond's chambers has many extraordinary elements; I have space to comment on only two of these.

While Sabine's visit to Claude's home suggestively uses her view from his council flat as part of its revelation of his modest financial circumstances, her visit to Edmond's Parisian chambers comparatively uses her view from his window, just as the lift she gives to Claude partners the lift she gives to Edmond. The setting is again important as a contribution to our ironic but sympathetic involvement with Sabine's plight: Edmond's inner office has light brown wallpaper, white woodwork and elegantly-curved shelves in one corner; but the most striking feature is the large tapestry that hangs on the wall behind him as he sits or stands at his desk. It is an old-fashioned form of wall decoration and it depicts a classical scene, a château or castle set in the middle of idealised parkland, some mounted figures in the foreground.[4] It symbolises Edmond's membership of a cultivated, almost aristocratic class; as Michel Serceau observes, 'the Parisian chambers of Edmond bear witness as much as the residences of his provincial cousins to the attachment to the styles of the past' (2000: 26). Sabine's arrival in his chambers panics Edmond and the scene uses as its framework his increasing efforts to avoid an embarrassing confrontation. When he first starts to explain himself, the telephone rings. He rushes towards it and the camera pans with him as he retreats behind his desk, as he does often in the scene; unfortunately for Edmond, the call extends his time with Sabine – his next client is going to be 15 minutes late. While he listens to the person on the telephone, he glances over at Sabine; this look motivates a cut to a medium shot of her. Sabine walks right, out of frame, towards the window and Rohmer cuts to a shot of her approaching it.

The full-length windows and floor-to-ceiling white curtains frame her dramatically as she looks out at the view, just as she did at Nicholas's wedding reception. Rohmer uses a point-of-view figure to show the view, but the bracketing shots do not show her face, only her back. Rohmer filmed the scene using only these windows as sources of light. As the film's sound engineer, Georges Prat, remembers, they waited for two days until the sunlight became appropriately autumnal (see Hertay 1998: 111–13). The decision to match the lighting schemes of the bracketing shots and the point-of-view shot allows the moment to impart a sense of mystery about Sabine's thoughts; without access to her face, we cannot be sure of what she is thinking. Nonetheless, although the film withholds the look on her face, the image of her standing by the window is quietly mournful. The decision to shoot in natural light for the interior, but set the exposure so that the view through the window is visible, also means that we can see what Sabine sees at the same time as we see her standing looking out. The inserted point-of-view shot through the window lasts three or four seconds – long enough for us to register it as embodying Sabine's view of a busy Parisian boulevard with eight-storey nineteenth-century apartment blocks, part of a central district, representative of a way of life from which Sabine is excluded.

As they talk, Sabine tries to leave four times; she reaches the door three times and each time Edmond manages to placate her and, therefore, avoid a confrontation. Only at the last attempt does her anger force her out of the door. Just as Sabine is pushing her way out, Edmond's next client, Madame Joindreau, comes in and Sabine collides with her. Though she apologises, the client insists that Sabine defer more obviously to her, pulling Sabine's arm and spinning her round. Understandably, this angers Sabine: 'I'd rather not see an old hag.' The client raises her hand to slap Sabine, who reacts by throwing the client's files down the stairwell, then stepping down herself. 'Who's that wild woman?' the client asks Edmond; 'Sorry, in our profession, we see all kinds.' He helps his client collect her papers and politely defers to her, doing what Sabine refused to do, united with her against Sabine. This is the film's second moment of separation from Sabine, and like the first it shows a side of Edmond which Sabine seems not to see.

The film ends with three short scenes. On a train, moving from right to left, from Paris to Le Mans, Sabine stands at a window looking out, smiling to herself about the scene she caused in his office. Then, inside Clarisse's shop, Sabine works with Clarisse. She blames Clarisse, perhaps clear-sighted at last: 'It was all your fault claiming it was love at first sight. It wasn't that at all.' Lastly, the film returns to the train. In a carriage, Sabine sits down opposite the young man who sat opposite her in the opening scene. They look at each other and smile. The music fades in. The end echoes the beginning, marking the artificiality of the construction. Though she has changed jobs and split up from Simon, Sabine is back on the train: we may wonder whether anything has changed in her, though the flirtation with the man sitting opposite looks hopeful. For Rohmer, the symmetry of the beginnings and endings in the first four *Comédies et proverbes* is 'a little bitter … disenchanted, ironic' (Legrand, Niogret & Ramasse 1986: 22). The repetition of the opening setting in the final scene encourages the feeling that the characters are trapped in their situations; however, as Rohmer points out, although the films end negatively, an ending of this sort 'leaves the door open for something more positive' (Hammond & Pagliano 1982: 220). By controlling the repetition and variation of elements such as train journeys, car journeys, views from windows and colours, Rohmer creates parallels and contrasts which point us to feelings and motivations that characters may not want to acknowledge openly. The overall effect is that the film shows Sabine's stubborn decision to marry to be wrong-headed, but it does so while exposing an insidious layer of class prejudice in contemporary France.

2. *Le Rayon vert*

There is a pronounced precision about *Le Beau mariage*: Rohmer prepared it meticulously, researched the project extensively and rehearsed the actors at length, directing their movements in detail.[5] However, by the time Rohmer had made his fourth *Comédies et proverbes*, *Les Nuits de la pleine lune*, which he shot, like *Le Beau mariage* and *Pauline à la plage*, on 35mm film stock with a finished script and schedule, he was frustrated with this way of working:

> For *La Collectionneuse* [1967], I hadn't written a script, but simply, day-by-day, loose pages, consisting solely of the dialogue. Since then, my films have become increasingly scripted. There's not a single moment of improvisation in *Les Nuits de la pleine lune*, where I even wrote the telephone responses that we don't hear. And so to avoid being pigeonholed in this Guitry-Pagnol category, I made, as a diversion, a holiday film last summer. I wrote absolutely nothing, not before, not after and not during the filming. (Quoted in Mauro 1985: 91)[6]

While editing *Les Nuits de la pleine lune* at the beginning of 1984, Rohmer decided to make a film that he would shoot on 16mm stock that summer in Biarritz. He had not written a script and nor would he ever. He only knew two things: that Marie Rivière would improvise the lead role amongst her family and friends and that her story would have some parallels with Jules Verne's short novel *The Green Ray* (1882).

Despite Rohmer's decision to embrace spontaneity, *Le Rayon vert* still evidences a structure based on the repetition of certain activities. Therefore, the discussion of *Le Rayon vert* that follows continues to focus on Rohmer's interest in daydreams, his use of movement/stasis oppositions as a dramatic method and his use of colours. The major framework of *Le Rayon vert* is the alternation between two types of scene: Delphine sitting down at mealtimes and/or at tables with groups of people who make her feel uncomfortable and Delphine walking around on her own. This chapter begins by describing the film's unusual production, before moving to sustained analyses of the two most significant mealtime scenes: the scene in which Marie Rivière and Béatrice Romand argue – the 'germ' of *Conte d'automne* – and the famous scene in which Rivière defends her vegetarianism. Following this, I discuss the depiction of Delphine ambling alone in places where she has gone to try to enjoy a holiday, first in Cherbourg, then in La Plagne and finally in Biarritz. Throughout the chapter, I return to the way in which Rohmer's filming of *Le Rayon vert* differs from his normal practices, for as well as being a story about a young woman struggling to enjoy her vacations, Rohmer's holiday film was a holiday from his usual way of working and, perhaps as a result, it is the film of his that seems to reflect most profoundly on his own artistry.

In working without script or a schedule, Rohmer renounced his usual control. As director of photography, Sophie Maintigneux, recalls, the gamble was to film a fiction film like 'a holiday film, to follow Delphine with complete freedom, and above all complete improvisation' (quoted in Durel 1986: 39). Rohmer had only four continuous collaborators working on location with him: Maintigneux, on photography; Claudine Nougaret on sound, simultaneously holding the boom and carrying the Nagra sound recorder; Françoise Etchegaray, acting as an all-round production manager, getting food, sorting out locations, liaising with officials; and Marie Rivière, the lead actress and the main collaborating improviser of the script. Rivière remembers that

> Rohmer hadn't actually written anything when he contacted me for this film. He told me the story of a girl who would be alone during the holidays. He explained some scenes, in Paris, in Biarritz and in the country. Then we quickly started to work on certain scenes, immersing ourselves in improvisation: the scene with the friends who 'counsel' Delphine at the start; the one with Vincent at the end. (Quoted in Carbonnier & Revault d'Allonnes 1986: 16)

Rohmer recalls, 'Le Rayon vert is completely improvised. Nothing was written. There is not a trace of writing. In certain cases, the actors improvised totally; they said what they wanted to say' (quoted in Legrand, Niogret & Ramasse 1986: 17). Rohmer depended upon chance meetings:

> It's a chance encounter with someone. Actually, I've found that throughout my life as a filmmaker I've met people who have inspired me. This isn't the first time. In particular, I'd met the actors in La Collectioneuse and above all Daniel Pommereulle, who, although he doesn't play the main role, is the spirit of the film. Actresses like Béatrice Romand, Arielle Dombasle, Pascale Ogier are very inspiring people with strong personalities. So, I need actors who are strong personalities. In the two last films [Le Rayon vert and Quatre aventures de Reinette et Mirabelle], it wasn't only that people could say their lines, but that they could project a romantic quality, albeit comic, and who bring with them a whole world to comic and dramatic situations. There, really, I am dependent on chance encounters. (Quoted in Legrand, Niogret & Ramasse 1986: 19)

Filming without a script or schedule imposed its own constraints. Instead of marking out positions on the set, Rohmer was forced to let performers, photographer and sound recordist improvise. He acknowledges the risk:

> There are things in improvisation that annoy me, odd habits, tics. It results in a kind of loss of time and content so that instead of giving more fluidity to the narrative, we get lost in completely pointless digressions ... So, I set off trying to avoid these pitfalls (which I haven't avoided completely, because at some points it appears forced). But I did try to avoid them, while filming as I usually film. In the end, I nearly succeeded because in my films there is normally a direction of the actors which isn't there. (Quoted in Ostria 1986: 34)

Rohmer admits that he was less able to control the actors' blocking, yet, in a film that reflects on the relative benefits of leaving things to chance and planning, he still imposes a structure on *Le Rayon vert* by alternating between Delphine ambling around and people talking at mealtimes, and by using intertitles to mark the days passing in July and August.

Le Rayon vert progresses in a linear way, staying with Delphine for all but one moment. The written dates introduce a diary-like element into the film's focus on Delphine but, especially in their sometimes abrupt introduction and in their acknowledgement of selection, they also signal the filmmaker's power of control over structure. Furthermore, the intertitles indicate the way that holidays often lack normal routines. The passing of time is not marked in the usual way, by work and weekends. It is not unusual on holiday to forget momentarily what day it is. For Delphine, though, the passing of days is significant because she is conscious of her holiday time disappearing; the intertitles mark the long period during which Delphine's unhappiness grows and the pressure on her to enjoy herself increases. Rohmer uses similar diary-like intertitles in two of his other holiday films, *Le Genou de Claire* and *Conte d'été*. In these cases, though, the intertitles signify the time passed as protagonists wait in one place for something to happen. Delphine does not wait around but her restlessness grows with her impatience as she feels the days of her holiday passing.

Comparing *Pauline à la plage*'s references to Matisse and *Les Nuits de la pleine lune*'s references to Mondrian with *Le Rayon vert*'s absence of visual references, Rohmer remarks that:

> When one makes a film of this genre, the image is less dominant than it is in other films. When one decides to give the actors freedom, one can't tell them: put yourself in this or that place. As a result, there are a lot more scenes with people sitting and scenes in which the frame changes, thanks especially to the use of the zoom lens. There is a style of reportage different to my other films. (Quoted in Ostria 1986: 35)

Filming improvised conversations around a table restricted Rohmer's use of shot/reverse-shot structures, though he argues that, seated at a table, people forgot about the camera and answered Rivière's questions more naturally. In one early sequence, the first mealtime scene, on 'mercredi, 4 juillet', Rivière and Rohmer collaborate as documentary interviewer and filmmaker. In a small urban garden, Delphine sits on the left of a table; an older man, a retired taxi driver (Basile Gervaise), sits facing the camera; his granddaughter (Virginie Gervaise) sits opposite him, with her back to the camera; on her right sits a young man (René Hernandez). They talk about the weather and then about holidays. Delphine asks the pensioner, from off-screen, 'What do you do for your holidays?' He replies: 'Me, nothing at all. I'm retired, on a pension. So I keep house. That's all I have to do.' Delphine interviews him: 'Don't you ever leave Paris?' He replies, 'Never.' The pensioner explains that he used to go to Jura, but 'I started taking holidays very late, because I worked a lot. I saw the sea for the first time when I was around sixty.'

The side framing of the retired taxi driver as he talks about his affection for Paris – he is a 'real Parisian', says the young man – includes a cluster of bright red roses by his head (Fig. 2.1). The image is beautifully composed: the wall behind the taxi driver is made out of grey breeze blocks, the rose bush and ivy climbing but not covering it; the combination of greenery, bright red roses and grey concrete sets off this conversation about Paris and the countryside. Moreover, throughout the scene, the background traffic noises are audible – at times

Fig. 2.1

prominent – on the soundtrack, adding atmosphere and heightening the presentation of an urban garden; the sound of scooters passing noisily in the background punctuates their discussion piquantly. When asked why he did not enjoy the mountains, the retired taxi driver chuckles that the ravines scared him. He insists on the charms of Paris – a park, the Seine: 'Who needs the sea? I get into water up to my ankles and I'm scared. I can't swim.' He laughs and with that Rohmer ends the scene.

The taxi driver's account of his lack of holidays surprises Delphine; his love of Paris and his final declaration that he cannot swim evoke a life different to the one she is living. His speedy, automatic delivery comes with a smile that hovers constantly on his face; despite his lack of holidays, he exudes warmth, contentment and a settled quality – things that elude Delphine. Rohmer describes this scene with the retired taxi driver as 'pure improvisation' (quoted in Legrand, Niogret & Ramasse 1986: 17) and in a scene like this he uses the techniques of Jean Rouch in *Chronique d'un été* (*Chronicle of a Summer*, 1961). *Le Rayon vert* does chronicle a summer, and Rohmer and Rivière work in a similarly collaborative way to Rouch and Marceline in *Chronique d'un été*; as Rohmer acknowledges, *Le Rayon vert* partly resembles a 'fictional documentary or a documentary fiction' (quoted in Philippon & Toubiana 1987: 9). Sophie Maintigneux worked as if shooting a documentary, with few lights, one gelatine and a zoom lens (Ostria 1986: 39). Having agreed some things with her, Rohmer encouraged Maintigneux to decide when to move the camera in following the improvised conversations (Ostria 1986: 35). Director and director of photography agreed beforehand that she should use the zoom to frame shots in response to the improvisations of Rivière, her friends and her family, which she did most evidently in this scene.

After the conversation with the taxi driver, Delphine visits her two sisters (Rivière's real sisters, Dominque and Isabelle Rivière), her brother-in-law (Claude Julien) and her niece and nephew (Laetitia Rivière and Alaric Julien). Rohmer stages the scene as if for a documentary, with the family sitting in a semi-circle and the camera (behind it, Rohmer, Maintigneux and Nougaret) closing the circle; in this scene, more than others, one becomes aware of the camera's ghostly presence. Delphine talks to her sisters about whether to join them in Ireland for a holiday. Delphine fiddles with a yellow feather as she expresses her reservations about Ireland, and while she talks Laetitia sneaks a glance at

Fig. 2.2

the camera. Laetitia tries to disguise her glance by directing her gaze up to the ceiling and turning her head round to look away. Having tested the reaction, she takes another look, this time confidently staring into the lens for about three seconds (Fig. 2.2). After this, in a moment of excitable triumph, she snatches the feather from Delphine, catching her aunt's attention. Delphine returns her attention briefly to Isabelle and the scene concludes with her decision not to join the family holiday.

As in the scene with the retired taxi driver, Rivière and Rohmer collaborate as documentary filmmakers: Delphine interviews Laetitia on her knee; when Isabelle's invitation distracts Delphine, Laetitia takes the opportunity to engage with the camera. This moment exemplifies the film's embracing of its quasi-documentary status; Laetitia's look at the camera puts pressure on the boundaries of *Le Rayon vert*'s fictional world: its existence as fiction is frangible.

The film combines this looseness with highly organised patterns in colour, setting and theme, and Rohmer often places the most improvised moments next to the most structured: the film cuts from this scene to show Delphine finding a playing card in the street, a Queen of Spades lottery card (Fig. 2.3). She passes a green lamppost and the violin music from the credits accompanies her find, thus linking the colour green, the cards and the music. A scene in which the film's fictional boundaries are challenged by the girl's acknowledgement of the camera precedes a short transitory scene in which the film's structure and the director's control is strongly re-asserted. That the film marks the first appearance of the motif of the playing card – a symbol of two kinds of games of chance: card games and the lottery – with the violin music from the credits indicates that Delphine's fate may be controlled by someone else.

Fig. 2.3

Le Rayon vert is a rare instance of a Rohmer film that uses music whose origin lies outside the fictional world; another instance is *Conte d'hiver*, discussed by William Rothman (2004). More frequently, Rohmer's films use music whose origins are within the fictional world, as in *Ma nuit chez Maud* (*My Night with Maud*, 1969), *Le Genou de Claire*, *Conte de printemps* and *Conte d'automne*. Both *Le Rayon vert* and *Conte d'hiver* are interested in fate, destiny, control and chance and both films use music to allude to the mysterious aspects of the author's intervention. *Le Beau mariage* and *Conte d'hiver* are examples of Rohmer films that use music that initially accompanies the title sequences, but which we then hear at moments during the film. *Le Beau mariage* repeats the music from the credits during Sabine's birthday party and this is the only piece of music we hear in the film. In *Conte d'hiver*, the central character, Félicie (Charlotte Véry), attends a production of Shakespeare's *A Winter's Tale*; during it, the tune from the opening credits, which we heard played on a guitar, is repeated on a flute. William Rothman writes of this moment: 'When the flutist plays this tune, we can recognise it, but it is not possible for Félicie to do so. Her experience of this moment and ours diverge. Recognising this tune, remembering the prologue, we feel that the film is revealing a sign to us, but not to her' (2004: 328). Similarly, in *Le Beau mariage*, the music has associations which are available to us but not to Sabine. *Le Rayon vert* differs from both *Le Beau mariage* and *Conte d'hiver* in that its music remains outside the fictional world, unheard by Delphine.

The intervention of the music and playing card marks the film's interest in control and chance. In one of the two major mealtime scenes, where she talks to her friends, Delphine hesitantly suggests that her belief in fate may be significant. This memorable scene revolves around a confrontation between Béatrice Romand and Marie Rivière. Both have distinctive individualities: Romand has an extraordinary power and energy; Rivière's tendency to yield to low spirits comes with the potential for both an airy silliness and a genuine searching for authenticity in social roles. The scene, which takes place on 'dimanche, 8 juillet', begins with Delphine, in a red jacket, walking past some large houses. Various green objects catch the eye: a dark green Mini, green trees and hedges, a green gate with a red sign on it. Then, as Delphine notices a small green poster on a lamppost, the music recommences. A close-up of the poster reveals its legend: 'Regain contact with yourself and others'; the poster promises, 'group or private sessions'.

Inside the garden, Delphine receives advice from three friends, Béatrice (Béatrice Romand), Françoise (Rosette) and Manuela (Lisa Heredia). As he does in the presentation of an argument between two female friends in *Le Beau mariage*, Rohmer works the confrontation between Béatrice and Delphine into the framings, costumes, settings and performances. Although Rohmer's commitment to record the actors' improvisations limits him, the scene has a precise shape. Therefore, to begin with, we see Delphine and Béatrice sitting on either side of a corner of the table (Fig. 2.4). Béatrice Romand wears a minidress of the brightest red yet seen; it differentiates her from the greenery of the garden and complements her loud and aggressive questioning: 'Why

Fig. 2.4

don't you go on holiday alone?' Béatrice's haranguing of Delphine takes place across the white triangle of the table's corner at the bottom of the frame. This corner points to the corner of the house in the middle of the frame; the line made by both separates the two women and marks the opposition between them. As Béatrice asks why Delphine does not go on a group holiday, the camera pans towards her, until it stops with the corner of the wall just visible on the left of the frame.

Contrasting the backgrounds, this pan imitates a shot/reverse-shot pattern, even though it remains one take, in which Rohmer captures the comic improvisations of Rivière and Romand. Both actors are intensely physical; even sitting down they both gesture and move in fascinatingly expressive ways. Romand, for example, repeatedly uses a teaspoon to punctuate her words. When Béatrice's suggestion of a group holiday fires up Delphine's defensiveness, the latter responds: 'Are you crazy?' Béatrice counterattacks with: 'Are you prejudiced? What's wrong with groups?' As their voices get louder, their words overlap and Béatrice picks up the spoon and waves it in front of her. When she subsequently pesters Delphine with 'You solve it by making an effort', Delphine throws her hands in the air and looks up in desperation, but Béatrice presses on (Fig. 2.5). Harassed by a monologue that Delphine finds increasingly hard to follow, her physical agitation comically increases: she raises her eyebrows, exaggerating a frustration felt more deeply than she might acknowledge; she shrugs her shoulders and speaks with long pauses and embarrassed laughs. Delphine repeatedly presses her chest or head when defending herself against Béatrice's attacks. Her outbursts pressurise Delphine, who occasionally recovers strength enough to turn sharply towards Béatrice, throwing up her hands and trying to talk; Béatrice speaks so loudly and quickly that Delphine's nervous interjections fail to find acknowledgement. When Delphine grabs her head and pushes up her hair, as if Béatrice gives her a headache, Béatrice almost screeches at Delphine: 'We're your friends, we want to help', she says, trying to recruit Manuela and Françoise, although neither has yet committed themselves (Fig. 2.6). Delphine opens her hands, then brings them together in a prayer-like gesture before clasping the side of her head, pushing her hands together, touching her chest and finally throwing her fingertips at Béatrice. Béatrice responds by taking up the spoon and pushing it into the space in front of Delphine, beating the air with it to emphasise her points. Rivière as Delphine simply fiddles ineffectually with the cake crumbs left on a plate, pushing them around and rubbing her fingers to brush them off.

Fig. 2.5

Fig. 2.6

The gestures of Romand and Rivière generate the interest of this scene but both actors also have particular ways of talking. Thus, for example, when Delphine says that the problem is that they only see each other now and again, and when they do Béatrice always does all the talking, Béatrice snaps, 'I've something to express and I express it.' Almost hysterical, Delphine replies: 'I have lots of things to express, but I don't express them.'

Romand responds in the most extreme manner yet: slowly enunciating each syllable loudly – Béatrice instructs Delphine: 'So, express yourself.' As she says this, she uses the spoon to point to Delphine, almost hitting her in the chest with it, extending her arm fully, as if grasping a microphone or passing a baton (Fig 2.7). 'We want you to express yourself'; Romand repeats the thrusting gesture with the spoon, but also marks the beat of each syllable with it: 'Nous sommes toutes écoutes' – 'We're all ears.' She over-pronounces each consonant and vowel, rolling her 'r's and spitting out the three 't's of 'toutes écoutes'; simultaneously, she leans forward, brushes her hair out of the way and cups her right hand to her ear in a sarcastic gesture of avid listening (Fig. 2.8). As Romand continues to enunciate slowly, she bounces the spoon on her fingers, leaking energy, before gesturing violently with it, Béatrice's vigorous confrontation penetrating Delphine's defences. Flustered by these attacks, our heroine returns to fiddling with the crumbs; Rohmer closes out this part of the scene with 'You mustn't stagnate'; he then cuts to Manuela.

Fig. 2.7

Fig. 2.8

Manuela is softer; but she, too, confronts her friend: 'Listen Delphine, in any case, you know it's finished with Jean-Pierre now. Either you meet someone new or you live with a memory.' Delphine hopes to find a 'new guy', but worries 'What can I do?' Manuela declares her supernatural powers: 'We can consult your stars, I can make the spirits talk tonight. I can make tables turn … You must have beliefs.' At this point, Delphine, in the framing of her and Béatrice that has been central, begins a fey speech about her beliefs with: 'Je crois, je crois, je crois, je crois.' As Rivière speaks, she holds her fingers flat against her upper chest, inclines her head to one side and looks up in a pose of exaggerated romance, getting carried away in a sweet but potentially irritating manner

Fig. 2.9

(Fig. 2.9). Delphine's dreamy vagueness is the complete opposite of Béatrice's pragmatism. While she gesticulates, Manuela sits like a fortune-teller or witch stroking a black cat (Fig. 2.10).

Rohmer describes how some scenes in *Le Rayon vert* were more difficult to film because the actors had to deliver lines that were essential to the plot, 'moments where

Fig. 2.10

actors vaguely knew where they were going' (quoted in Legrand, Niogret & Ramasse 1986: 17). When filming this scene, Rohmer told Heredia to intervene to keep the improvised discussion on the right track; it is appropriate, therefore, that Manuela professes that she can read cards to predict the future, even more so because Heredia was also the editor of the film:

She says things that move forwards in a precise direction. But at this moment here, I had spoken about it with Marie. It was she who had told me these stories of the cards; the stories with the colour green came from me. Everything is mixed up. As far as Béatrice Romand is concerned, she knew nothing. She arrived like that and all she knew was that the other one didn't want to go to a holiday club. (Quoted in Ostria 1986: 35)[7]

The film's editor, playing a friend of the protagonist, introduces the subject of superstitions and fate as explicitly as Rohmer did when he cut from the scene in which Laetitia stares at the camera to Delphine finding the playing card on the street.

The recurrence of green and red, the playing cards, the music and the green ray all relate to the film's interest in chance – Delphine declares to Manuela that she believes in 'things that crop up in life, things that happen all by themselves, things about love' – yet, paradoxically, it is through these structures and patterns that Rohmer asserts his control over his characters, even though he has attempted to loosen his control of the production generally. The motifs of the film revolve around chance, probability and superstition; Delphine's story centres on the relationship between leaving things to luck and intervening, improvising and planning. During filming Rohmer inevitably chose to keep some things that he chanced upon and discard others; furthermore, despite the flexibility and looseness of Le Rayon vert's production, Rohmer still imposed a structure. The horoscopes, the playing cards and the use of green were all planned (Carbonnier & Revault d'Allonnes 1986: 16), although, as the director recalls, Rivière told him the story about finding the cards, which he then incorporated. Manuela functions as Rohmer's agent in that she introduces the topics of superstition and belief, asking Delphine, 'Don't you believe in luck, in the cards, in the stars, nothing?' Delphine believes 'in things like playing cards you find in the street. Me, I find them.' While Manuela authoritatively confirms that she can read omens, reaching behind her to retrieve a copy of Elle, Delphine explains: 'What's weird is that I met a medium, a friend of mine, who told me that green would be my colour for the year. It's really weird but since then – perhaps I'm just noticing it – I keep running into green things.' Although Delphine and the film both allow for the possibility that maybe she is just noticing green things, Manuela teases her, suggesting that she will meet a little green man. Delphine shrugs if off, but Béatrice adds, 'Ah yes, it's the colour of hope', then asks Manuela to pass the magazine so that she can read the horoscopes: 'Unaware that you're just waiting for Prince Charming, you're alone and that seems to depress you. A vicious circle, but you're too stubborn to change.' The reference to 'Prince Charming' is a vernacular commonplace, but this film operates like a fairytale and Delphine at times acts like someone who believes in fairytale romances: 'I'm not stubborn', she gloomily protests, 'life's stubborn towards me.' On this, Rohmer cuts to a shot of the black cat stalking away along a narrow roof; it looks back once, then disappears.

Within this scene comes the film's only moment of separation from its protagonist and, as in *Le Beau mariage*, it conveys important information. While Delphine sits alone on some concrete steps in another part of the garden, Béatrice, Manuela and Françoise sit at the table. Françoise explains that Delphine's relationship with Jean-Pierre is finished, and she goes off to find Delphine; Manuela tells Béatrice that Delphine has been alone for two years. Although Delphine phoned Jean-Pierre earlier to ask him about staying in his holiday home and referred to him when talking to Isabelle about Ireland, this is the first time that the film reveals to us that her relationship with him is over.

Joining her on the steps, Françoise asks Delphine what the matter is; after some sobs from Delphine, Françoise invites her to join her family on holiday in Cherbourg. Rohmer had not planned to go to Cherbourg; the idea only came when Rosette invited them while filming this scene in Paris (Saada 1986: 25). For Rohmer, the Cherbourg sequence exemplifies his reliance on chance:

> We filmed an entire sequence in the house of people [Rosette's family] I didn't know and in a town [Cherbourg] that I didn't know either; I had refused to make an advance journey to get to know them, because there was a risk that the essential things would be said at that first meeting, to the detriment of filming, where the freshness of everything would have been lost. (Quoted in Mauro 1985: 93)

Once again, although the Cherbourg section relies on Rohmer's documenting of improvised group discussions around tables, it is also highly structured: eight scenes show Delphine's five days in Cherbourg with Françoise's family; in each scene her misery increases as her isolation from the family increases.

This progressive isolation is the key strategy of the 20-minute Cherbourg section. The first scene, on 'mercredi, 18 juillet', shows Françoise and Delphine meeting a young man near the port. While Françoise is pointing out various local sights, Delphine spots him; as she does so, she moves towards Françoise, as if hiding herself from unwanted attention. Delphine is nervous and giggly, shy and excitable; Françoise brazenly faces whomever they have spotted, her insouciance suggesting that flirting with young men frequently occupies her. Delphine wants to meet someone, but she stands apart from Françoise's social game of overt flirtatiousness; sincerity and authenticity prevent indifference; her friend's devil-may-care attitude alienates Delphine, who is unable to be light-hearted about romance. Françoise invites the young man, Edouard (Eric Hamm), over. He is a sailor, leaving for Ireland the next day.

Rohmer stages the scene in the corner of a walkway, bordered by a white rail and a low wall; in the background is the estuary. Françoise leans back against one side of a corner of the rail. Delphine leans back on the other side of the corner. An open panorama of the port forms the background for the threesome, but the rail and wall add structure to the image, breaking up the relationship between foreground and background. Within the corner of the rail, the actors move their bodies in response to each other and in re-

Fig. 2.11

sponse to the rail: Françoise leans back against the rail, confidently facing outwards, elbows resting on it as if she is leaning against a bar in a nightclub. In the long shot of Edouard, the rail leads the eye to him; as he approaches the women, he adopts a similar pose, sidling up alongside the rail and eventually leaning one side of his body on it as he faces Françoise. The corner has allowed Delphine and Françoise to face each other, but Delphine finds herself stuck between Françoise and Edouard (Fig. 2.11). Unlike the other two, she fidgets incessantly, her smiles resembling grimaces. Eventually, she

volunteers an excuse for not going out with him – 'Dining with the family.' Reaching a peak of uneasiness, she walks away from them both; Delphine does not want to meet someone casually like this.

The film cuts to the second Cherbourg scene: dinner in the garden. The camera set-up replicates that used for the meals with the taxi driver and with Béatrice, Manuela and Françoise. Delphine sits next to a handsome man in his thirties; he later appears wearing a red headscarf and is presumably one of Rosette's brothers. The other man, the father of some of the children we see, older and plumper than the one who appears in the red headscarf, sometimes wears a blue jumper; he arrives and places a tray of pork chops on the table in front of Delphine, inviting everyone to help themselves. Delphine tells the man in blue, 'I don't eat meat'. He appears baffled. Off-screen, someone asks if she does not like meat; Delphine says no.[8]

In 1984, vegetarianism was less common than now, although it may still be un-usual in France. Rohmer uses it for two reasons. Firstly, despite the valid arguments of vegetarianism, Delphine's refusal of meat is symptomatic of her whimsy; her delicate sensibility regarding vegetables and meat is not an affectation to her, but it separates her from people she meets. Secondly, although her refusal of meat surprises the family, they quiz her rudely about it. They do not plan to do so, but they inevitably group together against Delphine.

'Does she eat fish?', an off-screen voice asks; 'No, not much', replies Delphine. The camera pans to frame Delphine and the older man in blue, before coming round further to include a blonde-haired woman, presumably his wife. He asks if Delphine has any health problems. While she responds, Rohmer cuts briefly to a two-shot of the man in red and the dark-haired woman on his left, before returning to the previous framing of the blonde woman and the man in blue. The two shots compare couples who stare quizzically at Delphine and the combination of these shots directs attention to the family looking at Delphine, waiting for her to answer. The family interrogates Delphine because she does not conform to their sense of what is normal. They may think their questioning harmless, but Rohmer exposes the pressures of French familial conformity, demonstrating Delphine's isolation from a family who appear unaware of their hardness towards her. As with *Le Beau mariage*, *Le Rayon vert* stays close to the central character but sketches in a social context.

Delphine justifies her choices: 'At home, I eat grains, I cook things.' The blonde woman asks, 'Dairy products?' Delphine confirms this, then adds 'We don't need meat.' We see the third couple, Françoise and Hughes, who say nothing. The man in red says, unhelpfully but apparently innocently, 'Must be a problem when you're at other people's.' Delphine shrugs, 'Like here.' Everyone but Delphine laughs at the inadvertent gaffe that Delphine's neighbour made; the cosy chuckling excludes her. Even worse, the blonde woman off-screen comments, 'We can buy her what she likes.'

The references to Delphine in the third person highlight the power of accumulated knowledge that binds a family together; although they have welcomed Delphine to their holiday home, at the first sign of her difference to them they ignore her feelings. Despite the improvised gestation of the Cherbourg sequence, Rohmer efficiently sets forth Delphine's isolation within this family setting, and he does so by implying that she is not wholly responsible. With good intentions, Françoise embarrasses her at the port with the sailor; the family then carelessly gang up on her. Delphine begs her hosts 'Don't buy anything special for me.' 'Shellfish?' 'No, that's out too.' This provokes murmurs of disbelief and they continue as if they think she has not understood what shellfish is: 'Lobster? Crabs?' Delphine declines, 'No, they're animals.' The scene amuses – Marie Rivière is an accomplished comic actress – but it also censures the French bourgeois family in an almost Chabrolian way, although it is important not to over-emphasise this; Rohmer wants us to feel that these are social blunders we all could make.

The humour stems from Delphine's awkwardness in almost every situation; her whims easily irritate people. Only her morose, lonely wandering provides an escape from her prickly delicacy in groups. Yet Delphine has a vibrant physical presence and a keen sensibility for ephemeral beauty; her vegetarianism belongs to this. She tries to explain: 'Me, I don't think we should. It's especially red-blooded animals.' As she laughs nervously, the man in blue asks, 'So when a pork chop is put in front of you, what you see is the animal – is that it?' A cut to Françoise finds her arguing that a lettuce which wilts is also 'dead'. Cutting back to Delphine mid-sentence, the camera starts to zoom into a close-up as she elaborates, hesitating and pausing as she explains 'to me a lettuce is very far removed; it's much more remote from me than meat, than an animal'. The zoom into a close-up focuses on Delphine as intently as the rest of the family do; as she talks she sighs, blows out her lips, hunches her shoulders and looks off into the distance to her right. She talks self-consciously about what she thinks and, with the slow zoom forward, Rohmer and Maintigneux capture an extraordinary performance from Rivière: 'A lettuce

is more, it's a friend, it's lighter, it's … vegetables are airier, I don't know, they have…'
She stumbles; off-screen the blonde woman bluntly completes with '…no blood'.

The slow zoom into a close-up of Rivière intensifies our focus on Delphine as her justification becomes more abstract. The family pressurise Delphine in this scene, as much as Béatrice does in the earlier table conversation; and yet her distracted justification – 'a lettuce … is a friend' – is so humorously eccentric that we can understand the family's reaction. Rivière began her explanation softly. However, as the discussion continues her excitability increases; in particular, when the man in red comments that as a boy the sight of blood and meat at the butchers put him off meat (now he buys it in the supermarket), Delphine professes: 'That is the proof that it's completely a question of conscience, awareness of things. I think that's wrong because you eat meat, because you don't care what you're doing or how an animal is killed. That's wrong!' During Delphine's animated speech, Rohmer inserts several shots of family members hungrily devouring the pork chops, chewing the meat with concentration; as her justification becomes more proselytising, the camera ranges around the table finding bafflement on the faces of her hosts. The humour of her performance comes from the speed with which she rises to a pitch of excitement as she argues that everyone should give up meat: meat is 'heavy – I like to aerate myself'. Rivière's volubility stresses how out of place Delphine is here. The man in red offers her a bowl of flowers, but even these are refused by Delphine: 'To me a flower is poetic; it's a picture.' The scene ends and we cut to the following day.

The third Cherbourg scene takes place on 'jeudi, 19 juillet': in the foreground of a medium long shot, Françoise is on the swing in the garden, her boyfriend, Hughes, gently pushing her; in the background, Delphine is lying on the lawn, chatting with the eldest of the children. While Françoise and Hughes play on the swing with overtly sexual gestures,

Fig. 2.12

Delphine spends time with the children.There are three couples in Cherbourg, all of whom know each other well; Delphine is the odd one out. On his last push, Hughes playfully cups Françoise's breasts in his hands as a way of slowing her swing; she laughs up at him as he steps out in front and stops her. She gets up and they embrace; there's a palpable sense of a young couple lounging around on a hot summer afternoon feeling aroused (Fig. 2.12). As he receives her, he asks, 'Want to help pick strawberries?' Françoise answers him with another kiss and a nuzzle. As they leave, the young girl   takes the opportunity to play on the swing, asking Delphine if she wants a go: 'Not really', replies Delphine typically, 'swings make me nauseous.' Again, she provokes bafflement: 'You never went on a swing as a kid?' 'I told you, it makes me sick.'

Rohmer now reverses the deep-space relationship of foreground and background; Françoise and Hughes canoodle in the background, while Delphine and the child play on the swing in the foreground. The child questions Delphine annoyingly; she is naturally curious about the grown-up playmate and guest, but she adopts some of the prying tactics of her parents, continuing to ask questions of Delphine, who replies passively, sighing and touching her chest in a gesture of gloomy frustration. Visible in the background, Françoise and Hughes kiss. Delphine leans her elbow on a higher swing and clasps her forehead, as this persistent child asks, 'Do you like to sail?' She winces at this and lets out, 'Boats make me sick too, sweetie' (Fig. 2.13). Here, as elsewhere, the humour originates in Rivière's performance; as Delphine, she repeatedly comes close to a comic exaggeration of despair; yet, for all Delphine's self-dramatising, her emotions feel authentic.

Fig. 2.13

Rohmer cuts from this framing of contrasting couples to a richly expressive insertion that further lays stress on the contrast between Delphine and her hosts: a long shot of a table in the sun reveals that the other four adults, the two couples who harassed Delphine about her vegetarianism, are talking quietly amongst themselves (Fig. 2.14). This long shot of the family offers a view of togetherness that is also an exclusion. Sitting in a verdant garden, they may not realise that they exclude Delphine, but the insertion emphasises Delphine's situation to us. When Rohmer returns to Delphine and the inquisitive girl, a tall hedge and a blackcurrant bush surround them; as they eat blackcurrants, the girl asks: 'Got a boyfriend?' (Fig. 2.15). This is an innocent question for a girl who looks as though she is on the verge of puberty, but for Delphine it pries uncomfortably. She lies without hesitation: 'Yes, I have

Fig. 2.14

Fig. 2.15

a boyfriend.' Perhaps Delphine lies because she does not want to appear different to this girl; perhaps she hopes that a positive answer will prevent further questioning. It does not: 'Why didn't he come with you?' leads to further lies. The girl asks Delphine if she plans to phone her boyfriend; the shot ends with her replying, 'I've no plans now, things just happen.' A return to Françoise and Hughes, cuddling in the hammock, again pointing up the contrast between Delphine and this affectionate young couple, is followed by a shot of the four other adults at the table again, now playing Scrabble. Then, in ironic conclusion to this process of isolating Delphine, Rohmer cuts to a shot of Delphine sitting by a bucket, playing half-heartedly with a naked toddler (Fig. 2.16). There are three

Fig. 2.16

couples in Cherbourg, all of whom know each other well; Delphine is the odd one out. Delphine could be playing Scrabble with the adults, but she has retreated from persistent questions and taken refuge with a child too young to talk. The progression of these shots and the trenchant cutting between them highlights her unsociable moping.

On the following day, 'vendredi, 20 juillet', the two older girls are on the swings in their swimming costumes; the rest of the family are at the table in the garden. The table almost fills the box-like framing; on the far left sits the blonde woman, on the far right sit Françoise and Hughes, still absorbed with each other and apart from the others. Delphine sits between the younger man, who wears his red headscarf, and his dark-haired partner. The hostility to Delphine escalates in this scene. It is filmed in one shot and throughout it the

Fig. 2.17

camera again ranges around the characters, all of whom sit behind the table in a semi-circle; this is the fourth sequence of its kind, when the camera occupies a position outside the space, a reverse angle impossible without interrupting the improvisation. It begins as a medium two-shot of the man in red and Delphine who seem to be sharing a joke as Delphine seems unusually happy and relaxed (Fig. 2.17). The dark-haired woman asks Delphine if she wants to visit the beach tomorrow, to go sailing. The houseguest hesitates, then apologetically but unsurprisingly adds, 'Sailing, er – OK for the beach,

but sailing makes me sick.' Her refusal conforms to expectations about her inability to settle or feel at ease, but the hosts take it strangely: 'You get seasick? Pisces isn't your sign then.' 'No', confirms Delphine, 'I'm Capricorn.' Thus far, the family's reaction to Delphine's refusals remains polite; however, when Delphine observes that her neighbour in the red head-scarf is also a Capricorn, then asks the female astrologist what it means, the reply hints at ridicule: 'It's the sign of a goat climbing the mountain – all the way up.' Delphine suspects mockery; she purses her lips as the dark-haired woman adds 'but it's usually alone – that's a bit like you. Don't you think so?' Delphine agrees that it could be.

Presumably unaware of what they are doing, the family join against Delphine, circling around her quirks; given the opportunity to gang up again, both married couples direct their enquiries towards her. The husband in blue comments off-screen with blustering insensitivity: 'It's true, we haven't known you long, but we've the feeling that every time we propose something, it's "No, I'd rather not, no, not really".' His 'we've the feeling' horribly admits that these four have been discussing Delphine; the tactlessness contained in his politeness is so relevant to Delphine's experiences in *Le Rayon vert* that we might forget that the actors improvised this dialogue. Delphine defends herself, saying that she has 'been nice'. Initially, she does this jokingly, fiddling dreamily with first a lighter and then a cigar as she talks. But, as the attacks increase, the roving camera pans back and forth across the group, establishing that she is caught between the two couples as she was before, all eyes turned inwardly upon her. As the man in blue asks, 'what would really interest you?' Delphine looks close to tears. Beside him, the blonde-haired woman sits staring sulkily at Delphine. This framing of her prompts the most bizarre comment yet: when Delphine says she likes going for walks, the scene climaxes with the blonde-haired woman calling Delphine 'a plant', to which Delphine, astonished, responds: 'I am a plant?' The blonde woman nods and Rohmer cuts.

The abrupt cut away from this scene underlines the peculiarity of the insult. The surface holiday charm and relaxed meals do not disguise the intolerance of Delphine's whimsy, her apparent head-in-the-clouds romanticism. The family behave politely, never raising their voices; nonetheless a barrier exists between them and Delphine. Although only one-and-a-half minutes long, this single-shot scene feels longer. Panning around the five characters grouped at one end of the table, the ranging movement of the camera emphasises the way in which Delphine's hosts stare at her and press her.

Fig. 2.18

The cut introduces a single-shot scene: on the beach, the children and the three adult couples are all playing in the sea with a ball; the camera pans left then right with the ball. It then pans extreme right to reveal in long shot Delphine paddling morosely alone in a mini-skirt and long black shirt, unlike everyone else in bathing costumes (Fig. 2.18). The image amuses because it conforms to the picture that *Le Rayon vert* builds of Delphine, forever engaged with her own daydreams; but there is irony in the camera movement's revelation of where Rohmer has placed the actors for this short scene at the sea. The slow pan from the happy family playing together, oblivious to Delphine, isolated and fully dressed, comically confirms the conversation of the preceding scene and introduces the next.

Rohmer moves from Delphine isolated on the beach to her dawdling along a country path, buffeted by a wind that agitates the trees and bushes and provides – with the roar of the sea, which we hear but do not see – the soundtrack of this scene. She zigzags away from the camera along a path bordering fields and the nearby cliffs. Only her faded pink plimsolls off-set the greens of the grass, trees and bushes and the blues of Delphine's outfit – pale blue trousers and jumper, a blue jacket slung over her shoulder. Taking lolloping steps, she brushes against the hedges; Rivière's gait has a long stride, but she ambles rather than marches and the wind blows around her so strongly that she appears frail. When she comes to a crossroads in the rough track, she walks up to a gate and looks over it; in the distance, we can just make out the Normandy clifftops. She turns and wanders off in a new direction; the camera pans with her. Unsure of the direction she wants to take, after a few steps, she hesitates then wanders across the track, circling back until she sees a narrow path between two tall hedges, its tunnel-like entrance barely visible. She pauses, then walks away from the camera into the path. As she enters the path, she brushes the hedges above and beside her with her hand, engaging with the leaves and disappearing into the foliage.

Delphine continues to touch the overhanging ferns and flowers, smelling her fingers after brushing them along the hedges. Stopping to draw a flowery branch gently towards her, she smells its scent and then ambles on past the camera. Rohmer cuts to a shot of a rickety wooden gate; Delphine walks into shot and leans her arms on the gate, looking over it. A point-of-view shot follows: sea mist surrounds the field and trees, their tops blown roughly by the wind. When the film returns to Delphine, she turns slowly around and leans back to rest against the gate. A glance to her right introduces another point-of-view shot of tree tops blown vigorously. The noise of the sea has increased in volume. Two other shots follow, showing bushes being blown; then Rohmer returns to a shot of Rivière's head and shoulders: hair agitated by the wind, she sobs, looking up and around as she does so (Fig. 2.19).

Fig. 2.19

The moment reveals her misery to us, but it also reveals that the exact cause of her misery is unknown. We are not sure if she is moved to tears by the dramatic countryside and weather or if her sense of loneliness suddenly feels acute. Delphine's touching of the hedges connects with the later moment in the Alps when she touches the snow; she wants to connect with the natural environment and Rohmer conveys a wonderful sense of her absorbing her surroundings in a way that exemplifies her earlier declaration that 'lettuce is a friend'.

When Delphine returns she discovers that Françoise's family have also been for a walk, but their relationship with nature differs from Delphine's. As the latter approaches her hosts, Françoise and the blonde woman walk towards her carrying armfuls of wild flowers; Delphine accuses her friend: 'You're destroying nature.' When they offer her some she refuses them, saying, 'I don't cut flowers.' The film marks their blithe ignoring of her sensible ecological concern: the blonde woman does not wait for Delphine to finish talking.

Unhappy in Cherbourg, she returns to Paris with Françoise. There, she is approached by a pick-up artist, a *dragueur* in French, someone who casts a wide net; for Delphine, it is the crudest kind of encounter, one in which sexual availability is not disguised as romance. After this off-putting meeting, and arguably at her lowest point after her experiences in Cherbourg and Paris, Delphine decides to do what she had earlier scorned and visit Jean-Pierre's apartment in the Alps. Only 16 kilometres from the Italian border, in the extreme southeast of France, La Plagne is a ski resort, 2,000 metres up in the Alps, a long way from Paris and even further from Cherbourg, in the extreme northwest of France. Delphine's visit to La Plagne is important because she has been there before with Jean-Pierre; the locals know her as Jean-Pierre's girlfriend. When she arrives, though, she finds herself locked out of his apartment and decides to go for a walk.

Delphine likes rambling yet although people hike in the Alps in the summer, this was not what she had wanted to do. One consideration is that she is going somewhere out of season, to a ski resort in the summer. Delphine feels out of season with herself; she needs to, as the poster instructed, 'Regain contact with [herself] and others.' Her mountain walk similarly stresses her isolation. Delphine makes her way up the mountain without haste, eventually reaching a small plateau, with snow-capped alps in the distant background. On her right as she walks, a large expanse of snow and ice stretches away from her. Here she stops to look at the snow briefly then bends down and touches it, as if savouring it (Fig. 2.20). She rubs her hands together then walks away to a promontory on her left. Delphine's rambling walk in the mountains near La Plagne climaxes with this

Fig. 2.20

touching of the snow, perhaps a natural action for anyone finding snow in the summer, but expressive of her loneliness and her reaching out for something natural.

The film's expression of her contact with nature culminates in her seeing the green ray, but the walk in Cherbourg, the snow on the mountain and the waves flooding the cave later in Biarritz anticipate this conclusion. Rohmer planned these 'moments of solitude in nature' (1986), considering their progression important to the film's pace. Delphine's contact with nature is not a religious epiphany; the film does not suggest that her experiences give her a diminished sense of one's importance in the world and a simultaneous glorying of a feeling of connectedness to something larger. Delphine searches for something to lift her spirits and the film centres on Delphine's meandering; yet Le Rayon vert also explores the social habit and institution of the annual summer holiday, important in most Western countries, but especially important in France. It explores how we look to an annual holiday to vary our routine and to provide rest from work, but also to offer some form of emotional or spiritual nourishment. In its depiction of a lonely woman finding in natural surroundings a refuge from a society that she feels excludes her, Le Rayon vert has some parallels with Roberto Rossellini's Stromboli (1950) and a sustained comparison is tempting. One moment that prepares for Ingrid Bergman's experience on Stromboli's volcano occurs when she smells the grass growing from a wall and then puts it in her mouth; her contact with nature as she wanders alone finds an echo in Delphine's experiences. José Luis Guarner comments astutely that it is at the moment when Bergman's Karin touches the grass that she starts to realise that she cannot communicate with the people of the island: 'the only possible dialogue is between her and Stromboli' (1970: 40). Robin Wood sums up the quality of *Stromboli*'s ending in words that apply to Delphine and *Le Rayon vert*: 'If the actuality of her future is still unclear, she has grasped the need for wholeness of being, for a living relationship with the processes of nature and existence ... she has learned to distinguish her real needs from more transient and superficial (yet powerfully seductive) ones' (1974: 11).[9] In *Le Rayon vert*, Delphine's contact with nature relates to her concern for the environment and her vegetarianism, but it is also a variation of the film's expression of her loneliness and a preparation for her climactic vision of the green ray, the experience of which can be seen as a secular epiphany for Delphine.

She leaves La Plagne without staying the night, as if she has symbolically renounced her relationship with Jean-Pierre; after this she tells the truth about not being with him. Back in Paris again, she visits Françoise at work, then bumps into an old friend, Irène (Irène Skobline), who offers Delphine her brother-in-law's apartment in Biarritz. The intertitle 'mercredi, 1er août' begins a 7-minute sequence that follows Delphine on her own in Biarritz; throughout it, she never says anything and the only sounds we hear are background voices and the sea. Rohmer shows her on the large town beach of Biarritz, where the big swells of the Atlantic are too rough to swim in, and inside the apartment, where Delphine sits quietly on the bed eating before putting away the photographs that belong to unknown hosts. This long wordless sequence establishes the rhythm of Delphine spending time with herself on holiday in a loaned apartment in a town in which she knows nobody; in this, her third trip differs from her trips to Cherbourg and La Plagne. In both those places she knew people and both sequences began with her talking to someone. Biarritz is neither a place where she can socialise with a friend nor a place that holds memories of her relationship with Jean-Pierre. With its large crowds of holidaymakers, it absorbs her as an anonymous stranger.

'Jeudi, 2 août' begins the sequence which ends her solitude and which introduces the climax of Delphine's story. Rohmer heralds that introduction with an intense use of red and green. It begins with Delphine running along a beach's shallow surf in a white

Fig. 2.21

bikini, larger waves looming up behind her. When the Atlantic weather changes, a light mist hanging in the air, we see Delphine wearing jeans and a billowing red sleeveless mackintosh made out of plastic, a kind of large cape. She also carries a red bag as she walks horizontally along a cliff top, a low wall behind her. Hurrying down some steps towards the camera, her red cape stands out against the greenery of the cliffs. As she skips down more widely spaced steps at the side of a cliff, the film again marks out her red cape against the green moss of the cliffs, the grey stone steps and the grey-blue sea (Fig. 2.21). Delphine quickly descends onto a balcony while the camera holds its framing of her as she leans out across the wall, looking out to the foaming sea.

The waves crash loudly against the cliffs. This is the third of Rohmer's 'moments of solitude in nature' (1986). It ends with Delphine sitting on a wall, her hair wet and blown back, looking down as the waves flood loudly in and out of the cavern beneath her (Fig. 2.22). As with her walks in Cherbourg and La Plagne, her languid wandering along the cliffs in Biarritz expresses the way that she inclines towards melancholy. With her red cape marked vividly against the background sea and beach, her face is sad; when she looks down, Rohmer cuts to

Fig. 2.22

a point-of-view shot of the sea ebbing and flowing in and out of the cave, its huge roar dominating the soundtrack. There is a sense of her feeling awe at the power and the beauty of the natural world.

From here, Rohmer cuts to another promenade. The weather has warmed up slightly, though Delphine is yet to take off her red cape. For Alain Masson, this sequence of Delphine wandering evokes that of Kim Novak in *Vertigo* (1958) (1986: 44). Red and green are prominent in Hitchcock's film, but *Le Rayon vert*'s use of Delphine's red coat alludes more convincingly to 'Little Red Riding Hood'. Rohmer's film hints that a part of Delphine imagines – that maybe a part of all of us imagines – that men are either wolves or huntsmen and that there is a part of us that indulges such daydreams. As Delphine passes children poking around in rock pools, enjoying the Biarritz coastline at low tide, her red cape strikingly matches a man's red t-shirt. This sequence builds its intensity by focusing on red and green; it ends when she takes off her cape. In the next shot, wearing jeans and a jumper, Delphine clambers down some rocks barefoot and finds a playing card – a Jack of Hearts – on a rock. The violin begins again. The music and the playing card explicitly signal an approaching change in her fortunes. Rohmer cuts from the insert of the Jack of Hearts playing card to a shot of five people sitting on a wall. Delphine approaches from a path behind them. At that exact moment one woman asks another, 'You still reading Jules Verne?' Her words end the wordless sequence at Biarritz.

As Delphine approaches the five people the camera pans with her. She passes down a zigzag path, away from the group, although within earshot; one comments, 'Until I picked up this book and read *The Green Ray*, I found him paralysing. But now I think that *The Green Ray* is amazingly interesting.' Another woman speaks as Delphine walks out of their sight; the camera pans left with her as she passes them (Fig. 2.23). It then pans back right as she walks down in the opposite direction. The camera returns to the group of five people sitting on the low wall; Delphine looks up, evidently listening attentively, then sits down. Her wandering has led

Fig. 2.23

her by chance to find this group. One woman says: 'I read *The Green Ray*, I thought it was very good. It seemed to me a kind of fairytale, like a fairytale. The heroine is a fairytale heroine.' On that phrase Rohmer cuts to Delphine, who is turning her head as the woman continues: 'She's as simple as Cinderella or Snow White.' The film's structure falls into place: suddenly we realise that they are talking about our heroine and our film. The film cuts back to a frontal medium shot of three of the women as they continue talking about Verne's *The Green Ray* and its setting in Scotland. They ask the white-haired woman next to them if she has read it and she says that she has, but as a child. The woman who started the conversation explains her fascination with it in terms that apply to Delphine's story and the film that we are watching: 'I found it extraordinary, because it's a love story, a romance, with characters who are…' As she hesitates, the middle woman adds '…searching', and the first speaker agrees: 'Yes, searching for something.' They then ask the older woman if she has seen the green ray itself and surprisingly she says that she has seen it three times: 'At the last stage, there was a kind of pale green shaft like a sword blade, a horizontal beam, very pretty but extremely brief.' They comment that they will not see it today – too hazy; a shot of the setting sun confirms this. When the film returns to the group, one woman explains Verne's legend: 'That when you see the green ray you can read your own feelings and others' too.' A cut to a close shot of Delphine indicates that she has listened carefully to these last comments: 'That's what happened to his heroine, who never sees the green ray, but who finally reads her own feelings and those of the young man she's met.' When Rohmer cuts back to the group one woman asks the elderly man if he is familiar with the green ray. Amazingly, he stands up in front of them and offers to explain this 'phenomenon' in detail. This sequence represents Rohmer's most extreme intervention in the fictional world, one which has in other ways been established through improvisation; yet, as was the case with some of the other moments of imposed structure, it draws on the serendipitous. Rohmer cast some of *Le Rayon vert*'s performers before filming began; in other cases, he took what he found by chance. Such was the case with Dr Friedrich Günther Christlein, an elderly physics professor who taught at Munich University of Applied Sciences and who was on holiday in Biarritz. The motif of the green ray links the film's colour patterning with its evocation of predestined romance. Delphine wants to believe that a fairytale chance meeting will lead to love, but she also accepts, and the film clarifies, the make-believe quality of fairytale romances. At the moment when the relationship between the film's structure and its concern with daydreams and reality becomes most overt, Rohmer relies on a chance meeting with a scientist and that scientist's explanation of the reality of the green ray.

From Delphine overhearing the group discussing *The Green Ray* as the sun sets, Rohmer cuts to Delphine's third day at Biarritz, 'vendredi, 3 août'. On the beach a young Swedish woman, Lena (Carita), makes friends with Delphine. It emerges that the young woman loves travelling alone, but she does not perceive the differences between her extroverted outlook and Delphine's more reserved approach. Lena is explicit about the fictionality of her social performances and that openness repulses Delphine. Lena, for instance, actively intervenes in social situations; later on, when at a café, Lena invites two young men Joël (Joël Comarlot) and Pierrot (Marc Vivas) to join them at the table. Joël sits next to Lena and they immediately hit it off – they both know the rules of this kind of social game and are adept at playing it (Fig. 2.24). But as Joël and Lena flirt happily, Delphine resists attempts to engage in conversation and she eventually jumps up and leaves. Back at the apartment she asks a telephone operator for the number of Biarritz's station. The next day, when she goes to catch her train, she meets a sympathetic and attractive young man, Jacques (Vincent Gauthier).

Fig. 2.24

The casting of Joël was another instance of Rohmer leaving things open to chance; a friend of Arielle Dombasle's plays Lena, but Rohmer explains:

> The scene with the boy [Joël Comarlot] in Biarritz was completely improvised because he didn't even know what we wanted from him. I met him three minutes before filming, because the one who was supposed to come wasn't there. I found this boy on the beach, I put him next to the 'Swedish' girl and I said to him: 'Sit yourself down at this table and chat up these two girls.' (Quoted in Legrand, Niogret & Ramasse 1986: 17)

On the other hand, Vincent Gauthier had already been cast as the young man whom Delphine meets in Biarritz station and, as Marie Rivière mentions above, she and Gauthier had improvised scenes together before filming began. Their dialogue is exquisitely judged: the rhythm of their conversation is based on him asking her questions that she does not answer; this gives him space not to pressurise her to answer. Rohmer effectively contrasts this chance (but rehearsed) encounter with the planned (but improvised) encounter in the café; Jacques' warmth, diffidence, gentle voice and careful listening all stand out against Joël, prompting an unusual forwardness from Delphine.

Just as *Le Rayon vert* combines an extraordinarily documentary-like looseness with the most incredibly imposed, if not contrived, fictional patterns, so in its visual style the film evidences both a concern with verisimilitude and a disregard for it. *Le Rayon vert*'s interest in a natural light phenomenon connects to the grainy image, the result of filming on 16mm film stock. Using a 16mm camera facilitated the documentary-like production and therefore the realism of the film, yet the deliberate inclusion of visible grain foregrounds the image quality itself. The grain recurs throughout *Le Rayon vert*, notably during interior scenes and especially during the scene in Biarritz station. The grain transforms this scene, the fragility of the image conveying the sense that Rohmer and Maintigneux have only just managed to film with the light available inside the station, and enhancing the magical feeling of Delphine's chance meeting. The under-exposed quality of the image adds to the friability of Delphine's daydreams; ready to leave Biarritz, arguably at her most debilitated, a chance meeting reinvigorates her hopes.

She accompanies Jacques to the small port of Saint-Jean-de-Luz, south of Biarritz, only six kilometres from the Spanish border; as Alain Masson notes, her search has taken her to the extreme limits of France (1986: 44). They amble around the harbour and talk in a café; the centrepiece of this scene is Delphine's long speech about her attitude to men. The vital dynamism of the scene originates in the contrast between Marie Rivière and Vincent Gauthier's performances: Rivière's tendency to gesticulate vigorously suggests Delphine's vulnerable openness; in contrast, Gauthier remains still and attentive. Afterwards, as they walk along the promenade, Delphine sees a run-down beach shop called 'Rayon vert', its name spelled out in large green capital letters; at the same time the violin begins to play again.[10] The music stops as Delphine asks her companion to walk out to a promontory with her to watch the sunset. He agrees and they set off. The last scene builds to a climax that is not unanticipated, but is nonetheless more moving and beautiful than we could have expected.

As they sit waiting for the sunset Jacques starts talking, taking a chance by asking if she will come to Bayonne with him. She thinks he is 'kidding', but he insists not: 'I'd like it, that's all. It's simple. Let yourself go. Come on. Be nice.' Delphine studies him a while then says, 'We'll wait a little … Please be patient.' As they talk, their knees touch; rather than pulling her knee away, Delphine lightly brushes his knee with her hand. The screen fades to black; when it fades in we can see the sun touching the horizon. Off-screen Jacques asks, 'Wait for what?' At which point the violin music returns. Reversing to a shot of the couple reveals a warm, yellow light. She asks, 'Ever seen the green ray?' He has not and he does not know about it. As she explains the camera zooms slowly into a closer two-shot, with only their heads and torsos in the frame. 'Does it bring luck?';

Delphine will 'tell him later'. A shot of the setting sun occurs, then a return to the waiting couple. The alternation between setting sun and watching couple increases in speed; she starts to cry, sobs slightly; he puts his arm around her and wipes away the tears with his other hand. Delphine brings up her hand to clasp his; he whispers 'Look … wait.' They both do. Three alternations show the sunset and, at the last moment, a green ray. A final shot of the couple shows Delphine pointing and yelping excitedly (Fig. 2.25). Rohmer cuts to the last shot of the film: a slow-motion shot of the horizon, across which flies a barely perceptible bird. The violin music accompanies the sunset and leads into the final credits; Jean-Louis Valero's fugue, developed from the violin solo already heard, accompanies them.

Fig. 2.25

The end-credit shot of the sea is the final example of the grainy texture of the film. As I argue above, the frequently grainy quality of the images in *Le Rayon vert* is part of the artistry; the representation of natural light in a film whose title refers to a momentary light effect is wholly appropriate in its emphasis on transient epiphanies. Improvisations that produce extraordinary revelations of character, chance meetings with people who deliver perfect performances and scenes filmed with so little light that the grainy texture of the film becomes visible: all these connect to a film whose climax turns upon a chance meeting in a station and a chance vision of an atmospheric light effect. Planning and preparation relate to chance and luck and most stories balance hints about what may happen with surprises: in *Le Rayon vert*, intrigue about whether Delphine will meet any-one links to suspense about whether she will see the green ray; but this also connects to the development of the film, in particular to the questions that Rohmer had about whether he would be able to film a green ray and how he would film *Le Rayon vert*.

Rohmer took a chance by making a feature film without a script or schedule, deter-mined to make a film about chance meetings, yet despite its unusual production and its lack of conventional polish, the film presents a fictional world that has been stylistically fine-tuned. *Le Rayon vert* elaborates its central metaphor of the green ray through the striking repetition of green and red. Rhymes and patterns based on the repeated use of these two colours unify the film; awareness of that unity modifies our relationship to Delphine. All filmmakers balance marking out their field of interest with telling believ-able stories, but *Le Rayon vert* achieves a unique balance because Rohmer connects the film's stylistic patterning to Delphine's belief in astrology, to her finding the cards, to her seeing green things or talking about green and, finally, to Verne's novel and its legend about the revealing power of the green ray.

The rarity of seeing a green ray enhances the romance of watching a beautiful sunset and this appeals to Delphine's sentimental side, but Verne's legend appeals even more. By including the five holidaymakers discussing both Verne's *The Green Ray* and green rays, and by cutting to Delphine just as one of them describes Verne's heroine, Helena, as a 'fairytale heroine', 'as simple as Cinderella or Snow-White', Rohmer brings to the fore the connection between the film's investigation of chance and the intervention of its own creation. Subject and method are intricately related, as Alain Philippon notes:

> It is impossible not to see in this struggle between the failure and success of the encoun-ter [between Delphine and Jacques] (what we'll call here a very Rohmerian 'suspense') a fictional equivalent of the reality of filming: the moment of grace is also that of the unpre-dictable encounter between camera and actors, all the more reason for this in a cinema which gives them more than their due. (1987: 5)

Rohmer's strenuous attempts to document a green ray echo the fictional efforts of Del-phine in *Le Rayon vert* and those of Helena Campbell in Verne's *The Green Ray*, with all three the search for a green ray leads progressively westward: Verne's story ends with the heroine rescued from Fingal's Cave on the Isle of Staffa; Delphine's search ends in Saint-Jean-de-Luz; and Rohmer's filming eventually ended in the Canary Islands, where he sent Philippe Demard to capture a green ray, having failed to film one in France.[11] The appearance of the green ray is therefore the final example of the elements of the film which do not rely on chance, but rather impose a planned structure.

3. *Conte d'automne*

While Sabine in *Le Beau mariage* and Delphine in *Le Rayon vert* both daydream of finding a partner, the central character of *Conte d'automne*, Isabelle (Marie Rivière) is already married; she daydreams of finding a partner for her best female friend, Magali (Béatrice Romand). Like both films previously discussed, Rohmer's final part of his *Conte de quatre saisons* series explores the relationship between desires and reality; similarly, *Conte d'automne* strategically uses the repetition of movement, mealtimes and colours to construct perspectives on the characters and their world. However, while the linear story of *Le Rayon vert* focuses exclusively on Delphine's perspective and experiences, like *Le Beau mariage*, building its story on a single thread, *Conte d'automne* uses a structure whereby stories interact with and reflect back on each other, a mosaic-type design that allows Rohmer to enlarge *Conte d'automne*'s themes in extended metaphors. Marriage, and the characters' thoughts about it, form the film's central subject.

At the start, we assume that Isabelle has been married to her husband Jean-Jacques (Yves Alcaïs) for about 20 or 25 years: we might guess that she is in her mid-forties and that he is in his early sixties (born in 1938, painter Alcaïs is 18 years older than Rivière). Their ages are important because the film compares the younger generation with the older: their daughter, Emilia (Aurélia Alcaïs), appears to be in her early twenties and, in about three weeks, she will marry Grégoire (Mathieu Davette). Besides comparing Isabelle's established marriage with her daughter's impending one, the film contrasts Isabelle with her best friend, Magali, a single widow. Additionally, these relationships compare with two others: one being that between Magali's son, Léo (Stéphane Darmon), and his young student girlfriend, Rosine (Alexia Portal); and the other being Rosine's former relationship with her middle-aged ex-philosophy teacher, Etienne (Didier Sandre).

Isabelle ostensibly sets out to help Magali find a partner, both by inviting her to the wedding and then by placing an advertisement in the personal pages of a local newspaper; she successfully finds a suitable candidate and lunches three times with him before inviting him to her daughter's wedding. Rosine similarly plots to find Magali a partner, attempting to match her boyfriend's mother with her ex-lover Etienne, who is Magali's age. Rosine's meddling parallels Isabelle's efforts; by the end of the film, both Isabelle and Rosine find themselves more emotionally involved in their schemes than they had initially anticipated. Into this structure of parallels arrives Gérald (Alain Libolt), the handsome, divorced and middle-aged man that Isabelle recruits for Magali. Gérald's attempt to meet someone through the small ads contrasts with Etienne's relationships with younger women, in particular his ex-students. Using these relationships comparatively the film studies a marriage at an important point. The occasion is the wedding of the daughter produced by the earlier relationship, the event of which causes Isabelle to reflect on her own marriage. Although Emilia features less than Rosine, like her father, Isabelle's husband, she catalyses Isabelle's thoughts in the opening scene. This chapter focuses on those parts of the film that explore Isabelle's situation.

The patterns of *Conte d'automne* derive from three areas: transport, geography and wine-growing. From these Rohmer develops the film's motifs and metaphors. This chapter studies how the film establishes them in the opening two scenes in relation to Isabelle and Magali. It then traces their development in subsequent scenes, concentrating on Isabelle's meetings with Gérald and following this by looking at the climactic meeting between Magali and Gérald at the wedding in Isabelle's garden. As we saw in *Le Beau mariage* and *Le Rayon vert*, much of *Conte d'automne*'s interest resides in the elaboration of formal structures and the relation of them to questions about characters' thoughts. Rohmer's organisation and presentation of his actors' gestures can be as structured as the framing or colouring of shots; accordingly, this chapter scrutinises performances. The discussion of the two opening scenes that follows identifies the way that the film invites us to observe how Isabelle and Magali may be thinking about things that they are not discussing.

Perhaps even more than he did in *Le Beau marriage*, Rohmer importantly uses the geographical location of *Conte d'automne* and the film begins by emphasising its setting, opening with a shot of a quiet country road: on the left are pale stone walls, old and high with luxurious green tree-tops poking out over them, belonging to, presumably, either a large home or the village's ramparts; in the distance, a white car turns off the road; on the soundtrack, birds chirp; the sky is blue and sunny. The second shot shows a town sign announcing the village setting as Saint-Paul-Trois-Châteaux; behind the sign and map of the village, an old church dominates the background. While the first shot establishes the climate of the film's location, the second shot signals the film's setting, where Isabelle and her family live: the Rhône valley between Avignon and Montélimar. Magali and Isabelle, it will turn out, live on opposite sides of the Rhône with Isabelle on the eastern side, in the Drôme, in Saint-Paul-Trois-Châteaux, and Magali on the western side, in the Ardèche, near Bourg-Saint-Andéol. The following five shots, intercut with the credits, all give the impression of a warm and quiet Provençal country village at the middle of the day, with most people lunching or resting: three shots of narrow, shady village streets, a church in the background in one, a few people walking along in another; a shot through a bridge, in the background, an arch of light, a town square and fountain; lastly, a closer shot of another fountain with a hill in the background. The credits end and Rohmer takes us into the first scene with a long shot of a large and imposing house behind trees, a wall in the foreground. He then reverses the angle to a medium long shot of four people lunching in the garden under a tree, the wall behind them.

As he did in *Le Rayon vert*, so in *Conte d'automne* Rohmer uses the rhythm of mealtimes, particularly lunches, to set the pace of the film. *Conte d'automne* alternates mealtimes with the characters' restless movement up, down and across the Rhône valley. Two kinds of meal begin and end the film in the same garden: a small family lunch and a large wedding buffet. In between, various couples sit and eat or drink together: Magali and Isabelle, Jean-Jacques and Isabelle, Magali and Rosine, Isabelle and Gérald (three times), then Magali and Rosine again, joined by Isabelle. The particular expressive qualities of sitting down to talk, leaning back and folding one's arms or leaning forward, chin on hand, to listen attentively, repeatedly feature in *Conte d'automne*. Sitting down to eat or drink allows for many variations; positioning someone at a table isolates and emphasises the upper body and naturalises Rohmer's favoured shot of head, shoulders, arms and torso; standing up to walk away from the table can indicate displeasure, such as Rosine or Magali's move away when either one challenges the other. Similarly, when characters stand up from tables or low walls, it permits them to make speeches to or lecture whomever remains sitting.

The opening lunch scene sets up wine-growing as a source of narrative and meta-phoric interest. A medium shot of Emilia and her fiancé, Grégoire, follows the establish-ing shot of the table. Grégoire smells and tastes the wine, then declares that 'it is really good'. The first words of the film praise the quality of Magali's wine and the conversation subsequently turns to whether to use Magali's wine at the wedding. The second shot shows Isabelle and her husband, Jean-Jacques; off-screen, Grégoire remarks that in principle his parents are meant to supply the wine; Isabelle asks if his parents would mind if Magali supplied about forty bottles of wine. Emilia objects that 'it will complicate things', but Grégoire concedes that his parents will not mind, 'if it pleases your friend'; Emilia retorts, 'She's my mum's friend. Not mine.' This conversation makes Magali known as someone for whom Isabelle can do something; it also reveals her as a maker of good wine and holder of a bad temper. When Emilia explains, 'I'm on bad terms with her', her father replies, 'This is an opportunity to make up'; but, according to Emilia, 'Neither of us wants to'. Emilia's bad relationship with her mother's friend will find an echo in Magali's apparently difficult relationships with her own children – Léo, whom we meet, and her daughter, who remains off-screen in Orange, but from whom, according to Magali and Léo, she is estranged.

The predominant colours of the scene come from the pale cream and white buildings, the blue skies and the greenery. Emilia and her fiancé wear dark colours: she has on a

dark green t-shirt and he wears a dark red sweat-shirt; both dress more casually and youthfully than her parents do (Fig. 3.1). They also lean continuously back in their chairs, snuggling towards each other, while Isabelle and Jean-Jacques dress and sit more formally. Jean-Jacques wears a light blue shirt with the sleeves rolled up; his hair is completely grey. Isabelle wears a dress, the printed pattern of which comprises tiny black flowers on white material; the film continuously associates Isabelle with sharply-defined blacks, navy blues (jackets and bags) and crisp whites (jeans and skirts). The dark green and red of the younger generation are the hues associated with Magali and are the dominant autumnal colours of the film. In contrast to these colours, Jean-Jacques' pale blue shirt rhymes with the blue door behind him. In this scene, Isabelle's elegant black and white dress sticks out noticeably from the greens of the garden. Her hair is frizzy, not yet grey,

Fig. 3.1

but blonde; around her neck hangs a fine gold necklace; a thin gold watch encircles her wrist. Tall, slim, chic and elegant, Marie Rivière nonetheless projects the hint of fragility that Rohmer exploited in *La Femme de l'aviateur* and *Le Rayon vert.*

As the scene progresses, Rohmer increasingly presses us to notice Isabelle's attentive observation of her daughter and her fiancé. Having begun the scene with a long shot of the table and the four characters, Rohmer follows this with two pairs of shot/reverse-shots from the men's side of the table. They include both couples. He then cuts to a single shot of Isabelle, who has stood up to take a quiche from an adjacent table. Before she stands, Isabelle glances at Emilia and then looks down. When Isabelle gets up, the look that she directs to Emilia hints at thoughts of her daughter's animosity to her friend, perhaps also of her daughter's affection for her fiancé; her standing movement enlarges our sense of her annoyance. Marie Rivière is tall, and Rohmer uses her height expressively: she moves carefully, as if aware that sudden movements might have a big effect on those standing or sitting near her. She generally hesitates before rising from a table or taking a step in another direction; she characteristically also steps back or steps away from two people talking, a tactic of retreating which occurs more than once in the film. Here, while Emilia thinks nothing of arguing with her mother about Magali, Isabelle's glance across to Emilia, followed by her look down as she rises from the table, avoids confrontation. One cannot imagine Isabelle ever shouting or angry; nevertheless, standing reinforces her reprimand of her daughter: 'It bothers me that my best friend won't be at my daughter's wedding.' Panning, the camera follows her as she returns to her seat and passes the quiche to her daughter. Emilia receives it in a reverse-shot, but this time the camera has crossed the table to the women's side. Thus begins the sequence, when Isabelle returns to the table, of three pairs of shot/reverse-shots which end the scene, only now Isabelle appears on her own opposite Emilia and Grégoire, without her husband. We only see Jean-Jacques three times during the film (here, the middle dinner scene and the last scene); each time Isabelle remains distant and vague with him; as soon as she begins to argue with Emilia about Magali, the film moves to exclude him. Having isolated Isabelle from her husband, Rohmer will end this scene with two close-ups of her in which she says nothing, only attends to Emilia and Grégoire, whom we see in an intercut two-shot.

When Isabelle returns to the table Emilia provokes with 'she'll only come if we buy her wine'. After she says this, she looks up guiltily, almost as if she knows that she has pushed her mother too far. For Isabelle, 'That's enough'; but Emilia continues: 'I doubt she even owns a dress.' From what Magali eventually wears to the wedding reception we might judge this to be true; yet Isabelle exclaims: 'What a viper's tongue!' While reprimanding her daughter, Isabelle leans her head to the left, then straightens her back and leans forward as she pronounces that her friend is her business not that of her daughter's. Rivière's movements comprise simultaneously a nod of the head, raised eyebrows and a frown. She then sits back and, having made her point firmly, looks down for a second. Isabelle pushes the charitable part of this invitation: 'Look, it's a chance for her to get out for a change'; her daughter need not talk to Magali; the latter will not even congratulate her. Off-screen, Emilia responds, 'She doesn't want to.' Rivière bristles pointedly as she delivers her last line of the scene, 'How do you know?', characteristically pulling her left shoulder back in a more pronounced version of the two previous movements. Her shoulder's straightening resists, as if pushing away someone or something; the dip of the head, pulling it away from the shoulder while lengthening the neck, communicates to Emilia that she risks annoying her mother severely. Moving the conversation along, the daughter puts down the knife after cutting the quiche and adopts a conciliatory tone with, 'I won't say another word', resting her cheek on her hand and turning her head away from her mother.

Emilia's tone of voice intimates her smarting from her mother's reprimand; Grégoire notices this and asks Emilia, 'What have you got against her?' She hastens to say 'nothing', before describing how they had a fight two years ago: 'I stupidly agreed to work in her grape harvest. She has a filthy temper.' This comment allows Emilia to turn the conversation to humour and affection, redirecting Grégoire's focus back onto her: 'Worse than mine', she says. Snuggling her head into his neck she jokes 'see what you're in for?' A declaration to her mother exaggerates Emilia's reconciliation: 'OK, I'll let her kiss my cheek. No hard feelings [Sans rancune]'. Grégoire plays with the words rhyming 'aucune', meaning 'not any', with 'rancune'. 'Sans rancune' means, literally, 'without hard feelings'. This amuses Emilia vaguely but it also asserts a kind of superiority on her fiancé's part, the kind which Rohmer has often undermined and shown to be self-deceiving. Nonetheless, Grégoire's joke prompts Emilia to lean further towards him and kiss him affectionately on the cheek. With her head touching his, she calls him 'silly' but reiterates 'I love you'. Rohmer then cuts to the last shot of the scene, a return to the set-up twice used, for a close shot of Isabelle, sitting quietly observing Emilia and Grégoire. Something prompts a small smile; Rivière touches her lips with her fingers as she smiles and looks off-screen (Fig. 3.2).

Fig. 3.2

Any interpretation of this scene must concentrate on Marie Rivière's performance as Isabelle. To begin with, irony attaches to Emilia's comment 'see what you're in for?': Emilia and Grégoire, as a couple about to be married, cannot see what they are in for; Isabelle has more of an idea and Rohmer cuts to her, privileging her response to Emilia's comment to Grégoire. Isabelle's head and shoulders, isolated in a close shot, remain almost completely passive; she blinks three times and her eyes glance from Emilia to Grégoire. Rohmer then cuts back to the two-shot of the young couple, who are again touching arms; in fact, Emilia rests her right arm on Grégoire's left arm, which is almost hidden under the table. Constantly linking arms, they display a youthful enthusiasm for their relationship or, at least, an enthusiasm to be tactile while the relationship is in its youth. Emilia and Grégoire cannot predict what they are in for but the film explores that topic through its comparative study of Isabelle and Magali.

When Isabelle sits quietly in the two close shots in the opening scene she concentrates on Emilia and Grégoire's playful affection and physical contact with each other. The film emphasises her observation of her daughter's openly affectionate lounging against Grégoire. Their physical connection stresses both their continuous desire for one another and their lack of inhibition about displaying this desire in public. To address Grégoire, Emilia only has to turn her head to find her face inches away from his. Isabelle and Jean-Jacques' upright postures establish an opposing formality; seeing one's daughter so full of attraction for her fiancé might prompt one to reflect on one's own marriage. Isabelle's daughter is about to marry and leave the family. The child's departure might prompt a reassessment of the marriage that produced the child; without the children around anymore, wife and husband must return to each other.

To see Emilia happy must please Isabelle, but we might also be seeing her thinking about Magali's future or her own. Rohmer took us into the scene by beginning with the discussion about the wine, which included comments from all four people; he ends it by establishing Isabelle and her thoughts as his focus. This meal sets up the major concerns of the story: Emilia's immanent wedding; Magali the wine-grower, single and occasionally bad-tempered; Isabelle's concern for her single friend who does not get out much; and, perhaps, Isabelle's thoughts about her own marriage. Isabelle busily prepares to host her daughter's wedding party, but she also thinks of other things. Once she begins to look for a partner for Magali through the small ads, her imagination can expand the daydream. Isabelle is not conscious of wanting to find a lover and she might never express a dissatisfaction with her own marriage, but Rohmer's shift from a two-shot to a close shot isolates her withdrawal from the conversation into her own world; we cannot be sure of what Isabelle thinks, but we do notice that her thoughts hold her apart from her husband and her family. For the rest of the film, we follow either Isabelle's or Rosine's efforts to find a partner for Magali; we do not see Magali without either woman until the end of the story, when Gérald drives her to Pierrelatte station.

This scene's final shot finds its partner in the film's final shot, of Isabelle looking over her husband's shoulder as they dance at their daughter's wedding. Rohmer says:

> There are two essential shots in the film. The first is right at the beginning, when Marie Rivière announces that her daughter is getting married. She watches her daughter and smiles. We don't know what she's thinking. About her daughter's wedding? About Magali? In the same way, the last shot doesn't allow us to know what she thinks. I really care a lot about these two shots of opaque thoughts. We don't know what's at stake. But I hadn't anticipated these at the writing stage. It was during editing that I chose to keep them in the film, highlighting them more. (Quoted in de Baecque & Lalanne 1998: 34)

Rohmer continues, explaining his aims:

> I had the feeling that it would be better to organise it so that this story placed Marie Rivière in a world entirely separate from her real life and which didn't encroach upon her married

life. That it should be like a kind of daydream. Elsewhere in my films, where the tone is nevertheless not very dreamlike, one always finds a moment of absence from which it could only be a dream. Here, it would be this close-up of Marie Rivière's mysterious look at the beginning. From this point onwards, one can imagine that she imagines finding a lover for Magali and so on. (Quoted in de Baecque & Lalanne 1998: 35)

Rohmer's description of Isabelle ambiguously allows for two interpretations: one, that Isabelle, daydreaming during lunch, thinks about finding a lover for Magali; two, that Isabelle daydreams of finding a lover for Magali and that the film represents her daydream, her imagining of the series of events which comprise *Conte d'automne*. Although Rohmer says that his films are not conventionally dreamlike they do combine, as Pascal Bonitzer (1999) suggests, a deceptively straightforward transparency with a magical or enchanted quality; in all three films studied here, that magical quality is tied to the depiction of the central characters' thoughts and daydreams (Sabine's, Delphine's and Isabelle's).[12] William Rothman, writing of documentaries, notes how reality plays a role in all films:

> In no film is the role reality plays simply that of being recorded or documented. The medium transforms or transfigures reality when the world is revealed, reveals itself on film. And reality itself, in our experience, is already stamped by our fantasies. (1997: xiii)

In the close shots of Isabelle quietly sitting as she looks at her daughter, Rohmer shows us someone listening and responding to someone else; Marie Rivière moves her eyes and face to indicate Isabelle's attentiveness to her daughter's behaviour with her fiancé and her simultaneous absorption with other things. Despite Isabelle's declared interest in Magali, careful viewing confirms the impression that Rohmer focuses on Isabelle's thinking; and *Conte d'automne* gradually hints at Isabelle's innermost thoughts, those which she would not confess to anyone.

The second scene continues to develop the metaphoric value of geography, transport and wine-making; the following discussion outlines that development, first by examining transport and geography, which are linked, then by looking at geography and wine-making, which are also connected. A short sequence shows Isabelle driving to Magali's house on the other side of the Rhône. After Isabelle drives away from her house, we cut to a point-of-view shot from inside a car which traverses a bridge across the Rhône; on the right side of the road a sign indicates that Isabelle approaches Bourg-Saint-Andéol. Driving features prominently in the film – Léo takes Magali's car, Etienne drives Rosine home, Gérald drives Magali to the station. The film opens with an image of a car on a road and who will take whom home becomes an issue. Rohmer comments on his interest in the film's setting and on an experience of country living, the driving around:

> What pleases me in this film is that it doesn't take place in a town but in a region – the Rhône valley – where people live a few kilometres from each other. It's a very important element

of modern life in the country: people move around a lot. (Quoted in de Baecque & Lalanne 1998: 35)

In another interview, Michel Ciment asks Rohmer about why he chose the Ardèche and the Drôme. Rohmer replies:

First, the fact that people live in different locations and that they move, they intertwine. I like threads that intertwine and a plot is indeed like a web, with intertwinings, so it did reflect the subject of the film … the shape … is diamond-shaped. You have Avignon in the north and Montélimar in the south, and the Ardèche and the Drôme on each side. And inside this shape you have intertwining threads. (1998)

Rohmer's films often portray people on the move: in *Le Beau mariage*, Sabine routinely commutes; in *Le Rayon vert*, Delphine varies her routine with holiday travel: in both circumstances the characters' movements allow for digressions. Aware of the potential for the dramatic expressiveness of travelling, Rohmer films its various forms; in the countryside of *Conte d'automne*, the car dominates, functioning as a means of convenience and a way of showing restlessness.

Having decided which location to use, whether Le Mans, Biarritz or the Rhône valley, Rohmer makes the geography relevant to the characters and subjects of his films. *Conte d'automne* creatively uses several locations in the Rhône valley, all in either the Drôme or Ardèche. Isabelle lives and works in the ancient capital of Tricastin, Saint-Paul-Trois-Châteaux, a fortified town with old ramparts – which we see in the first shot of the film – and a twelfth-century cathedral, which, I suspect, is the location for Emilia and Grégoire's wedding. Gérald and Isabelle's first and last lunches occur at northern and southern points in Rohmer's exploration of the Rhône valley, Montélimar and Pont-Saint-Esprit. They lunch for the second time in a medieval hill village, La Garde-Adhémar, after which they wander around the herb garden at the base of its church. In addition to the visual appearance of road and town signs, *Conte d'automne*'s dialogue repeatedly refers to places. Rohmer often cuts from the mention of a place to an establishing shot of the place itself: to arrange the first meeting with Gérald, Isabelle phones him after receiving his brief letter; the telephone conversation ends with Isabelle saying, 'You'll be in Pont-Saint-Esprit. That's fine', and from the shot of Isabelle on the phone in the bookshop, Rohmer cuts to a travelling shot from the perspective of a car driving over a bridge across the Rhône and approaching on the left an old town whose landscape is sharply marked by two large square towers, presumably those of Pont-Saint-Esprit. Their second meeting follows directly from their first and Rohmer repeats the technique: after Isabelle declines to meet Gérald at home or in the evening he proposes lunch the following Saturday at La Garde-Adhémar; Rohmer cuts to a long shot of the hill village and follows this with a two-shot of them at lunch.

Not many viewers could identify where Saint-Paul-Trois-Châteaux or Bourg-Saint-Andéol are, but Gérald and Isabelle twice refer to the more infamous Tricastin nuclear power complex: they see it and comment on it when they walk in the herb garden after lunch in La Garde-Adhémar; then they argue about it in the café in Montélimar, just before she confesses to him. When Magali asks Gérald to drop her off, she asks him to drop her at Pierrelatte station, from where, she claims, she can catch a train to Orange to visit her daughter. Gérald himself works in Montélimar. This is where Rosine twice meets Etienne, where Isabelle confesses her plan to Gérald and where Rosine espies the conspiring pair bidding each other goodbye near Isabelle's car. Rosine and Léo appear to go to college in Avignon: when they meet in a café, an establishing shot shows Avignon's train station and ramparts. Through either road signs or a combination of verbal reference and establishing shots, Rohmer marks these places (Saint-Paul-Trois-Châteaux, Bourg-Saint-Andéol, Pont-Saint-Esprit, La Garde-Adhémar, Avignon, Montélimar and Pierrelatte) as settings, all of which are close together; Montélimar and Avignon, the northernmost and southernmost places that we see in the film, are only fifty kilometres apart. The director uses the characters' movements between these locations to suggest that their journeys form increasingly intertwining threads across the space; for example, it is significant that with their contrasting marital status, Isabelle and Magali live on opposite sides of the river, about eight kilometres apart. Isabelle pretends to be single when she meets Gérald and her crossing over to Magali's side of the valley echoes this narrative device; furthermore, it is equally resonant that, during her argument with Gérald about industrial development in the region, Isabelle insists that she prefers the Ardèche to the Rhône valley, the former being Magali's home.

When Isabelle drives to see Magali after lunch with her family, we see, in three point-of-view shots taken from her car, that she drives first across the A7 motorway – the 'Autoroute du Soleil', which runs the length of the Rhône valley. Tricastin is on her left and Pierrelatte is on her right; she then crosses the canal that runs between Donzère and Mondragon and which presumably serves the Tricastin nuclear power station; in the last of the three shots, she crosses the Rhône with Bourg-Saint-Andéol shown on her right. There is no shot of Isabelle in the car, but we feel as if we are looking first south and then north with her as she crosses to her friend's house. David Heinemann compares these three travelling shots, which he calls 'anonymous', with the trio of shots that opens *Conte de printemps*:

> Both sequences introduce us to characters just as they cross from their ordinary routines to events of dizzying possibility. This disembodied floating – gazing out at the passing world without really being in it – shows an outer journey while mirroring an inner one; it represents both a detached view of the world and a consciousness moving though space. (2000: 52)

Heinemann's comments rightly characterise Isabelle's 'detached' or 'disembodied' mood, though he incorrectly calls the shots 'anonymous': the preceding shot has shown Isabelle at the wheel of her car as she leaves her house. Furthermore, the three shots all contain landmarks or signs: the first shot allows us to notice that Isabelle is crossing the busy Autoroute, the nuclear power station visible a few miles south; the second shot of the bridge being approached, with the canal to its right, contains a legible sign telling us that Isabelle crosses the canal (similar in function to the second shot of the film, which announces the village setting of Saint-Paul-Trois-Châteaux); the third shot to which Heinemann refers shows the Rhône river and the church tower of Bourg-Saint-Andéol. In a film in which a married woman pretends to be her single best friend, Isabelle's crossing of the Rhône to Magali's side marks the beginning of an adventure for her, a daydream of romantic intensity, a passing, as Heinemann notes, from 'ordinary routines to events of dizzying possibility'.

The film contrasts Isabelle's mode of transport with that of the other plotter – whereas Isabelle drives, Rosine rides a bicycle. When Isabelle arrives at Magali's home, she finds Rosine about to leave on her bicycle. Magali introduces them, then Rosine cycles off, after which Magali tells Isabelle about Rosine's former relationship with her philosophy teacher, Etienne, and her current relationship with Magali's son, Léo. Rohmer constructs intriguing sets of parallels between these three women, not only between the two plotters. In her appearance, Alexia Portal's Rosine looks vaguely like a younger version of Romand's Magali: both women have dark, frizzy hair, though they dress differently, with Rosine usually in black. At Magali's, she wears black jeans, a thin black belt and a pale yellow sleeveless top. Portal convinces as a young woman who, despite being still in love with him, suspects that a relationship with her former philosophy teacher and ex-lover, Etienne, a man who confesses that he prefers younger women, is unlikely to be long-lasting. Successfully embodying conflicting emotions, Portal ensures that Rosine's calculations often appear naïve, born out of her reluctance to be forthright with herself. In her actions, then, Rosine resembles Isabelle: both women plot to find a husband for Magali and the film develops similarities and differences between the two plotters through things like transport and geography.

At lunch, Emilia commented spitefully that Magali rarely leaves her vineyard. The setting of the country as opposed to the city allows for Magali to be busy with her work and yet isolated, without colleagues at the vineyard she inherited from her father. Rohmer structures his film *Les Rendez-vous de Paris* (1995) around chance meetings and arranged meetings; people bump into one another unexpectedly in places that lots of people visit. In an urban context cafés, museums and parks exist as public spaces in a way that open countryside does not; in the area in which Magali, Isabelle, Rosine and Gérald live, defining what constitutes a public space presents difficulties. Although Rosine and Etienne unexpectedly see Isabelle and Gérald in Montélimar, this is not the norm. In contrast to the city, where one might often find oneself surrounded by others, only the wedding reception offers an opportunity for meeting people in a crowd, as when Etienne encounters a former student of his, an attractive young woman in red, whom Rosine perceives as a rival.

The first time we see Magali separated from her vineyard – either the vines themselves or her large house and sprawling garden – occurs when she attends the wedding reception at the end of the film. People come to visit her: Isabelle drives; Rosine cycles.

One can move from north to south by train, say between Pierrelatte and Orange, although Magali waits without success for a train; to cross from east to west in the countryside that Rohmer films, as Isabelle frequently does, some mode of private transport (a car or a bicycle) is essential. Rohmer turns these movements into a thematic pattern that climaxes at the wedding reception. Rosine's bicycle indicates her youth; it allows her to move around independently and we only see her in a car when Etienne gives her a lift home from the wedding. Although the film shows both Rosine and Isabelle moving independently around the countryside – and that is important to their sense of themselves, and to their plotting – unlike Isabelle, Rosine cannot offer lifts: one needs a car to do so. Rohmer emphasises the giving and accepting of lifts in *Conte d'automne*: Isabelle accepts a lift from Magali to the vineyard, in her battered white Renault 4; Rosine accepts a lift from Etienne and declines a lift from her supposed boyfriend, Léo, but only after her match-making has failed – significantly, Etienne scolds her, like a teacher, in his car. Gérald gives Magali a lift to Pierrelatte station, in an example of a car forcing people together in an uncomfortably cramped and enclosed space, in which one is largely unable to change one's physical position: when Magali becomes angry, she cannot stand up and walk away; she has to demand that he drop her off.

If Rosine's plot parallels Isabelle's plot, Magali's situation compares with that of Isabelle. Tom Ryan (Andrew *et al.* 2000) proposes that the two older women are bored, but Ryan's claim does not bear scrutiny: Magali is lonely, but there is no evidence that she is bored; Isabelle is not bored, but she finds herself at a time in her life when many things that were previously pressing have settled into routine. Her life is pleasant, but runs smoothly and unhurriedly enough to allow her to find time, even during the build-up to her daughter's wedding, to arrange to meet a man through the small ads; she has the time and the imaginative space to conceive her plot to help Magali. She is not bored, but perhaps she harbours a nagging feeling, potentially inconsequential, that her life, though charmed and happy, lacks spontaneity.

Settled middle-class elegance infuses Rivière's Isabelle; despite living in the country, her hair, posture and clothes all evoke sophistication, only set off by accompanying traits of fragility. Béatrice Romand's Magali carries an opposing set of characteristics: robustness, intensity, intransigence, obstinacy. At Magali's, Isabelle wears a pair of white jeans, a patterned blouse and a navy blue jacket. Always carrying or wearing stylish accessories, she brings to Magali's home a large and impractical floppy straw hat, the function of which as a shade from the sun will be negated by the wind that keeps blowing it off. In contrast, Magali's costume evokes practicality: faded blue jeans, thick brown leather belt and an old green top, unbuttoned at the neck. Furthermore, whereas Rivière's hair is thin, blonde and loosely wavy – when she lunches with Gérald, she is concerned about the strong breeze that disarranges her hair – Romand's hair explodes in the wind; thick, dark and tightly curled, its chaotic movements resist the wind. Yet Rohmer also plays against these physical differences: Rivière's refinement comes with longer limbs and larger hands and she can appear prone to hesitancy and self-doubt, the fear of being clumsy; Romand's intransigence conceals vulnerability. In *Conte d'automne* Romand and Rivière play characters whose behaviour recalls Sabine in *Le Beau mariage* and Delphine in *Le Rayon vert*; however, now Rivière is more confident and Romand is more vulnerable.

The contrast between Isabelle and Magali is elaborated when they visit the vineyard. During this scene, which uses three locations, the symbolism of wine-making also develops substantially. As the two friends amble along the path between vines, the film connects Magali to her work and her land: she repeatedly handles the leaves and grapes, and soon walks amongst the vines.[13] In her faded green top and denim jeans, hair swirling around her head like a bush, she merges with her vine and the landscape around it; Isabelle's crisp white trousers, navy blue jacket and straw hat contrast with this. Delivering her speech about the ageing of Côtes-du-Rhône, Magali wanders into her vines until only her upper body is visible. Isabelle, meanwhile, hesitates on the path, clean blue and white colours sharply isolating her from the green surroundings (Fig. 3.3). She follows Magali, but her height and costume separate her from the environment. Shades of green dominate the image; Isabelle stands dramatically apart from these.

Fig. 3.3

Magali emphasises that she produces two times less than her neighbours do because 'what I want to do is prove that a Côtes-du-Rhône is a wine that will age well, a bit like Burgundy. I've got lots of bottles, but I'm holding them to age them more, even though it's risky.' Isabelle asks, 'For how long?' and Magali confesses that she does not know, but 'meanwhile they're ageing very well'. After asking this, Isabelle overtakes Magali, the camera panning with her, ninety degrees away from its original position, until the married woman challenges her single friend: 'You don't have to sell me those forty bottles.' Off-screen Magali replies sulkily, 'That's not it', to which Isabelle responds by turning around to face her. Isabelle has pushed ahead of Magali, put some distance between them, then turned to confront her friend about her reticence and her withholding of her wine, and perhaps herself: her 'You don't have to sell me those forty bottles', in the context, also refers to the taking of other kinds of risks. Rohmer's camera accompanies Rivière, contributing to the tension between the two friends by separating them.

The two-shot that followed them up the path and into the vine transformes into a medium shot of Isabelle when the camera pans around with her. In what becomes a separating shot/reverse-shot pair, Rohmer reverses the angle, after Isabelle turns around and cuts to Magali, who stands alone in the vine. She remains a part of the vine physically, but the camera isolates her as she explains to her friend the reasons for her doubts and hesitancy, her anxieties about its vintage and her willingness to try it at the wedding: 'To tell the truth, it'll be an experiment.' Béatrice Romand often delivers her lines humorously by enunciating slowly and exaggerating the correct pronunciation of each syllable. In this instance, though, her characteristic delivery stresses melancholy; she raises the pitch of her voice towards the end of her first phrase, continuing to pick off leaves from the vine absent-mindedly but in an agitated, nervous way, not yet looking up. As she says, 'I doubt if that wine will get better', Romand continues fiddling with the leaves, keeping her eyes lowered. As she finishes her line with 'Not that vintage. I don't think so', she looks up at

Fig. 3.4

Isabelle. This is normal when people converse: she passes the conversation back to Isabelle, indicating that she has finished talking. However, director and actor underline Magali's unhappiness in this shot: isolated in the vine, eyes open wide, mouth unsmiling, head tilted and hands fiddling in front of her, Magali looks sad (Fig. 3.4). Her 'vintage', which she thinks has reached its best, refers, for us and for her, to her worries about ageing. Rohmer cuts after this sentence about a vintage not improving any more and the feeling of Magali's sadness, moving to a different location and a different type of shot.

At the second location Isabelle and Magali both walk through the vines, Magali leading the way, saying, 'over there, that's my neighbour's property', and gesturing with her left hand, palm open. Isabelle follows Magali through the windy fields, hat initially in

Fig. 3.5

hand, but then placed on her head. Throughout this dialogue, Marie Rivière has to hold onto her hat to avoid losing it to the wind, while Romand's hair swirls wildly around her head (Fig. 3.5). Bringing a hat indicates a degree of preparation, but the failure to control it also suggests preparation going awry. Isabelle listens to her friend say, 'see how well it's kept', then replies, 'Not at all like yours.' Rohmer then cuts to a point-of-view shot of the neighbour's tidy vines, while Magali acknowledges that 'there are no weeds between the vines'. Revealing that she 'got criticised this year', Magali justifies her stub-

bornness: 'If you don't want weeds, you have to use herbicide, which spoils the taste of the wine.' Magali's reason for not using herbicide indicates her willingness to take risks for the sake of the quality of the outcome: she risks a poor harvest as the weeds may strangle the grapes and she accepts that she should have done more spring hoeing.

Jean-Marc Lalanne points out that Magali's reluctance to use herbicide as an intervention in her wine echoes the same principle in her personal life, in that she does not want to intervene artificially to create a situation, while 'Isabelle, on the other hand, is like the neighbour's vine. Her principles are those of organisation and intervention' (1998: 43). As well as demonstrating her unwillingness to intervene, Magali's opposition to herbicide supports her claim that she 'honours' the land, does not 'exploit' it, and indicates her willingness to take risks to ensure the quality of the harvest. Not using herbicide to control weed growth, like waiting for wine to mature, may lead to nothing.

As the two women continue to amble, Magali observes that letting weeds grow brings advantages: close shots show some corn rocket and the wild snapdragon, the name of which Isabelle later remembers during her walk with Gérald in the church's herb garden at La Garde-Adhémar, just as he starts to doubt her act. Isabelle turns around and takes the lead through the vines, explaining as she walks, in a key explanatory line for her character: 'It's not my memory; it's my attention span. When I'm in the countryside, I don't like to focus on things … by my nature I'm a dreamer, in the city or the country.' After Magali declares herself an artisan, Rohmer cuts to a shot of her Renault driving up a steep path.

Once out of the car, at the third location, Isabelle and Magali walk up a hillside. In the background, we can see the rich, dark greens of a wooded valley and, in the distance, the mountains; Isabelle comments on these, 'the Ventoux hills', the film again orientating us. Magali cautions Isabelle, who wanders away from the path towards the slopes, asking 'Where does that lead to?' 'It's steep, don't fall', Magali warns her friend. Away from her vines, Magali hesitates but Isabelle is more adventurous; she has the security of her marriage. Wandering down the slope, Isabelle asks Magali about a bush, whether it is juniper. The more knowledgeable wine-maker corrects her, 'it's cade'. 'Are there snakes here?', Isabelle asks. A cut to Magali shows her standing characteristically, hands on hips, legs spaced apart, head tilted in amusement as she asks, jokingly, if Isabelle means 'vipers'. As they discuss being scared of animals or of bees and wasps, Magali stays near the path, but Isabelle wanders into the bushes on the slope and gets entangled in a briar. Magali rushes over to help her (Fig. 3.6).

Fig. 3.6

Rohmer's use of metaphor deepens when Isabelle gets tangled up after straying from the path.[14] With her close-fitting t-shirt and jeans, practically and safely dressed as Isabelle is not, Magali offers few opportunities for entanglement; she unhooks the branch from her wayward friend's blouse, telling her to be more careful next time. They return to the path and their dialogue again verifies Rohmer's resourceful fascination with construction and metaphor. After Magali unhooks Isabelle, the latter exclaims 'what dexterity!', but Magali responds by conceding her weaknesses and confessing her vulnerability: 'Yes, but I've got no grip. I'm bad at things that take strength … Luckily, there's Marcel. But he's old, he's going to retire … OK, make fun of me, but I need help.' The scene ends with this allusive acknowledgement by Magali that she would like someone around.

Set during late summer and early autumn, *Conte d'automne* begins with a discussion about the quality of a wine and ends with a song celebrating the grape harvest. Rohmer asserts that: 'With me, the season is never indeterminate. If I decide to set a film in winter, it's because of things that only occur in winter' (quoted in Daney & Bonitzer 1981: 31). Examples of the seasons being used as metaphors or symbols are not hard to find in art, literature and song. Typically, autumn has been used figuratively in two ways: the first is to evoke the autumn harvest providing fruitful plenty; the second is to allude to maturity, ripeness turning to decay. Rohmer uses both of these traditional associations to develop *Conte d'automne*'s story and, as writer and director, he finds several ways of expressing his autumnal themes.[15] Rohmer also explains how he always tries to discover a second theme for his films during the writing stage, often finding that the actors or the locations inspire this second theme: 'For example, in *Conte d'hiver*, there is the story of this girl who searches for the father of her child, but also her belief in reincarnation. And for me, the film exists at exactly the moment when this second theme appears' (quoted in Burdeau & Frodon 2004: 20). The 'second theme' of *Conte d'été* is the music, and yet Rohmer explains that he only decided to make the lead character a musician because the actor himself was a guitarist (Amiel & Herpe 1999: 14). A 'second theme' of *Conte d'automne* is the wine and yet, similarly, Rohmer only decided to make Magali a wine-maker when he was looking for locations and discovered that many of the women he met in the region worked in vineyards. While exploring the area Rohmer found two adjacent vineyards, one unkempt with straggly weeds but no herbicide, the other neatly laid out and whistle-clean. He decided to film in the vineyard of one of the women he met, and ended up incorporating into the script some of the things that she said about the use of herbicide (Amiel & Vassé 1998: 12). Magali's decision not to use herbicide is relevant to her character in several ways: she confesses to Isabelle that her neighbours were not happy about her refusal to use herbicide and this difficult relationship with them, her refusal to intervene and her correlating acceptance of disorder all complement her character appropriately.

Choosing to make Magali a wine-maker allowed Rohmer to make the quality of her wine both a part of the story and a metaphor for other issues related to maturity. However, Rohmer had also to decide that Magali's connection to the land would distinguish her artisanal business from a corporate enterprise. Artisanal wine-growing allows for sophistication of taste to become part of the story more than organic carrot production would; Magali can produce something that is 'vraiment bon' to both Grégoire and Gérald, the latter of whom demonstrates a refined palate. Uncertainties about the quality of a harvest guarantee that autumnal warmth and ripeness are part of the story, while doubts about the ability of Magali's wine to age well connect expressively to wider questions of waiting; relevant anxieties about waiting for something or someone are intertwined with the question of whether a Côtes-du-Rhône will improve with age, not an issue with established *appellation contrôlée* wines (Magali does not make Châteauneuf-du-Pape or Gigondas, distinguished Rhône valley wines). Rohmer exploits a full range of variations of the autumnal theme: Isabelle and Magali's discussion is about wine that ages well and the benefits of not intervening; Rosine later remarks that some women remain young; it is a film about a middle-aged woman meeting a man, but a part of it concerns a middle-aged man, Etienne, who is only interested in younger women.

The sophistication of Rohmer's work comes from its capacity to impart a feeling of things not being talked about but felt by both characters: Isabelle knows that she will have to persuade Magali to come to the wedding reception; Magali resists persuasion. Magali must know that her friend will try to act as a Good Samaritan to her, matching her charitably but awkwardly with an inappropriate man. She fears this awkwardness; perhaps she also fears being exposed as one of few single women at the wedding reception. The conversation between Isabelle and Magali is ostensibly about the forty bottles of wine that Magali will supply for the wedding, yet many of Isabelle and Magali's lines have a substantial resonance as indirect admissions about their lives. Magali's doubts about her wine echo her anxieties about meeting anyone and it is significant that her wine and its ageing quality will be the focus of the conversation between Gérald and Magali when they eventually meet at the wedding. Rohmer makes the wine references felt as part of an extended yet unobtrusive metaphor: the story's parallels and echoes endow the film with its richly ironic humour yet two constants in Rohmer's art prevent this controlled structure from seeming contrived. The first is the use of settings as both locations and prompts for Rohmer's themes; the second is the type of performance his films elicit.

His actors delicately finesse the film's comic structure and fill out the emotional and psychological richness, often subtly hinting at their characters' awareness of a line's resonances. The emotional intelligence that Rohmer's characters reveal – especially the women – allows them to combine innocent declaration with wry acknowledgement. In their comic delivery of Rohmer's intricately patterned dialogue the actors are able to suggest that the characters know at some level that something like the wine symbolism is functioning as both a genuine topic of conversation and an indirect expression of deeper feelings. This is also a result of Rohmer's detailed control of the script as apparently innocuous lines of dialogue often resonate beyond their immediate context. For example, elements introduced in the scene at Magali's vineyard develop further when Isabelle pretends to be a wine-grower during her meetings with Gérald. At their second lunch, at La Garde-Adhémar, Magali's earlier comment to Isabelle about her lacking strength finds its partner when Isabelle knocks over the salt and pepper shakers. Embarrassed, she apologises: 'Sorry, I'm clumsy.' Gérald politely disagrees, but she then explains that 'I'm better at big tasks than small ones, because of my large hands'. The line is part of the small talk of two strangers, but it recalls, as a further contrast between the two women, Magali's earlier line. The 'big task' that Isabelle is 'better at' refers to her ability to arrange something like this between Gérald and her friend, something for which Magali confesses she lacks strength and for which she says that she needs help.

The film continues to develop its use of wine-growing, both when Isabelle and Gérald first meet for lunch and then finally when Gérald and Magali meet at the wedding. During their first meeting Isabelle and Gérald talk about themselves and Isabelle, pretending to be Magali, describes her friend's past: 'My dad died five years ago. I took over his busi… his vineyard.' Isabelle almost slips up, but her revelation that she is a wine-grower distracts him for he says, as if pleased at finding common ground so soon, that he too is the son of a wine-grower. When Gérald asks whether Isabelle produces 'Côtes-du-Rhône or [Coteaux-du-]Tricastin', the latter being the name of both a local area and wine as well as the name of the power station, she tells him that she produces Côtes-du-Rhône. This discussion leads to the conversation about their backgrounds and the discovery that until decolonisation in the 1960s both their families had been wine-growers in the French colonies in the Maghreb. Both families had moved to La Drôme, the area where they live. This explanation is historically realistic; of the wine grown in the Coteaux-du-Tricastin region Jancis Robinson notes: 'The region was substantially re-developed by *pieds noirs* returning from North Africa in the late 1960s' (1999: 717). It is further evidence that Rohmer integrates wine-making into the plot at an extraordinarily dense level of detail.

Fig. 3.7

When Gérald and Magali eventually meet, at Emilia and Grégoire's wedding reception, their encounter takes place as he tastes her wine (Fig. 3.7). 'Like it?' she asks. 'It has aged well', he replies. He then looks at the label to check the year that it was made. '1989', he exclaims twice, surprised by its age and quality: 'For a local wine that's exceptional ... as good as the Gigondas I had yesterday.' Gérald's compliments about the wine provoke her to confess: 'Forgive me for bragging – it's my wine.' She turns away from the table to face him; he does the same, making face-to-face introductions possible: 'Je suis viticultrice', she smiles broadly, removing her sunglasses.[16] Gérald then smiles and says that he is the son of wine-makers who returned to France from Algeria. The whole film has been leading to this conversation: Gérald and Magali discussing the quality of her wine. Gérald knows from Isabelle that Magali is a wine-maker, but he does not know, though he may suspect, that this is her wine being served at the wedding. We cannot know for sure what Gérald knows about the wine he is drinking before he praises it, though the film has opened with Grégoire praising Magali's wine as 'vraiment bon', and it seems unlikely that Gérald takes advantage of prior knowledge and performs a piece of flattering theatre for Magali. The optimism that infuses their first meeting grows from the good fortune that leads him to compliment her wine before he knows whose wine it is. Romand and Libolt's performances in this scene are entrancing. Auspiciously for a flirtatious first meeting we can detect the soft warmth between the pair, the spark of attraction that suits the sharply sunlit autumnal clarity. Isabelle chose the right letter and the right man to meet Magali. This wedding reception introduction differs substantially from the one that takes place in *Le Beau mariage*, but then Dombasle's Clarisse and Romand's Sabine both act more like Rosine than Isabelle.

Libolt and Romand ensure that their conversation develops with an easy wonder that distracts us from remembering that Gérald has prepared for this meeting. Magali smiles continuously and offers, as a partnering return to his description of his parents' move from Algeria to France, 'mine from Tunisia', chuckling at her own haste in replying: 'They left me that vineyard.' Gérald confesses regretfully that his parents gave up wine-growing for business; 'but I miss the countryside', he says, looking around. Magali appears more excited than we have yet seen her. She looks down, bites her lip, hesitates before telling Gérald, 'You know…', and she turns her back to the camera but her face to Gérald, 'few people can say what you said – you delighted me.' We have already had some indication of Gérald's knowledge of wine in the restaurant with Isabelle, but he modestly insists that 'not only connoisseurs can appreciate it'. Gérald implies, as the subtitle awkwardly translates that 'anyone can tell it's good'; but Magali takes his word and reverses its sentiment, complimenting him by implication: 'Yes, but the opinion of a connoisseur is flattering.'

The dance scene that concludes *Conte d'automne* also concludes the film's use of wine-growing, while re-introducing Isabelle's husband, with whom she dances. He dances well and appears attentive. There are no villains in Rohmer's films; we have just not seen his story. As Isabelle dances with her husband, her daughter and her new son-in-law dance playfully with them, all laughing in the glow of the evening lights. The words of the song appear on screen. It is a spirited song, performed as an upbeat celebration by the band, and the family dances to celebrate the daughter's marriage. Appropriately, the song celebrates the passing of time and links our growth with the harvesting of rich fruits. Isabelle has brought Gérald and Magali together (they have left separately but have arranged to meet soon); she is dancing with her husband at her daughter's wedding party. For most of this scene, Marie Riviére smiles over Yves Alcaïs' shoulders; in the last shot she loses her smile and looks down. Rohmer concludes the film with this lingering poignant image of Isabelle resting her head on Jean-Jacques' shoulder (Fig. 3.8). She looks sad, distant and regretful. Isabelle may only feel sad at the thought of her daughter leaving the family home, but we remember her earlier embrace with Gérald in the living room. As Isabelle tried to find a partner for Magali, she may have begun to experience niggling, barely acknowledged and never articulated

Fig. 3.8

feelings that climax in the excitement of her embrace with Gérald. Riviére's last glance downwards allows for the possibility that Isabelle has enjoyed flirting with Gérald, more than she would be willing to say.[17] However, although Isabelle seems to be thinking of something, possibly Gérald, Rohmer refuses to confirm these feelings.

Alcaïs, as Isabelle's husband, is a handsome man; dancing at the end of the film with his wife lends his character an air of sprightly sophistication. However, the most conspicuous thing about him is his thick grey hair; next to Isabelle, he looks the eighteen years older than her that he is. Rohmer undoubtedly thought of this during casting because Alain Libolt's Gérald is younger, closer to Isabelle's age. Although Rohmer wants us to notice these things, age differences do not account for Isabelle's actions. In Gérald Isabelle discovers a diversion from routine, something for which she did not know she was looking. While Rosine wants to extract herself from her relationship with Etienne, even though he continues to attract her, Isabelle constructs, as George Eliot writes of Rosamond in *Middlemarch*, 'a little romance which seeks to vary the flatness of her life' (1988: 810). Isabelle loves her husband but the film acknowledges that, again as Eliot writes, a marriage's 'demand for self-suppression and tolerance' can produce 'vague uneasy longings' (ibid.); in her plot to find Magali a partner Isabelle stumbles across an opportunity to daydream of romance. A married woman who perhaps feels the flatness of her routine ostensibly does nothing adulterous. For Isabelle, as she confesses to Gérald 'it's a little game that amused me, even though it's a bit dangerous'. Pascal Bonitzer argues of the portraits of marriage and adultery in Rohmer's *Six contes moraux* that the phantom of adultery serves to reinvigorate desire within marriage (1999: 120). The revival of a marriage is not the subject of *Conte d'automne* though. Isabelle appears happy in her marriage; yet although no reason for Isabelle's unhappiness emerges, Rohmer's film worries at the institution. From outside, from Magali's viewpoint, say, this marriage looks fine, stable and harmonious, but Rohmer offers a privileged view of Isabelle. Without using fantasy or melodrama he allows us to perceive gradually that Isabelle may feel dissatisfied.

Through the construction of two parallel plots to find Magali a partner *Conte d'automne* is able to compare the situations of an older woman and a younger woman. Although I have not discussed Rosine and Etienne's roles here, I want to end by citing a significant conversation that takes place between them during the third scene of the film.[18] This scene introduces Etienne and vividly illustrates Rosine's conflicting feelings towards her former lover. When Etienne says that affairs with students lead only to regrets or to friendships that are far from innocent, Rosine accuses him: 'You love that. You thrive on ambiguity.' Etienne's response summarises one of Rohmer's central concerns: 'Maybe for the titbits of life, the part that is half dreamt and half lived. But for the basics [le part solide], and I don't say one's more profound than the other, I hate ambiguity. If I live with a woman, she'll be younger than I am, but the age difference will be reasonable.' Etienne's comments on a part of life that is 'half dreamt and half lived', for which ambiguity might be acceptable, describe the feelings of several Rohmerian characters. In *Conte d'automne* they characterise Isabelle's uncertain relationship with Gérald; she enjoys the ambiguity of their relationship until it threatens the solid part of her life, her marriage.

As I have discussed above, Rohmer extensively researches his locations and, in effect, his actors, using both as productive sources. The director acknowledges that his films contain elements of 'of absolute *cinéma-vérité*, of documentary-fiction' (quoted in Daney & Bonitzer 1981: 32). Nevertheless, while Rohmer gives solidity to what he can firmly represent, he creates drama and intrigue out of what is 'half dreamt and half lived' by the characters, showing us, in Pascal Bonitzer's words, an 'enchanted reality' (1999: 35). *Conte d'automne*'s intrigue stems from ambiguity about Isabelle's feelings for Gérald and from Rosine's feelings for Etienne. The youthful intensity of feelings which Rosine experiences does not disappear, but the part of our lives that is more solid begins to take more of the time previously devoted to being 'half dreamt and half lived'.

Although Rohmer insists that the 'opaque' last shot of the film 'doesn't allow us to know what she thinks', it tempts us to conclude that the film shows satisfaction in long-term relationships as difficult if not impossible. The vitality of the film, however, develops less from one conclusion than from its comparisons of relationships; hints about Isabelle's unhappiness – depressing hints – come within a tale about Magali's possible future happiness. The story of *Conte d'automne* is potentially that of a melodrama like *The Reckless Moment* (Max Ophuls, 1949) or *Brief Encounter* (David Lean, 1945), but Rohmer pulls back from the certainties of unhappy marriages and trapped wives. Isabelle does not appear unsettled in her marriage, yet we see Gérald throw her stability off-balance. She drifts into the flirtation with him thinking that she controls her intervention into Magali's life and that by not meeting Gérald in the evening she avoids commitment, but his declarations to her disturb her equilibrium.

The last frames of *Conte d'automne* are sensitive to Isabelle's feelings for Gérald and sensitive to the complexity of marriage, friendship and love. One could argue that the film concludes that marriage might not be as satisfying as Emilia hopes for. Magali might envy the security and confidence that Isabelle's marriage affords her but Isabelle, despite being apparently happy and secure in her relationship, might envy Magali's freedom. However, *Conte d'automne* ends both optimistically and pessimistically: Magali and Gérald attract each other spontaneously and genuinely; Isabelle is not depicted as trapped in a marriage that suffers from an acute power imbalance. *Conte d'automne* demands recognition that she might be dissatisfied, though she might never act on these feelings. While Magali longs for a relationship, Isabelle, in contrast with Rosine, feels her youth – and therefore the possibility for youthful dalliances – disappearing permanently. Marriage offers stability and opportunities to avoid loneliness, but being single offers the potential for the spark and excitement of romantic entanglements; the first heady flush of romance is denied to Isabelle, but not to Magali. Although Isabelle responds giddily to the headiness she experiences with Gérald, it ends quickly. The ending does not confirm that marriage guarantees happiness, but nor does it show it as an institution that necessarily traps women. The film studies social norms and values; it does not prioritise the exposure of an oppressive ideology. Like all of Rohmer's films, *Conte d'automne* offers a shaded insight into the kind of restlessness we can experience with the constraints and flatness of our routines; perhaps it is more common that we might daydream of our responses to a sense of frustration and vague disappointment, less common that we might have an affair. Just as he does in *Le Beau mariage* and *Le Rayon vert*, in *Conte d'automne*, Rohmer brings these daydreams to life.

Conclusion

Rohmer's organisation of his material means that his films have an impressive vitality and richness, even in something apparently so loosely produced as *Le Rayon vert*. It can be hard to isolate what is most important in Rohmer's films as every detail seems to have a function beyond its immediate context; and he works out his subjects into all dimensions of a film. There are many parts of the three films studied here that would reward further attention. The scene in Edmond's chambers in *Le Beau mariage*, for example, with its astonishing confrontation between Dussolier and Romand, is one of the most complex in that film. The whole Biarritz sequence in *Le Rayon vert* could be productively examined at length, particularly the wordless 7-minute sequence following Delphine alone on the crowded beach, much of which was filmed just by Rivière and Maintigneux; more could be said about the role of Lena and the scenes featuring her and the two young men in the café, or the role of water as a purifying – or at least a clarifying – element (Delphine emerges from the sea and tells the truth, to Lena, for the first time in the film). One could also look at the delicate brilliance of the Garden Café scene in *Conte d'automne*, during which Isabelle reveals herself to Gérald. The film's longest scene and its dramatic peak, the shifting mood and temper of it turn upon Libolt and Rivière's subtle performances and Rohmer's intricate use of shot/reverse-shots.

In that scene, as in all three films, the moving force which dominates is the relationship between what characters say, what they do and what they think about. *Le Beau mariage*, *Le Rayon vert* and *Conte d'automne* are all critical of and yet sympathetic towards heroines who sometimes behave in a frustratingly blinkered way: Sabine's stubborn decision to marry Edmond; Delphine's refusal to socialise; Rosine and Isabelle's meddling; Magali's intransigence. However, Rohmer renders these traits in contexts that reinforce our understanding of these characters. Within the dynamic co-ordination of settings, performances and framings, the three films dissect characters' feelings and motivations, revealing the sources of contradictory behaviour. A sustained and energetic control of the films' style ensures our ironic but sympathetic involvement with the heroines, even those, like Sabine in *Le Beau mariage* and Delphine in *Le Rayon vert*, who occasionally behave in a silly manner. The result is that anyone who tries to draw straightforward moral lessons from Rohmer's work is liable to miss a viewpoint that his films make available. Rohmer's films do not offer moral judgements on people or actions; they explore, as Tamara Tracz comments, 'the dilemma' (2003).

Too often, Eric Rohmer's films have been received as examples of an elegant but ultimately straightforward realism. His association with André Bazin and with the *nouvelle vague* has meant that critics have often not looked beyond the apparently transparent presentation of actors and settings, particularly within the critical discourses which have valued fragmentation and disruption over coherence and consistency. This study has hopefully demonstrated the complexity and richness of Rohmer's films and, in particular, his visual style. Rohmer's moving films about ordinary life touch on major philosophical and personal issues, yet they can seem so slight that it is easy to miss their subtly suggestive meanings. Rohmer's careful scrutiny of behaviour and the sophisticatedly ironic method of storytelling he uses, by which means we observe follies but never condemn them, results in a compassionate and humane art.

NOTES

1 Durgnat writes: 'Human relations, or intrigues, are conducted through so much explanation that conscious and reflected-upon principles and decisions all but replace action and feeling as the substance of the film. Reflexivity, even objectivity, begins within the characters, and criticism inevitably resembles a commentary upon a running commentary' (1988: 198). See also his 'Eric Rohmer: The Enlightenment's Last Gleaming' (1990).

2 Rohmer in *Télérama*, 1013, 15 June 1968, quoted in Crisp 1988: 51. For discussion of Howard Hawks's use of stars, see Gerald Mast (1982). As Mast explains, Hawks's films shift 'the emphasis away from the external incidents and toward the underlying psychological and emotional interactions beneath the incidental surfaces' (1982: 300). Rohmer talks extensively about Hawks in Serge Daney and Pascal Bonitzer's interview, saying 'it is Hawks who has served me as a secret model' (1981: 30).

3 Maria Tortajada similarly observes Rohmer's use of the same actors in different roles: 'The parts of Marie Rivière in these two films [*Le Rayon vert* and *Conte d'automne*] are diametrically opposed: as Delphine, she stays on the side of authenticity, ideal love and transparency; as Isabelle, she manipulates as the third person who mediates between the couple' (2004: 234, n.1). However, despite this apparently diametric opposition between Delphine and Isabelle, *Conte d'automne* gives an ironic ending to its story of Isabelle's mediation between Magali (Béatrice Romand) and Gérald (Alain Libolt), because although the married woman manipulates the situation to help her friend, she is surprised by the chance attraction that she feels towards Gérald.

4 There is, as John Gibbs pointed out to me, a contrast between this wall hanging and Sabine's poster. One could also mention the poster on the wall of her Parisian apartment, which advertises an exhibition of work by her lover, Simon Leghen.

5 Béatrice Romand recalls: 'For *Le Beau mariage*, I thought that there would be some freedom, but no! The places were marked on the floor to a millimetre' (quoted in Higuinen & Lalanne 1998: 41).

6 Part of this quotation is cited in Hertay (1998: 77). Alain Hertay also repeats what Rohmer says about his films becoming more and more written during the 1970s and his working more with experienced actors rather than non-professionals as he had done with Patrick Bauchau, Haydée Politoff and Daniel Pommereulle on *La Collectioneuse*.

7 *La Femme de l'aviateur* credits Lisa Heredia in the cast list, while *Le Beau mariage* and *Les Nuits de la pleine lune* both credit Lisa Heredia as assistant editor; *Le Rayon vert* lists her in the cast as Lisa Heredia; however, *Le Rayon vert*, *Quatre aventures de Reinette et Mirabelle*, *L'Ami de mon amie* and *Conte de printemps* all credit her as Maria-Luisa Garcia, editor of each of the four films.

8 Sophie Maintigneux confirms that the performers improvised this scene of Delphine explaining her vegetarianism to a bemused family: 'Nobody knew what was going to happen. I had a pile of magazines at my feet and I loaded the camera as I went along. It so happened that these people didn't know that Marie is a vegetarian, and one of them, suddenly, brought out some

pork chops' (quoted in Durel 1986: 39).

9   Rohmer wrote a review of *Stromboli* for *Cahiers du cinéma* on its release, reprinted in *The Taste of Beauty* (1989). He begins his criticism by saying that '*Stromboli* is the story of a sinner who receives God's grace' and that it is a 'grand Catholic film' (1989: 124). Thirty years later, in 1983, during an interview with Jean Narboni, Rohmer says: 'Rossellini is the one who turned me away from existentialism. It happened in the middle of *Stromboli*. During the first minutes of the screening, I felt the limits of this Sartrian realism, to which I thought the film was going to be confined. I hated the way it invited me to look at the world, until I understood that it was *also* inviting me to look beyond that' (Narboni 1989: 9). Despite Rohmer's comments on *Stromboli*'s religious aspect (and it is a mistake to take his words too literally), as subsequent critics have noted, the film is ambivalent about Karin's experiences, just as Rossellini himself was. Tag Gallagher (1998) describes Rossellini's varying responses, while in the 1974 interview with Gallagher and John Hughes that is published in *My Method*, Rossellini declares unequivocally that he does not believe in God and nor did he when he made *Stromboli* (1995: 230, first published in *Changes* 87, April 1974).

10 Rohmer found this shop as Delphine finds it, 'by chance' (Ostria 1986: 35).

11 *Le Rayon vert* credits Philippe Demard for the sunset. Rohmer explains: 'I waited a whole year to photograph it [in France], and we never did get it, so I had to send a technician off to the Canaries to shoot it there! But also, of course, the ray is a bit like Hitchcock's MacGuffin, a motor for the story' (quoted in Andrew 1987: 26).

12 In his book on Rohmer, Pascal Bonitzer develops this idea: 'We should note by the way that "ontologically" cinema shares the same dual nature of dream and reality, of an "enchanted" reality, as that in which Don Quixote travels. In principle, cinema records reality – landscapes, houses, men, women and animals, Clermont-Ferrand, Lake Annecy, the Talloire villa, the lanes of Le Mans, the Cergy-Pontoise area, etc (to mention only Rohmerian settings). But on screen, whether we want it or not, these elements of reality find themselves recruited to serve the dream, the fiction, the film which we have come to enjoy in a darkened room. To be a cinema hero, to live things as if in a film: this basic Quixotic desire has been experienced by all cinema spectators (1999: 35).

13 Fiona A. Villella (2000) also notes the 'innate connection between Magali and her vineyard' that Rohmer establishes in this scene, as does Michel Serceau, who writes: 'Isabelle comes and goes from the house to the bookshop, to Magali's property, to her meetings with Gérald. She isn't engraved into this environment, where she merely resides. The visit to the vines reveals her lack of knowledge of nature' (2000: 81).

14 Tom Ryan also notes that 'the women's ennui is suggested by their constant movement around the vineyards rather than through their conversation ... Nor is it by chance that, wandering away, Isabelle catches her blouse on a thorn' (Andrew *et al.* 2000).

15 Bert Cardullo notes the 'double meaning' of *Conte d'automne*'s title: 'not only have the valley's grapes ripened, but four of its inhabitants – the principal figures in *Autumn Tale* – have come to that mature age of 45 or so when the reality of winter, or the fact of mortality, first comes into view' (2004: 178).

16 Maria Tortajada, in an article on Rohmer's exploration of 'ideal' love and pragmatic love, points

to this moment as significant: 'What structures the meeting is the emphasis upon the couple's looks, which is of course highly significant because the perfect model of love at first sight shows the pair looking directly into each other's eyes experiencing love's transparency' (2004: 236). For this reason, Romand's removal of her sunglasses, the shading of her eyes to see more clearly and the turning of her back to the camera are all significant.

17 Several commentators, including the director, have noted this shot. For example, Fiona Villella writes: 'Isabelle's anxiety in the final shot confirms a longing, restlessness and questioning that Rohmer explores with such masterful subtlety' (2000). Editor Mary Stephen says that she chose this one out of three or four shots and that Rohmer then approved her choice, sending written instructions to exhibitors that the houselights of the cinemas be kept down until the last frame of the film (Mousoulis 2000). *Cahiers du cinéma* used the final frame as the lead photograph in their special issue on *Conte d'automne* (September 1998, 527).

18 For a more substantial discussion of Rosine and Etienne's roles see my article in *Undercurrent* (2006).

BIBLIOGRAPHY

Amiel, Vincent and Herpe, Noël (1999) 'Eric Rohmer on *Conte d'été*', trans. Pierre Hodgson, in Michel Ciment and Noël Herpe (eds) *Projections 9: French Filmmakers on Film-Making*. London: Faber and Faber, 13–17.

Amiel, Vincent and Vassé, Claire (1998) 'Entretien Éric Rohmer: Des gestes proches du dessin', *Positif*, October, 11–15.

Andrew, Geoff (1987) 'Rohmer's Return', *Time Out*, 11–18 March, 24–6.

Andrew, Geoff, Terry Ballard, Rose Capp, Rolando Caputo, Adrian Danks, Darron Davies, Philippa Hawker, Tina Kaufman, Bill Mousoulis, Tom Ryan, Brad Stevens, Fiona A. Villella and Jake Wilson (2000) 'Rohmer Talk', compiled by Bill Mousoulis, *Senses of Cinema* 5. On-line. Available at: www.sensesofcinema.com/contents/00/5/talk.html (accessed 16 June 2003).

Anger, Cédric, Emmanuel Burdeau and Serge Toubiana (1996) 'Entretien avec Éric Rohmer', *Cahiers du cinéma*, 503, May, 45–9.

Bergala, Alain (1986) 'Retour à Stromboli', *Cahiers du cinéma*, 387, September, 22–4.

Binet-Bouteloup, Marie (1982) 'Éric Rohmer tourne *Le Beau mariage*', *Cahiers du cinéma*, 332, February, 35–7.

Bonitzer, Pascal (1999) *Éric Rohmer*. Paris: Editions de l'Etoille/Cahiers du cinéma.

Burdeau, Emmanuel and Jean-Michel Frodon (2004) 'Entretien avec Éric Rohmer sur *Triple Agent*', *Cahiers du cinéma*, 587, March, 16–23.

Carbonnier, Alain and Fabrice Revault d'Allonnes (1986) 'Tête à clap! Marie Rivière', *Cinéma*, 368, 17 September, 16.

Cardullo, Bert (2004) *In Search of Cinema: Writings on International Film Art*. Montréal: McGill-Queen's University Press.

Clédar, Jean (2006) *Éric Rohmer: Évidence et ambiguité du cinéma*. Paris: Le Bord de l'eau éditions.

Crisp, Colin (1988) *Eric Rohmer: Realist and Moralist*. Bloomington: Indiana University Press.

Daney, Serge (1982) 'J'vais m'marier', *Cahiers du cinéma*, 338, July/August, 56–8.

Daney, Serge and Pascal Bonitzer (1981) 'Entretien avec Éric Rohmer', *Cahiers du cinéma*, 323–4, May, 29–39.

De Baecque, Antoine and Jean-Marc Lalanne (1998) 'A mes acteurs, je serai fidèle toute ma vie: Entretien avec Éric Rohmer', *Cahiers du cinéma*, 527, September, 32–37.

Durel, Michel (1986) 'L'Heure bleue', *Cinématographe*, 122, September, 39.

Durgnat, Raymond (1988) '*L'Ami de mon amie* (*My Boyfriend's Girlfriend*)', *Monthly Film Bulletin*, 55, 654, July, 198–9.

____ (1990) 'Eric Rohmer: The Enlightenment's Last Gleaming', *Monthly Film Bulletin*, 57, 678, July, 187–8.

Eliot, George (1988 [1871]) *Middlemarch*. London: Penguin.

Etchegaray, Françoise (1986) 'À la poursuite du rayon vert', *Cahiers du cinéma*, 387, September, 26–7.

Gallagher, Tag (1998) *The Adventures of Roberto Rossellini*. New York: Da Capo.

Goudet, Stéphane (2004) 'Entretien Éric Rohmer: "On dit" ou l'Histoire hors champs', *Positif*, 518, April, 23–7.

Guarner, José Luis (1970) *Roberto Rossellini*. London: Studio Vista.

Hagberg, G. L. (1994) *Meaning and Interpretation: Wittgenstein, Henry James, and Literary Interpretation*. Ithaca: Cornell University Press.

Hammond, Robert and Jean-Pierre Pagliano (1982) 'Eric Rohmer on Film Scripts and Film Plans', *Literature Film Quarterly*, 10, 4, 219–25.

Heinemann, David (2000) 'Reinventing Romance: Eric Rohmer's *Tales of the Four Seasons* – Freedom, Faith and the Search for the Grail', *Film Comment*, 36, 6, November/December, 50–4.

Hertay, Alain (1998) *Éric Rohmer: Comédies et proverbes*. Liège: Editions du Céfal.

Higuinen, Erwan and Jean-Marc Lalanne (1998) 'En campagne des femmes: Rencontre avec Béatrice Romand et Marie Rivière', *Cahiers du cinéma*, 527, September, 38–41.

Klevan, Andrew (2000) *Disclosure of the Everyday: Undramatic Achievement in Narrative Film*. Trowbridge: Flicks Books.

La Fontaine, Jean de (1982 [1678]) *Selected Fables*, trans. James Michie. London: Penguin, 87–88.

Lalanne, Jean-Marc (1998) 'L'annonce faite à Magali', *Cahiers du cinéma*, 528, October, 43–4.

Legrand, Gérard, Hubert Niogret and François Ramasse (1986) 'Entretien avec Éric Rohmer', *Positif*, 309, November, 15–23.

Leigh, Jacob (2006) 'The Caprices of Rosine or the Follies of a Fortnight: Parallel Intrigues in Eric Rohmer's *Conte d'automne*', *Undercurrent*, July. On-line. Available at: http://www.fipresci.org/undercurrent (accessed 1 July 2006).

Magny, Joël (1995) *Éric Rohmer*. Paris: Rivages.

Martin, Adrian (2000) 'Some Kind of Liar: *A Summer's Tale*', *Senses of Cinema* 5. On-line. Available at: www.sensesofcinema.com/contents/00/5/summer.html (accessed 5 September 2002).

Masson, Alain (1986) 'Le Capricorne souverain de l'onde occidentale, sur les *Comédies et proverbes*', *Positif*, 307, September, 43–5.

Mast, Gerald (1982) *Howard Hawks, Storyteller*. Oxford: Oxford University Press.

Mauro, Florence (1985) 'Secret de laboratoire: Entretien avec Éric Rohmer', *Cahiers du cinéma*, 371–2, May, 90–3.

Mousoulis, Bill (2000) 'Interview with Mary Stephen', *Senses of Cinema* 5. On-line. Available at: www.sensesofcinema.com/contents/00/5/stephen.html (accessed 5 September 2002).

Narboni, Jean (1989) 'The Critical Years: Interview with Eric Rohmer', trans. Carol Volk, in Eric Rohmer, *The Taste of Beauty*. Cambridge: Cambridge University Press, 1–18.

Nogueira, Rui (1971) 'Eric Rohmer: Choice and Chance', *Sight and Sound*, 40, 3, 118–22.

Ostria, Vincent (1986) 'A L'improviste: Entretien avec Éric Rohmer', *Cinématographe*, 122, September, 33–7.

Philippon, Alain (1987) 'L'Heure juste', *Cahiers du cinéma*, 392, February, 5–6.

Philippon, Alain and Serge Toubiana (1987) 'Le Cinéma au risque de l'imperfection: Entretien avec Éric Rohmer', *Cahiers du cinéma*, 392, February, 8–13.

Robinson, Jancis (1999) *The Oxford Guide to Wine*. Oxford: Oxford University Press.

Rohmer, Éric (1982) 'Le cinéma des cinéastes [interview by Claude-Jean Philippe and Caroline

Champetier]', tx: France Culture, 30 May, extracts included on *Le Beau mariage* DVD, Arrow Films.

___ (1986) 'Microfilm: Interview with Serge Daney', tx: France Culture, 7 September, extracts included on *Le Rayon vert* DVD, Arrow Films.

___ (1989 [1983]) *The Taste of Beauty*, trans. Carol Volk. Cambridge: Cambridge University Press.

___ (1998) 'Projection privée [Interview with Michel Ciment]', tx: France Culture, 17 October, extracts included on *Conte d'automne* DVD, Artificial Eye.

Rosenbaum, Jonathan (1999) 'Master of Realty: *Autumn Tale*', *Chicago Reader*. On-line. Available at: http://www.chicagoreader.com/movies/archives/1999/0899/08209.html (accessed 31 January 2006).

Rossellini, Roberto (1995) *My Method: Writings and Interviews*, edited by Adriano Aprà. New York: Marsilio Publishers.

Rothman, William (1997) *Documentary Film Classics*. Cambridge: Cambridge University Press.

___ (2004) '*Tale of Winter*: Philosophical Thought in the Films of Eric Rohmer', in William Rothman, *The 'I' of the Camera: Essays in Film Criticism, History, and Aesthetics* (second edition). Cambridge: Cambridge University Press, 325–39.

Saada, Nicholas (1986) 'Entretien avec Sophie Maintigneux: Chef opérateur', *Positif*, 309, November, 24–5.

Serceau, Michel (2000) *Éric Rohmer: les jeux de l'amour, du hasard et du discours*. Paris: Les Éditions du Cerf.

Tortajada, Maria (1999) *Le spectateur séduit: le libertinage dans le cinéma d'Éric Rohmer et sa fonction dans une théorie de la représentation filmique*. Paris: Kimé.

___ (2004) 'Eric Rohmer and the Mechanics of Seduction', *Studies in French Cinema*, 4, 3, 229–38.

Tracz, Tamara (2003) 'Eric Rohmer', *Senses of Cinema*. On-line. Available at: www.sensesofcinema.com/contents/directors/03/rohmer.html (accessed 16 June 2003).

Verne, Jules (1965) *The Green Ray*. London: Arco Publications.

Villella, Fiona A. (2000) 'Magical Realism in *Conte d'automne* (*Autumn Tale*, 1998)', *Senses of Cinema*, 5. On-line. Available at: www.sensesofcinema.com/contents/00/5/autumn.html (accessed 16 June 2003).

Wood, Robin (1974) 'Rossellini', *Film Comment*, 10, 4, July/August, 6–11.

2.3 VOICES IN FILM
Susan Smith

ACKNOWLEDGEMENTS

I would like to thank Douglas Pye and John Gibbs for inviting me to contribute to this exciting new *Close-Ups* series – and Yoram Allon at Wallflower Press for enabling this venture to come to fruition. I am also grateful to my colleague Martin Shingler for giving me the opportunity to present part of this research at the excellent 'Sounding Out' conference that was held at the University of Sunderland in September 2006. The discussions on the voice that were generated during the course of that event were most stimulating and I am very appreciative of the feedback that I received from other delegates. Writing on the voice has been an extremely rewarding experience and one that, as well as helping to open up further areas of study for me, has allowed me the great pleasure of returning to films that I have long admired and arriving at a deeper understanding of them. It has also given me the chance to study the vocal artistry of a range of stars whose achievements – particularly in the case of Greer Garson, Ronald Colman and Robert Donat – have rarely received the recognition they deserve within the discipline of film studies. And it is the rich contribution made by these and other stars to the act of speaking (and, in some cases, singing) in film that this study is above all dedicated to acknowledging.

INTRODUCTION

There is a memorable moment in *Love Me or Leave Me* (Charles Vidor, 1955) where the singer Ruth Etting (Doris Day), now in the depths of despair following her marriage to her controlling manager Marty Snyder (James Cagney), is reunited with her former arranger and would-be lover Johnny Alderman (Cameron Mitchell) in a Hollywood recording studio, during which encounter she proceeds to sing the number 'I'll Never Stop Loving You' to his accompaniment on the piano. Judged in purely visual terms, the staging of this scene is fairly unremarkable as we are shown these two actors sitting by the piano amidst the nondescript setting of an otherwise empty and rather drab-looking sound studio. Yet despite the sterile blandness of the surroundings (the only exception to this being a small section of red and yellow piping that is visible on the wall behind Ruth and Johnny as they stand talking during the initial part of their encounter in the studio), the scene itself is utterly engrossing as we witness the frustrated longings that these two characters have for each other finding some form of partial if still inhibited release during the course of the song. Offered by Johnny to Ruth as a re-declaration of his love for her, the song is performed by Day with a self-absorbed intensity that speaks volumes about her character's yearning to escape from the unhappiness of her marriage to Snyder while simultaneously suggesting – through her habit of staring straight ahead into the distance (rather than at Mitchell) for much of the time – Ruth's extreme difficulty at this point in owning up to her feelings for Johnny. Indeed, in accounting for the effectiveness of this scene, one could argue that it is, if anything, the stark contrast between the overall banality of the *mise-en-scène* and the rich texture of Day's singing voice that ultimately makes this moment so profoundly moving: the drab emptiness of the recording studio comes to embody a quality of emotional barrenness and desolation to Ruth's life that her singing now begins to challenge and defy.

It is a private playing out of feeling – both between these two characters and within Ruth herself – that is completely lost, however, on the figure of Georgie (Harry Bellaver), the loyal stooge sent by an already suspicious Snyder to watch over Ruth as she re-establishes her professional partnership with Johnny. Sitting just outside the recording studio and able to look on at the two of them through the open vista provided by a large transparent screen, this figure would seem – again in purely visual terms – to occupy a quite privileged position as, acting as an extension of Snyder's jealous, controlling gaze, he carries out this surveillance on Ruth's first meeting with Johnny after a substantial period of absence. Yet, separated from these two characters by the soundproof screen and without access to the loudspeaker system that is so prominent during the live recording session that Snyder secretly intrudes into later on, Georgie's inability to hear the impassioned intensity of Day's singing renders him unable to grasp the significance of the emotional drama that is being played out before him, his disconnection from what is going on being confirmed by the aimlessness of his behaviour as he sits, in the dimly-lit background, idly flicking through a magazine during the height of Day's performance.

Johnny's greater proximity to Ruth, as he sits watching her from his position at the piano while she performs the song, does ensure the presence of a more active, alert form of male looking in this scene. In his case, though, the worried attentiveness of his gaze is motivated very differently by feelings of concern regarding the emotionally damaging effects of Snyder's influence over her and by a desire to gain some reassurance, through her performance, of her ongoing self-belief in the value of her singing. And while it is made clear that the number that Ruth sings is one that has been written and chosen for her by Johnny, any notion of him acting here as the author of her desire is swiftly dispelled by Day's ability to take such complete ownership of the song. Performing it with the utmost intensity and conviction, she manages to transform this male figure's verbal affirmation of his unstinting feelings of love for her character (feelings which he has to rely on her to vocalise through the act of singing) into a most moving exploration and rediscovery of Ruth's own sense of selfhood.

There is a particular logic to starting this study with a discussion of this moment from *Love Me or Leave Me* for, having already written about that film as part of my analysis of the musical's fascination with the great female singer in *The Musical: Race, Gender and Performance* (2005), my use of it here is indicative of the extent to which this study emerges as a natural outgrowth from and complement to that earlier work. As a connecting link between these two volumes, this most simply staged of songs (which has no need to depend for its moving effect on the more elaborate techniques and glamorous settings of the big production number) is consequently of interest not just for what it reveals about the expressive power and resilient strength that the great female singer's voice may come to assume in the Hollywood musical, but for what it suggests more broadly about the capacity of the human voice to bring a quality of feeling and texture of meaning to the medium of film that may not be possible to convey through the visuals alone. It is this special cinematic contribution that the voice is capable of making – in both its singing and speaking, verbal and non-verbal aspects – and the creative possibilities that can arise when filmmakers choose to capitalise on the more individualistic properties of certain actors' voices that this study is devoted to exploring. In doing so, it will continue to develop and expand the earlier book's investigation into the expressive qualities of the female voice while simultaneously complementing that with a now much greater emphasis on the relationship between masculinity and the voice. In shifting its focus of interest in this way and in choosing to centre its analysis around a number of key vocally-charged moments in a range of films, it is hoped that this study will in turn offer a valuable counterbalance to some of the more theoretically-driven work in this area. For while much of this has often been keen to stress the importance of acknowledging what Barthes refers to as the 'grain of the voice' or 'the body in the voice as it sings' (1977: 181 & 188) and 'the voice's autonomy from language, indeed from signification' (Dunn & Jones 1994: 1), in practice there has been little detailed, sustained attention given to understanding how an actor's voice actually sounds in the precise context of a particular film and the richly varied, often highly subtle ways in which its distinctive characteristics may be used to shape the poetics of the text in question.

1. Growing up in Minnelli's films: articulating resistance and loss in *Father of the Bride* and *Gigi*

Voicings of unrest in *Father of the Bride* (1950)

'I would like to say a few words about weddings. I've just been through one. Not my own, my daughter's. Some day in the far future I may be able to remember it with tender indulgence, but not now. I always used to think that marriage was a simple affair. Boy and girl meet, they fall in love, get married, they have babies, eventually the babies grow up and meet other babies and they fall in love and get married, and so on and on and on. Looked at that way, it's not only simple, it's downright monotonous. But I was wrong. I figured without the wedding. Now, you fathers will understand. You have a little girl. She looks up to you. You're her oracle. You're her hero. And then the day comes when she gets her first permanent wave and goes to her first real party. And from then on, you're in a constant state of panic. If the boys swarm around, you're in a panic for fear she'll marry one of them. If they don't swarm around, why of course you're in another kind of a panic and you wonder what's the matter with her. So you don't worry about it. You say to yourself, "I've got plenty of time to worry about that. I'll just put off thinking about it." And then suddenly it is upon you! It was just three months ago, exactly three months ago that the storm broke here. It was an ordinary day, very much like any other day. I had caught the commuters' train home, as usual. It was late, as usual...'

In choosing to begin *Father of the Bride* with this speech by Spencer Tracy – who, in his role as Stanley Banks, is shown sitting in his armchair and addressing the camera very directly – Minnelli and his screenwriting team of Frances Goodrich and Albert Hackett manage to signal right from the outset this film's very distinctive sensibility as a domestic comedy and its desire to draw us into a subversive pact of understanding with its male protagonist. Occurring in the immediate aftermath of Stanley's daughter's wedding, this opening monologue by Tracy is delivered in a flat, jaded, wounded tone of voice that perfectly captures his character's overwhelming feelings of desolation and loss. Indeed, as the camera (accompanied on the soundtrack by a rather weary, off-key version of the bridal march music) moves across the room, taking into account the various remnants of the wedding reception that lie scattered on the table and floor before momentarily coming to rest on a view of Tracy's feet and legs (just prior to the start of his speech), it is almost as if his character is being presented here as part of the discarded leftovers from his daughter's wedding, a figure who feels his purpose and value to his daughter are now redundant and whose sense of self-will has, as a result, been greatly depleted. In pausing on this view of Tracy – as his right arm reaches down to his left foot and begins to massage it – the camera itself seems to catch something of his character's lethargy. Then, in unison with his act of pulling his left foot and leg up onto his right knee while lifting the empty shoe up with his other hand, it tracks up to reveal the actor's

Fig. 1.1

upper body and face. As Tracy continues to rub his left foot slowly for a moment, he throws us a brief wary glance (Fig. 1.1), the tentative nature of which, in not assuming a right to immediate intimacy or seeking to impose his gaze upon us too strongly all at once, proves all the more effective in securing our attention and trust, attracting our curiosity as it does and drawing us gradually into an alignment with him that feels quite natural and unforced. The quiet, low pitch of Tracy's voice and the informal style of his address as he begins to speak develop this sense of unforced intimacy and closeness of rapport with the audience. The effectiveness of this becomes all the more apparent when one contrasts it with the highly self-conscious, full-on mode of address adopted by Steve Martin as he tries all too hard to win over the audience's affections during the equivalent opening sequence in the 1991 remake of *Father of the Bride* (directed by Charles Shyer and with some reworking of the original script by him and Frances Shyer).[1]

In the initial mood of despondency that characterises this opening address by Tracy, his voice in fact seems quite close in tone to that of the cynical, world-weary narrator of *film noir* and this parallel is strengthened by the role that his voice-over subsequently plays both in giving further vent to his character's anxieties about Kay (Elizabeth Taylor) and in allowing this male figure to achieve a degree of retrospective control over a situation he otherwise feels quite helpless about. In helping him to impose some form of pattern and order on the emotional turmoil and chaos of the wedding preparations, his voice-over narration can be understood, more particularly, as offering him a form of compensation for those moments (as during the engagement party) where his voice is undermined within the narrative. Yet while Tracy's voice-over narration bears close resemblance, in its anxiety-ridden tone, to its counterpart in *film noir*, in being so predicated on the father's unwavering devotion to his daughter and so dedicated to expressing his concerns about what will happen to both her and their relationship once she is married, it differs quite radically in motivation from the *noir* male's much bleaker construction of the woman as dangerous, threatening other. That Stanley's anxieties are triggered by a realisation of his daughter's growing up could potentially problematise this by inviting his reaction to be read in terms of a fear of her emerging sexuality and independence. And yet, as I hope to demonstrate, a close reading of Tracy's various vocal responses within the film tends to suggest a rather different, more complex set of motives. In exploring the father's reaction on being confronted with the fact of his daughter's growing up, we will begin not with an analysis of the voice-over narration itself but by considering the significance of other moments of vocal release that occur at certain moments within the narrative. Although such utterances lack the more measured control and authority associated with Tracy's voice-over narration, they can nevertheless be understood as forming part of *Father of the Bride*'s overall concern with giving vent to frustrations and anxieties that – as the film's various visual images of claustrophobia and containment suggest – are otherwise liable to remain thwarted and unresolved. Indeed, one could argue that it is precisely in these more unguarded, undisciplined moments of vocal release that both Stanley and the film as a whole perhaps come closest to admitting what they want to say.

The first instance of such diegetic vocal release occurs early on in the flashback section of the narrative during the scene at dinner where Stanley and his wife Ellie (Joan Bennett) discover that their daughter Kay is in love with Buckley Dunstan (Don Taylor), a young man whom Tracy's character comically struggles to recall as he unflatteringly casts his mind back over the various boyfriends of hers that he has encountered in the past. As a dreamy-eyed Kay (who has talked incessantly about Buckley throughout Stanley's subjective musings) responds to her father's question of whether she is going to marry 'this character' with the words 'I guess so', the following exchange takes place, culminating in Stanley's outburst:

Ellie: And just when are you planning on getting married?
Kay: Well, I, I really don't know yet, Mother. It all depends on Buckley's plans. It may be months, it may be a few weeks, it may be any time at all. We can't tell yet. But there's one thing. We won't be pinned down. Buckley's very decided about that sort of thing. He just won't be pinned down.
Stanley: [Sarcastically] I hope that, er, Buckley won't think I'm too nosy if I ask a few simple questions?
Kay: Okay, Pops, I suppose we have to go through this. It seems to me that…
Stanley: [Interrupting her] Who is this Buckley anyway?
Kay: Now listen, Pops…
Stanley: And what's his last name? I hope it's better than his first one!
Kay: Now listen…
Stanley: Where the devil does he come from? And who does he think is going to support him? If he thinks I am he's got another thing coming!

The scenario that arises here in some ways bears striking resemblance to the scene that takes place at the dinner table in Minnelli's earlier musical film *Meet Me in St Louis* (1944). On that occasion the father, Mr Smith (Leon Ames), was also shown discovering (in that case through the confusion caused by the long-distance telephone call from Rose's (Lucille Bremer) boyfriend) that his eldest daughter is, to put it in his words, 'practically on her honeymoon' to a man he has never even heard of, his discovery moments before that he is the last one to find out having prompted him to turn to his wife (Mary Astor) and ask: 'Anna, I'm curious. Just when was I voted out of this family?' It is an exclusion from the emotional life of the family that the grandfather (Harry Davenport) had earlier construed in more explicitly conspiratorial terms when, on hearing the second youngest daughter Agnes (Joan Carroll) ask with regard to the same matter: 'Everybody knows but Papa?', he replied with an air of mischief in his voice: 'Your Papa's not supposed to know. It's enough that we're letting him work hard every day to support the whole flock of us. He can't have everything.' In justifying the father's exclusion in terms that make clear the family's expectation for him to provide for them in his role as breadwinner (a role that is construed as sufficient privilege enough as to warrant exempting him from the rest of the family's domestic affairs), the grandfather's response here gestures towards another link between Mr Smith and Stanley whose own angry reaction to the news of his daughter's forthcoming marriage is rationalised (in the final two lines of his outburst) in terms of an assumption that he will be required to offer financial support to the young couple.

This concern about the economic pressures associated with his patriarchal role is something that finds further outlet for expression during Stanley's angry diatribe against his future son-in-law later that same night and also during his 'man-to-man' talk with him the next evening where he launches into a lengthy monologue about the responsi-bilities involved in being a married man that ironically lasts so long as to leave no time for Buckley to tell him about his own financial situation. But whereas the harassed Mr Smith's preoccupations with his work responsibilities and financial commitments seem to disable him from any close engagement with even his youngest children (one of his few exchanges with Tootie (Margaret O'Brien) during this scene being to ask her to re-mind him to spank her for leaving a roller skate on the stairs for him to fall over on his way down to dinner), in Stanley's case, the shock of his discovery during *Father of the Bride*'s parallel dinner-table scene is made all the more devastating because of the very devoted nature of his involvement with his daughter. Her centrality to the happiness of his domestic life was demonstrated very clearly at the start of the flashback sequence where it was the vibrant sound of her voice calling out 'Pops! Pops! Hi, Pops' as she came down the stairs to greet him that had the effect of animating and breaking through the more mundane nature of his daily return home to the suburbs routine. The great pleasure he takes in this welcome by his daughter invites an even more specific point of contrast with Mr Smith whose own disgruntled reaction on hearing his two eldest daughters singing *Meet Me in St Louis*'s title song on his return home from work could not be more different: 'For heaven's sake stop that screeching!'

Commenting on the significance of Stanley's reaction to the news of his daughter's forthcoming marriage to Buckley, James Naremore argues that 'Stanley's anger and suspicion are prompted by a fairly obvious Freudian need to keep Kay to himself...' (1993: 97). Yet when considered within the precise context of the scene itself and Tracy's performance during it, there seems to be nothing necessarily 'obvious', inevitable or indeed adequate about the supposedly Freudian nature of Stanley's motivations here. It is certainly reasonable to infer that his initial expressions of hostility towards Buckley are triggered in part by his sense of shock on realising how this figure has taken over the centre ground that he had previously occupied in his daughter's affections. But to read his reaction here as motivated purely by feelings of jealousy and possessiveness (and the possibility of unconscious desire for the daughter that a Freudian reading of this kind implies) would be to ignore the extent to which the father's displacement from such a position (from being what he had described in his opening address as 'her oracle, her hero') now provides him with a viewpoint from which he is able to recognise the subservience inherent in Kay's newfound attraction to this other man as, justifying their views entirely in terms of Buckley's decisions and plans, she ominously subordinates her will to his. This alternative motivation to Stanley's behaviour becomes clear during the final stage of the dinner-table conversation when, following Ellie's intervention and her attempts to calm him down by saying 'You don't give Kay a chance', he responds to his daughter's even more fulsome eulogy about Buckley:

Kay: Now listen, Pops. I'm 20 and Buckley's 26, and we're grown people. And as far as
          your supporting Buckley, I'll tell you this right now. He's the kind that wouldn't let
          anyone support him. He'd rather die first. That's the kind of a person he is. He's a
          wonderful person. He's the kind of a person that's absolutely, I mean, absolutely
          independent. Buckley wouldn't come to you for help, not even if, even if we were
          starving in the gutter. And his name is Dunstan. That's what it is. Buckley Dunstan.
          And he's a wonderful businessman. I mean a really wonderful businessman. And he
          has a wonderful job.
Stanley: Doing what?
Kay: Oh, I don't know, Pops. He makes something. Does it really matter what it is? He's
          the kind of a person that can do anything, anything at all. He's, he's absolutely,
          terribly wonderful. [She leaves the room upset.]
Ellie: Stanley, you've hurt her.
Stanley: Do you know, while she was talking, all I could think of was a little girl in brown
          pigtails and dirty overalls, flying at the boys when they pushed her too far. It seems
          like such an incredibly short time ago.

Stanley's earlier anger and frustration having subsided, his final words here become infused with a much more melancholic, introspective quality as, now shifting his attention away from Buckley, he wistfully reflects on the change that has taken place in his daughter. His reference to her as 'a little girl in brown pigtails and dirty overalls, flying at the boys when they pushed her too far' is especially revealing given the image that it conjures up of a very feisty, independent individual whose guts in standing up to the boys is so at odds with the display of deference to Buckley that he has just witnessed in the adult Kay, the only determined stance of independence that she now seems able to celebrate being that of her husband-to-be, not hers. That Stanley's distress at the news of his daughter's marriage to Buckley is motivated not just by feelings of resentment at being displaced by the younger man but by a recognition of the loss to Kay's own sense of selfhood that her growing up now entails is also gestured at in the scene later on where he is shown lying in bed at night, unable to sleep, his face restless and wracked with worry. On that occasion it is his act of picking up and staring at a framed photograph of Kay as a little girl dressed in dungarees and standing in front of a horse that finally seems to prompt his next and most vehement outburst against his future son-in-law.

As well as hearkening back to his earlier wistful recollection of Kay as a little girl, this image of her as a horse-loving 'tomboy' acquires an additional resonance due to the echoes it offers of Elizabeth Taylor's memorable, star-defining performance in *National Velvet* (Clarence Brown, 1944) where the actress (then only 12 years old) played a young girl who, against all the odds, fulfils her dream of winning the Grand National by riding her beloved horse Pie in the race. For those of us aware of Taylor's role in that film, her associations with this more active, spirited girl persona help shape and inform our understanding of this and other moments in *Father of the Bride*, giving added imaginative life and conviction to Stanley's reflections on his daughter's identity as a little girl and encouraging greater empathy with his feelings of loss on witnessing Kay's transformation into a more subdued bride-to-be. While *National Velvet* is itself quite notable for the space it gives to the expression of the female's unconventional side and for its ability to acknowledge, albeit with a degree of acceptance, the likely containment of those energies as she grows up and moves towards married life, what makes *Father of the Bride* so significant is the way that it uses Tracy's voice to register a sense of how the female's transition into patriarchal marriage may in fact be experienced as a profound loss for the father too. Unlike his male counterparts in *National Velvet* and *Meet Me in St Louis*, he seems extremely appreciative of the vibrant, subversive qualities of the female child and the freedom that her youth affords, and much more sensitive to what the relinquishment of all this entails. To admit to such a notion outright would, in the context of the ideological conformity of 1950s American society, be extremely difficult but what is fascinating about *Father of the Bride* is the way in which one senses the film as on the verge of some kind of admission of this fact.

The potential for voicing such concerns finds one of its most vivid demonstrations during the scene at the Dunstans where Stanley, on becoming drunk, talks incessantly about Kay. In his chapter on the film, James Naremore refers to this sequence only briefly as one of several instances where Stanley unsuccessfully tries to act out his 'father of the bride' role: 'Growing ebullient and woozy, he monopolises conversation with long-winded stories about his daughter' (1993: 100). Yet, as when summarising Stanley's earlier hogging of the conversation during his 'man-to-man' talk with Buckley in terms that obscure, among other things, the importance of that moment in enabling Tracy's character to unburden himself of the responsibilities and pressures that he has shouldered throughout his married life,[2] Naremore overlooks the crucial contribution that this scene at the Dunstans makes to what I have been arguing is a coherent and subversive pattern of vocal release within the film. Initially triggered by Mrs Dunstan (Billie Burke) who asks to 'hear all about our new daughter' and by Ellie's modest disclaimer that 'there's nothing to tell, really', it begins with Stanley recounting 'the time Kay was a baby and Ellie left her in front of the grocery store in her carriage and went home and forgot all about her'. This is followed by a sequence at the dinner table where, now noticeably more drunk, Stanley reminisces about his daughter learning to swim: 'She was five years old when I gave her her first swimming lesson. She was absolutely wonderful. Not frightened a bit. You know how Ellie is about the water, but Kay takes after me ... Well, anyway, she just, er, she just took like a duck to water. Just like a … [he tails off]. When she was about six I started taking her out to the raft with the other kids and throwing her in [he laughs]. Yeah, she'd just plop in. "Diving" she called it [he laughs again].' Then, following another dissolve, this sequence concludes with an even drunker Stanley: 'She was only 15 when the boys started crowding in. They were all over the house. I used to come home at night and find a stranger sleeping on the sofa in the living room and one on the hammock in the porch … And then all of a sudden she seemed to lose interest in them. And then…' It is at this point that Ellie, deeply uneasy about her husband's inebriated state, breaks into his drunken musings and asks the Dunstans to tell them 'all about Buckley' at which point Stanley, to his wife's even greater embarrassment, falls asleep.

Considered within the context of the earlier moments we have already studied, this scene is notable for the way that it begins by using the license provided by alcohol to give fuller, freer vent to Stanley's feelings of admiration and enthusiasm for the younger Kay. Having done so, it then takes the opportunity provided by his much more inebriated state in the final section (as Tracy slows down his speech and slurs his words more heavily) to register his growing sense of weariness and ineffectuality as that stage of his daughter's life passes and she becomes subject to the attention of boys. The oppressiveness of this latter scenario is reflected in the image that Tracy's words conjure up of the house crammed full of her young male admirers, the sense of suffocation and claustrophobia evoked by which contrasts quite markedly with the vitality and fluidity of the picture he paints in his account of Kay learning to swim as a child. In his emphasis on her fearlessness, then, Stanley's reminiscing during this sequence at the Dunstans' dinner table is consistent with his earlier reference to her as 'a little girl … flying at the boys when they pushed her too far', although in this case the sense of gender freedom summoned up by his account is enhanced all the more by the positive connotations of the water imagery. The delight he takes in recounting his act of 'throwing her in' to the water is also suggestive of the pleasure and release that he, not just Kay, was able to find in such moments of play, the more liberating effect of which he can here only articulate and recreate through the inhibition-loosening powers of drink.

As the possibility of obtaining further vocal release within the narrative becomes more difficult as the momentum of the wedding preparations builds, the voice-over becomes increasingly important in enabling this private, resistant register of thought to find some form of continuing outlet and expression. This is nowhere more apparent than during the actual wedding scene itself where the voice-over (working against what Naremore regards as the film's tendency to go back on itself by offering a celebration of the very wedding – and consumerist culture – it had earlier been so critical of) punctuates the soundtrack in ways that manage to disrupt the conventional flow of the church ceremony, infusing the scene with its own distinctive tonal colouring. Thus, as the Reverend Galsworthy (Paul Harvey) begins to read out the wedding service, Tracy's voice-over can be heard striking up on the soundtrack in a manner that, intruding into the vicar's speech and drowning out his words, serves to remind us of the theatricality and mechanics associated with this whole event and the performative nature of Stanley's role in it:

All I could think of was the part I had to play. I knew I had a cue coming. When the Reverend Galsworthy got to the place where he asks: 'Who giveth this woman?', I had to say, 'I do.' It was my only line in the show and I wanted to get it right. Then I was supposed to drop back a step, turn and join Ellie in the front pew. [Cut from a medium shot of Tracy's face to a view of him from behind as he begins to move one of his feet around the floor.] I couldn't remember what was immediately in my rear. I began to explore. I didn't want to trip or fall. People are so quick to attribute such things to alcohol. [Cut back to a longer frontal shot from over the Reverend Galsworthy's shoulder.] While I was still exploring, it was on me.

As well as managing to maintain this more sardonic form of commentary (which also punctuates much of the early section of the wedding reception sequence) the voice-over is crucial in enabling the film to offer a continuation of Stanley's earlier meditation on Kay. This begins near the start of the wedding scene when, on witnessing his daughter's assurance in pausing at the back of the church, Stanley can be heard expressing his admiration for her, via the voice-over:

Kay overwhelmed me. She waited for the proper moment with the calmness of a general watching his forces deploy into battle. Buckley, on the other hand, had the haggard look of a man who had just completed a dangerous bombing mission.

Fig. 1.2

Given the traditional notions of femininity that are ordinarily associated with a church wedding and considering Taylor's own appearance as a radiantly beautiful bride in the shot that accompanies this piece of voice-over narration (Fig. 1.2), Stanley's use of such a 'masculine' war metaphor is quite striking. What it embodies, in effect, is a much more unconventional view of his daughter than that which he had expressed in the previous scene when, momentarily overwhelmed on seeing her in her wedding dress for the first time, he described her as looking 'like the princess in a fairytale'. In now likening his daughter's poise and assurance to that of a general marshalling his troops on the battlefield, this later voice-over is suggestive of how, as the reality of Kay's marriage and what it implies looms ever closer, Stanley instinctively responds by seeing her in ways that are once again rooted in an admiration for her active, independent side. The significance of the view of Kay that Stanley constructs as he stands waiting to take her down the aisle both complicates and informs, in turn, that other key moment of voice-over narration which occurs later on in this scene when Tracy, now looking on as the young couple prepare to say their wedding vows (Fig. 1.3) can be heard responding to the vicar's question, 'Who giveth this woman to be married to this man?':

'Who giveth this woman?' 'This woman?' But she's not a woman. She's still a child. And she's leaving us. [Cut to a shot showing Stanley and Ellie in the front pew, with the camera then moving in closer to Tracy's face.] What's it going to be like to come home and not find her? Not to hear her voice calling 'Hi Pops!' as I come in? I suddenly realised what I was doing. I was giving up Kay. Something inside me began to hurt (Fig. 1.4).

Fig. 1.3

Emerging at the very point that marks Kay's formal transition into adulthood and married life, Tracy's voice-over here perfectly illustrates the importance of this device in giving expression to the male protagonist's overwhelming feelings of resistance and loss on being confronted with the reality of his daughter's growing up, his sceptical reiteration of the first part of the vicar's question – 'Who giveth this woman?' – and then just the two words 'This woman' serving to register something of his immense difficulty and struggle in coming to terms with this change. As such, it constitutes one of the

Fig. 1.4

most crucial examples of where Tracy's voice-over, switching from its otherwise quite sardonic, deadpan tone, is able to infuse this domestic comedy with an elegiac, introspective quality. The positioning of these forms of voice-over at or towards the end of certain scenes and at critical moments where Stanley's emotional bond with Kay has been eroded or undermined all help, along with the properties of the vocal delivery itself, to endow such moments with a rhetorical weight and insight that far outstrips their literal duration. A Freudian reading of the kind alluded to by Naremore might, of course, construe Stanley's denial of Kay's womanhood here as a sign of possessiveness born out of a reluctance to admit to his daughter's grown-up sexuality and attractiveness to other men. Yet the very measured, thoughtful, understated nature of Tracy's vocal delivery does much to impart a maturity of reflection and a sense of integrity and dignity with regard to his character's feelings for Kay that seem ill catered for by readings based on the idea of unruly, impassioned paternal jealousy. The tenderness of Tracy's voice as he utters the words 'But she's not a woman. She's still a child. And she's leaving us' also manages to convey a deep feeling of paternal warmth and protectiveness towards Kay and a concern for her vulnerability on entering marriage that suggest that it is more than just his own self-interests that are at stake here. Indeed, it seems no coincidence that this voice-over strikes up at the very point where Kay's more subordinate, passive role as object of patriarchal exchange between father and fiancé is made clear. Following on so soon from that earlier voice-over commentary that took place as Stanley and Kay stood waiting at the back of the church, his rebuttal of the Reverend's question with 'but she's not a woman. She's still a child…' strongly resists any temptation on our part to read his words here as a denial of her adult status *per se* (the mature qualities of which he has just extolled) or as indicative of some wish to see her as still a child in some mere diminutive sense (his likening her to a war general having evoked an admiration for her stature that goes very much against this). Rather it comes across as symptomatic of some underlying anxiety and unease as to what the notion of being a woman in adult patriarchal society stereotypically involves.

As the film moves towards its climax, and the dialectic between vocal release and physical/emotional containment that is established elsewhere in the film finds its striking culmination in the wedding reception scene where Stanley's route to Kay is constantly blocked by the hordes of guests who get in his way, his failure to reach her in time before she leaves for her honeymoon prompts one final melancholic reflection on the

Fig. 1.5

voice-over: 'She was gone. My Kay was gone. And I'd been too late to say goodbye to her', he says as he arrives at the front door only to see the car containing the newly-married couple driving away (Fig. 1.5). The positioning of this voice-over at the very conclusion of the flashback section of the narrative endows it with an added sense of finality and loss. At the same time it also marks a kind of endpoint with regard to how far the film is able or prepared to go in articulating such male concerns, its foregrounding of Kay's telephone call to Stanley from the train station at New York in the final scene enabling it to move instead towards a happier form of resolution more in keeping with its generic status. It is left instead to the elegiac properties of Tracy's final voice-over to invest Stanley's words with a significance beyond what they can actually say, their tonal affinity with his earlier musings on his daughter as a little girl inviting us to read such lines as 'She was gone. My Kay was gone' not as a last vestige of paternal possessiveness but as a final, resigned acknowledgement of the passing of the younger, more vibrant Kay.

Exploring the possibilities and limits of song: the search for an authentic male voice in *Gigi* (1958)

In turning to *Gigi*, it is fascinating to explore how such male preoccupations with the girl's growing up find further scope for inflection in this musical adaptation by Alan Jay Lerner and Frederick Loewe of Colette's short story about an adolescent female being trained in the ways of a courtesan in early twentieth-century Paris. In one sense, it is possible to see the film's generic status as allowing for a much fuller working through of the kind of male anxieties that we have already explored in relation to *Father of the Bride*. Yet while the satisfying nature of the resolution provided at the end suggests that this may ultimately be true, a key mark of *Gigi*'s achievement lies in its readiness to confront and expose the potential difficulties and challenges that the exploration and articulation of such male concerns pose to it as a musical form.

It is possible to find signs of this problematising tendency at work in *Gigi*'s opening sequence where Maurice Chevalier's ability to offer – through the song 'Thank Heaven For Little Girls' – a much more optimistic, upbeat perspective on the girl's growing up than his male counterpart could do at the beginning of *Father of the Bride* can be read as symptomatic of his character's very different position here. For unlike Stanley, whose feelings of paternal devotion towards his daughter gave him such a stake in her earlier identity, before the pressures and changes wrought by her growing up, Chevalier's Honoré Lachaille is motivated by his role as the promiscuous lover figure. As such he values the little girl precisely for the fact that she *will* grow up and mature, seeking to define her worth quite differently in terms of her future sexual allure:

Each time I see a little girl
Of five or six or seven,
I can't resist the joyous urge
To smile and say

Thank heaven
For little girls!
For little girls get bigger every day.

Thank heaven for little girls.
They grow up in the most delightful way.

Those little eyes so helpless and appealing
One day will flash
And send you crashing through the ceiling!

Thank heaven for little girls!
Thank heaven for them all,
No matter where, no matter who.
Without them what would little boys do?

Thank heaven…
Thank heaven…
Thank heaven for little girls.

The genial warmth of feeling that Chevalier exudes throughout his performance of this song does point to the possibility of the music being able to bring out a more caring, avuncular, even fatherly side to his character – particularly during that moment leading up to the song where he can be heard commenting with genuine affection in his voice: 'How adorable they are!' on seeing a little girl dressed in white pass by. But for those of us already familiar with his role in the film, a knowledge of Honoré's exploitative approach towards his mistresses elsewhere in the narrative tends to severely problematise his musical homage to little girls who seem to be celebrated here not for themselves and the qualities they embody but for the supply of beautiful women they will offer him and other men in the future. In terms of the song itself, Honoré's lack of real insight into the special qualities of the girl figure is betrayed by such lines as: 'Those little eyes so helpless and appealing', the rather saccharine nature of which – in construing her according to notions of vulnerability and passivity – seems so diametrically at odds both with this film's portrayal of Leslie Caron's character Gigi and Minnelli's more long-standing investment in the anarchic qualities of the female child in *Meet Me in St Louis*. The suggestions of sexism inherent in some of Honoré's earlier remarks prior to the start of the song – as when describing his profession as that of 'lover and collector of beautiful things' – adds another layer of qualification to his celebratory view of the girl's growing up by making clear the kind of objectifying treatment to which she will then become exposed. His follow-up comment – 'Not antiques, mind you. Younger things. Yes, definitely younger' – on seeing an elderly woman walk past develops this a stage further by pointing to the double standards to which she will eventually become subject once the moment of transformation and her youthful phase of beauty have passed.

That the transition alluded to in the song's lyrics may not be entirely a matter of celebration for the female herself is reinforced visually by the contrasts that Minnelli establishes throughout this sequence between the vitality and freedom of movement associated with the group of girls playing on the grass and the more negative forms of containment associated with their adult counterparts. Categorised rather like laboratory specimens by Honoré according to their married or unmarried status, these are shown (respectively) either seated together in gossiping huddles or rather unhappily confined to their carriages. Honoré's own observation on seeing two courtesans ride past in a carriage – 'Oh, what a poor, defenceless pair in those pathetic rags they wear' – is delivered with an irony that is meant to signal his belief in the greater prosperity accruing to women who choose (instead of getting married) to assume the role of mistress to men like himself. Yet the sense of attenuation and loss that is conveyed through the rigidity of these two women's poses and the stony impassivity of their expressions invite us to recognise at what cost such material wealth and glamour has been bought.

Chevalier's charisma – so full of easygoing charm and relaxed informality in front of the camera – does much to defuse any more stringent critique here of his character. Indeed, it is important in terms of establishing the credibility of the world we are about to enter and of understanding the younger male protagonist's difficulty in freeing himself from it, that we are able to feel something of the attractiveness of a figure like Honoré whose resistance to marriage and the pleasure he takes in the freedom this offers him are in other respects quite in tune with the kind of outlook one finds elsewhere in Minnelli's films. However, unlike in *Father of the Bride* where Tracy's opening direct address to the camera is indicative of that film's desire to develop a close and subversive bond of involvement with his character, in *Gigi* Chevalier's equivalent act of introducing himself to us at the start of the film serves to establish his role as more that of a jovial host who is capable of offering us a knowing insider perspective on the habits and mores of early twentieth-century upper-class Paris, yet in a way that does not require us to become bound into an exclusive alignment with his character. So, whereas Tracy's initial address and ensuing voice-over narration are crucial in enabling the story of the daughter's impending marriage to be filtered through Stanley's point of view, in *Gigi*, the positioning of Chevalier's song at the beginning and end of the narrative results in a framing device that instead tends to function as an outer casing for a musical text whose inner core is dedicated to offering a much more serious exploration of the impact wrought on the younger male by the girl's growing up.

This process of pulling us back from Honoré and the compromised form of utopian outlook that he embodies continues with his next number, 'It's a Bore', which is sung by him and his nephew, Gaston Lachaille (Louis Jourdan), as they ride in a carriage *en route* to their next social engagement. In adopting a contrapuntal structure to this song – whereby Gaston rebuffs every attempt made by his uncle to convince him of the joys of living by stressing the predictability and monotony of their existence – the composers establish very quickly the importance of this younger male figure in offering a dissenting, alternative male voice to that of Honoré. At the same time the half-spoken style of singing used by Jourdan throughout this number is most effective in conveying the sense of his character as someone caught in a kind of limbo state between speech and song, struggling to escape from the tedium and restrictions of the everyday world represented by the former, yet too tied down by it to be able to discover and enjoy the more liberating potential offered by the latter. That Gaston's inability to participate in the joyful optimism of this song is the result of some deep-seated disillusionment on his part with the kind of rich, frivolous playboy lifestyle that his uncle advocates and extols is made clear during the reprise of this number later on. On that occasion, the general celebration of life that was offered in the song's first rendition is replaced by a much more masculinist set of lyrics as Chevalier's character attempts to persuade his nephew of the need to uphold a code of male honour now threatened by Gaston's discovery that his mistress Liane (Eva Gabor) has been unfaithful to him.

Honoré:	Just imagine your chagrin
	When she sees you wander in
	And you find her with that slippery señor
	What a moment supreme
	When she totters with a scream.
Gaston:	What will she do?
Honoré:	Scream.
Gaston:	What did yours do?
Honoré:	Scream.

Gaston:	What do they all do?
Honoré and valet:	Scream.
Gaston:	It's a bore.
Honoré:	But think of the bliss
	Of the pleasure you will miss
	When she topples in a heap
	And you leave her there to weep on the floor.
Gaston:	It's a bore.
Honoré:	You must catch her if you can.
Valet:	For the dignity of man.
Honoré:	Take advantage of the chance.
Valet:	You owe it, sir, to France.
Both:	This is war!

Considered in the context of this second version of the song, Gaston's expressions of boredom become quite explicit admissions of discontent with the sexist, patriarchal rules and conventions underpinning Honoré's outlook on life, although at this stage he can only voice his resistance to this with an air of defeatism that seems as yet unable to construe an alternative way forward: 'All right. But it's a bore!' he sings/says in frustration before proceeding to participate in Honoré's ruthless unmasking and humiliation of Liane at Honfleur.

The attempt to find some alternative form of musical expression that is free from Honoré's influence and that of the broader social realm he represents finds its response in the form of a shift elsewhere in the film to a more interior mode of singing. This begins with the song, 'She is Not Thinking of Me', that is sung by Gaston at Maxim's (just prior to the reprise of the 'It's a Bore' number) and during which he first gives vent to his suspicions about Liane's infidelity. The decision by Minnelli and the composers to present this song in the form of an interior monologue is crucial in signalling Gaston's growing detachment and alienation from the world represented by Maxim's (Fig. 2.1). This is particularly evident in the case of the first and last parts of the song that are sung by Jourdan in voice-over mode, the timing of which,

Fig. 2.1

in occurring during the two sequences where Liane sits at the table next to Gaston, is especially effective in highlighting the oppressiveness of this kind of courtesan style relationship to his character. Even during the middle sequence where he appears to sing out loud, the tight framing of the camera on him, coupled with the indications provided in the background that his singing is going unnoticed by those around him, combine to maintain an aura of interiority to his soliloquising here, the self-absorbed nature of which has the effect of yet further reinforcing the extent of his disconnection from the world around him.

While this interior singing monologue is expressive, on one level, of Gaston's increasing discontent with the social milieu that surrounds him, in being so obsessed with his mistress's infidelity, these voice-over musings nevertheless suggest much about his inability, at this stage in his development, to extricate himself from a world with which he is otherwise so disillusioned. This is reflected in the vocal delivery itself, the more positive impulses of which – as evidenced by the upward searching momentum of the opening section of each verse and the warmer emotional colouring that Jourdan gives to such lines as: 'So disarming/Soft and charming' and 'She's so gracious/So vivacious' – are consistently offset by the half-spoken style of the singing. In helping to convey the tone of ironic suspicion and indignation that runs throughout the song as it moves towards a reiteration of its main title refrain, this tends to reinforce all the more how imbricated Gaston still is in this superficial world of social gossip and intrigue. In showing the ease with which Gaston is able to move between a voice-over style of singing and an open mouthing of the lyrics – as he switches to singing out loud when Liane goes off to dance with Honoré only to revert immediately to the singing voice-over mode when she returns to the table – Minnelli further qualifies any idea of the song enacting an outright withdrawal from such a society by this male figure. In allowing him to shift so effortlessly between these two modes of singing, the director instead invites us to recognise how well-practised Jourdan's character is in the whole game of dissembling and deceit that he is so critical of in his mistress. The stylistic self-consciousness that characterises Minnelli's presentation of Jourdan's singing during this number even goes so far as to invite certain parallels to be drawn between Gaston's behaviour here with regard to Liane and that of the other guests whose earlier backbiting about the various couples shown entering the restaurant was also staged by the director with a degree of theatricality and artistic contrivance. This involved suspending the music as the guests stop and stare at the couples on their initial entrance and presenting their gossip in the form of a Brechtian-style chanting chorus, all of which seems designed to reflect the artifice and mechanical nature of these characters and the world they inhabit.

This ability to oscillate from one mode of singing to another and, by extension, from an inwardly resistant form of self to a socially well-practised and contrived style of behaviour, finds its spatial counterpart in Gaston's habit of alternating between the superficial world of high society parties and sexual intrigue on the one hand and the more secluded setting of Mamita's (Hermione Gingold) apartment on the other. Although this latter space is itself implicated in the whole tradition of courtesan-style relationships that Gaston is so dissatisfied with (a fact that Minnelli never allows us to forget through his colouring of the walls and the furniture upholstery in a very bold, striking red), in being inhabited by two females whose respective youth and old age place them outside of the kind of narrow categorisation of women that Honoré outlined in the opening sequence, it offers Jourdan's character the possibility of a much freer, less socially restrictive form of interaction with the opposite sex than that which is available to him through his relationships with mistresses like Liane. 'It's the one place in Paris where I can go and relax' admits Gaston on explaining to Honoré, just moments prior to their first rendition of 'It's a Bore', why he chose to go there rather than to a formal tea party at the embassy a few days before. His decision to forgo that planned engagement and instead seek out the comforts offered by his 'old friend' Madame Alvarez (referred to elsewhere in the narrative as Mamita) thus serves to initiate a pattern of sudden cancellations and departures that finds its first on-screen realisation only minutes later when Gaston stops the carriage and, after bidding his uncle goodbye, sets off for Mamita's apartment, once again having decided not to go ahead with his next luncheon appointment.

This alternation between these two spaces finds its significant focal point in the form of the staircase that leads up to Mamita's apartment. As the site where Gaston's moments of vacillation and crisis are often acted out, it foregrounds a series of ascending and descending movements on his part that (as with the competing tendencies inherent in his half-speaking style of singing) encapsulates that tension in his character between an upward striving for a more meaningful sense of self on the one hand and a lapsing back into a more socially-conditioned mode of being on the other. As the film proceeds to demonstrate, though, the possibilities for escape and fulfilment that are offered by the staircase and apartment space are rendered increasingly problematic as Gigi's training to be a courtesan begins to take hold. Indeed, the extent to which Gaston's world is turned upside down by this change is reflected in rhetorical terms by Minnelli and Lerner's decision to reverse that earlier pattern as Gaston now finds himself impelled in the second part of the narrative to make a series of hasty departures *from* (rather than impromptu visits to) Mamita's apartment.

This process of reversal begins during the sequence later on in the film where Gaston, on returning to Mamita's apartment following a period of absence in Monte Carlo, becomes upset and leaves on seeing a now more grown-up-looking Gigi appear in her new high-collared white dress. Although Mamita attributes his angry departure here to Gigi's forthright and unrepentant rejection of his criticisms of how she looks ('With all the talk there is about you, Gaston, I've never heard it said you had any taste in clothes') it is this display of defiance on the younger female's part that, if anything, seems to be what draws him back. This is suggested during that brief interlude in the action where, as Mamita leaves the room and goes into the kitchen, the camera lingers behind to show Gigi watching Gaston from the window as he stands in the street below. As Gigi begins to smile in knowing anticipation of his change of heart, Minnelli cuts to a view of Gaston pausing beside his car and breaking into a smile of amusement that recalls his previous reactions to those earlier moments of verbal sparring between him and Gigi. But if this display of feisty independence seems to provide Gaston with a form of reassurance about Gigi's innate strength of character that enables him to come to terms with the changed nature of her appearance here, then Mamita's talk with him – during which she explains her refusal to allow him to take Gigi out in her new dress on the grounds that her granddaughter would be 'labelled' by her association with him – propels him into a much deeper state of crisis as he is forced to confront the drastically changed conditions under which he will be allowed to continue his relationship with Gigi. 'I understand responsibility to Gigi better than you, Gaston. I'll do all I can to entrust her only to a man who'll be able to say: "I'll take care of her; I'll answer for her future"', Mamita tells him as she tries tactfully to make clear the two sisters' readiness for him to provide for Gigi as his courtesan. The implications of her words prompts Gaston to leave the apartment in anger once again but not before expressing his feelings via an outburst that, in its construing of Mamita's words as a declaration of her intention to save Gigi for marriage, seems marked both by a refusal to confront the reality of the offer she is making him here and also a recognition of the damaging consequences for Gigi's reputation that her going out with him would entail:

> But forgive me if I wonder, madame, whom you are keeping her for? Some underpaid bank clerk who'll marry her and, er, give her four children in three years? ... To see her married in white in some dingy little church to a plumber! Who'll give her nothing but a worthless name and the squalor of good intentions? Very well, madame. Very well! If that's your ambition, inflict your misery in the name of respectability. I pity you! I pity you all!

As in *Father of the Bride*, then, the male protagonist's shock on being confronted with the consequences of the girl's growing up finds outlet in sudden verbal outbursts of anger wherein he gives vent to his anxieties and frustrations. In this case, though, the musical elements provide the opportunity for a much more extensive exploration of the male protagonist's feelings as Gaston is shown walking through the streets of Paris and engaging in a singing form of soliloquy that marks a further development in the film's overall strategy of using Jourdan's voice to bring out a deeper state of interior reflection in his character:

> She's a babe! Just a babe!
> Still cavorting in her crib;
> Eating breakfast with a bib;
> With her baby teeth and all her baby curls.
> She's a tot! Just a tot!
> Good for bouncing on your knee.
> I am positive that she
> Doesn't even know that boys aren't girls.
>
> She's a snip! Just a snip!
> Making dreadful baby noise;
> Having fun with all her toys;
> Just a chickadee who needs her mother hen.
> She's a cub! A papoose!
> You could never turn her loose.
> She's too infantile to take her from her pen.
>
> Of course that weekend in Trouville

In spite of all her youthful zeal,
She was exceedingly polite,
And on the whole a sheer delight.
And if it wasn't joy galore,
At least not once was she a bore
That I recall.
No, not at all.

Hah!

She's a child! A silly child!
Adolescent to her toes,
And good heaven how it shows.
Sticky thumbs are all the fingers she has got.
She's a child! A clumsy child!
She's as swollen as a grape,
And she doesn't have a shape.
Where her figure ought to be it is not.

Just a child! A growing child!
But so backward for her years
If a boy her age appears
I am certain he will never call again.
She's a scamp and a brat!
Doesn't know were she is at.
Unequipped and undesirable to men.

Of course I must in truth confess
That in that brand new little dress
She looked surprisingly mature
And had a definite allure,
It was a shock, in fact, to me,
A most amazing shock to see
The way it clung
On one so young.

She's a girl! A little girl!
Getting older, it is true,
Which is what they always do;
Till that unexpected hour
When they blossom like a flower...!

Oh, no…!
Oh, no…!
But…!
But…!

There's sweeter music when she speaks,
Isn't there?
A different bloom about her cheeks,
Isn't there?
Could I be wrong? Could it be so?
Oh where, oh where did Gigi go?

Gigi, am I a fool without a mind
Or have I merely been too blind
To realise?
Oh, Gigi, why you've been growing up before my eyes.
Gigi, you're not at all that funny, awkward little girl I knew!
Oh no! Over night there's been a breathless change in you.
Oh, Gigi, while you were trembling on the brink
Was I out yonder somewhere blinking
At a star?
Oh, Gigi, have I been standing up too close
Or back too far?
When did your sparkle turn to fire?
And your warmth become desire?
Oh, what miracle has made you the way you are?

Gigi…!
Gigi…!!
Gigi…!!!

Oh no! I was mad not to have seen the change in you!
Oh, Gigi!
While you were trembling on the brink
Was I out yonder somewhere blinking
At a star?
Oh, Gigi, have I been standing up too close
Or back too far?
When did your sparkle turn to fire?
And your warmth become desire?
Oh, what miracle has made you the way you are?

The song is thus structured in a way that is designed to reflect the main stages in Gaston's conversation with himself as he initially alternates between hot-headed denials that she has grown up and quieter, more reflective passages wherein he begins to concede to the reality of the physical change that has taken place in her before eventually moving towards a more outright celebration of her newly-emerged womanhood. In enacting this process, the song would therefore seem to ably demonstrate the transformative, problem-solving powers of the musical number as Gaston is shown discovering, during the course of his performance, a more tender, lyrical, romantic form of voice. Yet while Jourdan's ability to now infuse his half-spoken style of singing with a genuinely musical form of feeling is movingly indicative of an emerging potential in his character that points forward to Gaston's later process of change and self-discovery, there are other aspects relating both to the song and its location within the narrative that (as with the opening number) invite a more cautious reading of this male celebration of the female's transformation. Indeed, given the film's vibrant portrayal of Gaston's relationship with Gigi earlier in the narrative and the strategic positioning of certain verbal disclosures both before and after the title song, it is possible to understand the overt trajectory of this number – whereby Gaston goes from strenuous denial to sudden realisation and then full-blown celebration of the fact that Gigi has grown up – as masking over other more deep-seated and unresolved forms of disavowal and evasion in his character.

This aspect to the song becomes evident when we compare the first part of its lyric with Stanley's third piece of voice-over narration during his daughter's wedding in *Father of the Bride*. For while, in both cases, the male's reaction on being confronted with the fact of the girl's growing up is to try to deny this by emphasising her child-like status instead, in Gaston's case his construing of Gigi in such terms carries with it none of those feelings of veneration that Stanley displayed for Kay as a little girl during his corresponding voice-over commentary. Tracy's insistence: 'But she's not a woman. She's still a child' thus finds its more dismissive counterpart in the opening lines of the fourth and fifth verses: 'She's a child! A silly child!' ... 'Just a child! A growing child!' The marked difference in tone in this is also reflected semantically through the pejorative shift in meaning that occurs as a result of the replacement of Stanley's word 'still' with Gaston's 'Just'. In portraying Gigi in these more reductively infantile terms, Gaston resists the fact of her growing up in ways that tend to invalidate and deny the more subversive vitality that he had earlier been shown taking such pleasure in during one of his impromptu visits to her grandmother's apartment and then during their seaside holiday together at Trouville. That Gigi's verbal sparring and ritual cheating during their games of cards *are* a source of immense pleasure to Gaston (offering him, as they do, a very playful dismantling of the class and gender power structures inherent in his social position) is admitted to quite explicitly by Gaston during the scene where he decides to accept Mamita's invitation to stay for dinner rather than go to his next social engagement at the Eiffel Tower. On that occasion he responded to Mamita's cautionary observation that Gigi 'takes advantage' of him (on hearing her granddaughter answer him back just as she leaves to take his message of apology to his uncle) with the words: 'Oh let her, let her, Mamita. It amuses me.' Then, on hearing Mamita scold Gigi in the very next scene for her excited questioning of Gaston about what it will be like at Trouville (having won the right to go to that seaside resort with him by beating him at cards), he proceeds to override Gingold's objection once again: 'Believe it or not, Mamita, I have a better time with this outrageous brat of yours than anybody in Paris!' he explains before proceeding to sing: 'Let her gush and jabber. Let her be enthused. I cannot remember when I have been more amused.'

'The Night They Invented Champagne' number that follows is itself important in demonstrating the invigorating effect that Gigi has on Gaston as she is shown drawing first Mamita and then him into a performance characterised by relaxed informality and a fluid interchanging of partners and choreographic movements. This celebration of Gigi's vitality and her ability to rejuvenate Gaston continues during the seaside holiday episode at Trouville. The opening sequence of this – in showing the 'rough and tumble' nature of Gaston and Gigi's antics as they play in the sea – can even be understood as offering a vitally alive version in the narrative here and now of Stanley's alcohol-induced reminiscence in *Father of the Bride* of the times when he taught Kay how to swim as a child by throwing her into the water. The freedom from gender roles that Gigi's youthful vitality embodies is again highlighted during the tennis-game sequence where her energetic running from one side of the court to the other to retrieve the balls sent over by Gaston is comically contrasted with the rigid, mechanical behaviour of Honoré's would-be mistress. Unlike Gigi, the latter stands rooted to the spot, only hitting those balls that come within arm's reach, her highly restricted movements in turn prompting her male partner to hit the balls across very tamely while bowing deferentially and apologising profusely when he hits a ball too wide.

Given the joyful sense of abandonment characterising these moments of play, it is all the more noticeable that Gaston should seek to understate the impact of all this when reflecting on the changes taking place in Gigi during the first part of the title song. On beginning to concede certain signs of her emerging maturity he construes his acknowledgement of this in ways that now privilege notions of restraint over the very feistiness of spirit that had made the holiday so memorable ('Of course that weekend in Trouville/ *In spite of all her youthful zeal*/She was exceedingly polite/And on the whole a sheer delight') while the extent of Gigi's rejuvenating impact on him during that holiday is also subjected to a degree of denial ('*And if it wasn't joy galore*/At least not once was she a bore…'). It is possible to interpret Gaston's tempered recollection of the impression made by Gigi on him during their holiday together as a reflection, in part, of the very different criteria by which the female comes to be viewed and judged once she is deemed to have grown up, the recognition of which here results in the male protagonist himself subjecting Gigi to this kind of discourse of containment. But for a deeper understanding of Gaston's motives in downplaying and dismissing Gigi's vibrant girl-like qualities during the first part of the title song (both when resisting and acknowledging the fact of her having grown up) we need to cast our mind back to the scene immediately after the Trouville episode. This is the one where Alicia (Isabel Jeans) calls Mamita to her apartment and berates her sister for allowing Gigi to spend the weekend at the seaside with Gaston on the grounds that such a display of 'lack of tact' might ruin any chances that her great-niece has for becoming his courtesan. On hearing a stupefied Mamita attempt to defend her decision on the basis that 'it was a most congenial weekend', Alicia then offers the following telling retort: 'So congenial that Gaston returned Monday morning, cancelled all engagements and left Paris that same evening for Monte Carlo!' Although her own pressing preoccupation with the possibility of Gigi becoming Gaston's mistress prompts her to gloss over the significance of this behaviour by Gaston (she responds to Mamita's bemused question 'But why?' with 'It doesn't matter why! It may be a blessing in disguise. It gives us time' [that is, 'for Gigi's lessons']), as an audience we are left to ponder the implications of this disclosure.

It is possible, of course, to read Gaston's sudden cancellation of all his engagements and his speedy departure for Monte Carlo as forming part of that overall pattern of erratic behaviour that began (at least in on-screen terms) with his abrupt termination of his carriage ride with Honoré during their initial performance of the 'It's a Bore' number. Considered in that broader context, it is suggestive, at the very least, of how the experience of being with Gigi during that weekend has made him even more resistant and unable to contemplate a return to the tedium of his usual social routine. Yet the drastic nature of his actions here – in removing himself completely from Paris – also points to the possibility of a more extreme form of emotional upheaval being generated in him by his time with Gigi and one that, in not being resolvable on this occasion by a visit to her apartment, could be interpreted as implying an element of denial or evasion with regard to his feelings for her. That there is more to Gaston than meets the eye is tantalisingly hinted at on his return to Mamita's apartment from Monte Carlo. On that occasion, Minnelli chooses to present the initial encounter between Gigi and Gaston at the doorway from a more enigmatic camera viewpoint than usual as the tassles of a nearby curtain are allowed to intrude into the left-hand side of the frame, hindering any potentially more revealing glimpse of Gaston's reaction on seeing her again.

The possibilities raised by Alicia's earlier disclosure find their moment of realisation in Gaston's own revelation – during the scene where Gigi turns down his offer to provide for her as his courtesan – that he discovered he was in love with her while he 'was away from [her] – in Monte Carlo'. Given that this solitary trip occurred immediately *after* his holiday with Gigi and *before* being confronted with the change in her on his return, such a disclosure daringly points to the possibility that Gaston's love for Gigi pre-dates the physical transformation she undergoes during his absence and is rooted in a valuation of precisely those qualities of vitality and active femininity that he had come to enjoy and appreciate in a more sustained, intense fashion during his time with her at Trouville. These suggestions of an off-screen emotional crisis taking place in Gaston all help to explain the extremity of the reaction provoked in him on seeing Gigi appear (on his return from Monte Carlo) in her elegant new white dress. His initial reaction on being asked by Gigi how she looks – 'You look like an organ-grinder's monkey!' – is particularly revealing in the light of those earlier verbal disclosures since, in comparing her appearance to that of a subservient performing animal, it points to an underlying anxiety on his part about the loss of independence and identity that her transition to adulthood may involve. His follow-up question – 'What's happened to your little Scotch dress?' – develops this a stage further by suggesting his desire to reclaim the younger, feistier version of Gigi that this garment represents while his criticism of 'that ridiculous collar!' on the grounds that 'it makes [her] look like a giraffe with the goitre!' also alludes to his fear of the distorting, constraining impact that her growing up may entail (Fig. 2.2).

Fig. 2.2

This whole incident involving the white dress has its authorial roots in Colette's original story but the sequence as a whole takes on an added significance and coherence in the context of Minnelli's work where clothing is often used to register the oppressiveness of social, especially gender, roles. In terms of other examples of this from elsewhere in Minnelli's films, one thinks especially of the scene in *Meet Me in St Louis* where Esther (Judy Garland), barely able to breathe, is shown being forced into a corset by her sister in preparation for the Christmas Ball and also of the one in *Father of the Bride* where Stanley is shown standing in front of a mirror while trying to squeeze himself into the now very tight suit that he wore for his own wedding. This use of costume to suggest the suffocating nature of gender roles was also demonstrated earlier in *Gigi* during the sequence where, on receiving intensive training on how to be a courtesan, Caron's character is shown reluctantly trying on an excessively large dress chosen by her aunt, the ruffle of which appears so big as to almost completely obliterate her face (Fig. 2.3). In demonstrating the swamping effect of this garment (and the role it represents) on Gigi, it is as if the director thus seeks, through the device of comic exaggeration, to prepare us for the significance of Gaston's later reaction to the more elegant white dress.

Fig. 2.3

Considered in the light of these various verbal disclosures and vocal outbursts, then, Gaston's insistence in the title song that 'She's a child! A silly child! … Just a child! A growing child!' can be understood not simply as a denial of her adult sexuality *per se* but, rather more complexly, as an attempt to disavow his already established feelings of love for the pre-transformed version of her. These feelings, now complicated and brought to heightened awareness by the more overtly sexualised nature of her appearance that he is presented with on his return, can only be disclaimed through this denigratory reduction of her former identity to that of 'silly child'. There is one moment where the more elegiac acknowledgement of loss that one associates with Tracy's voice-over in *Father of the Bride* does manage to break through, though. This occurs mid-way through the song when Gaston's sudden moment of realisation that Gigi has grown up is greeted by him with the words: 'Oh, no…! Oh, no…!!', the extra pronounced stress that Jourdan places

Fig. 2.4

on the second rendition of this line being especially effective (along with the closer view now provided of this actor's intense facial expression) in conveying his deep sense of resistance and dismay (Fig. 2.4). A sense of loss still lingers on, too, in the wistful tone of the closing section of this verse: 'Could I be wrong? Could it be so?/Oh where, oh where did Gigi go?' Then, as Gaston moves down from the little bridge and stands in front of the lake that he had previously seen Gigi sitting in front of on his return from her grandmother's apartment earlier on in the narrative, his contemplation of how she is now no longer 'that funny, awkward little girl [he] knew' ('Oh no! Overnight there's been a breathless change

Fig. 2.5

in you') finds its poignant confirmation in the image of a group of white swans in the water behind him: elegantly beautiful (in a manner that recalls Gigi's first appearance in her white high-collared dress) yet hemmed into a little corral that separates them from the rest of the lake and the two other swans visible at the far side of the shore (Fig. 2.5).

The romantic possibilities opened up by Gaston's realisation of Gigi's transformation do offer him a form of compensation clearly unavailable to Stanley, however, and this is reflected in the second part of the song where Jourdan's groping delivery of the word 'But… But…' appears like an attempt to console himself as he begins to contemplate the advantages arising from a different, more mature version of Gigi: 'There's sweeter music when she speaks/Isn't there?/A different bloom about her cheeks/Isn't there?' Yet while the rest of the song ultimately moves towards an outright celebration of Gigi's growing up that is more in keeping with the kind of rose-tinted perspective offered by Honoré on the girl's transition to womanhood during the film's opening number, in their emphasis on the suddenness of Gaston's discovery the lyrics at the same time avoid the possibility that is gestured at elsewhere of a longer, more complex process of emotional upheaval and self-discovery taking place in the male protagonist. In romanticising the moment of Gigi's transformation, the lyrics also evade the more negative consequences arising from such a change that Gaston had earlier given voice to through his outburst over Gigi's new dress and which Mamita had sought to confront him with when outlining the changed terms and conditions under which he would now be allowed to continue his relationship with her granddaughter. That the film is alert to the limitations of Gaston's romantic vision is registered with immediate, telling irony at the end of the number when, with the sumptuous strains of the 'Gigi' theme music still reaching their crescendo on the soundtrack as he climbs back up the stairs to the apartment, he is shown adjusting with disconcerting alacrity to his former way of life on being met at the door by Mamita:

Gaston: Mamita, are you alone?

Mamita: Yes.

Gaston: Good. I have an important business matter to discuss with you.

In a shift that recalls Gaston's ability to move all too easily between a potentially more serious, meaningful inner self and a superficially performative social one during his earlier singing of 'She Is Not Thinking of Me' at Maxim's, the film thus delineates, with unsettling abruptness, the restricted nature of his emotional development here. In doing so, it shows how the tender, lyrical feelings that had earlier been brought to the point of conscious articulation by Gaston's realisation, during the title song, that Gigi has grown up, are then suddenly stymied and replaced, on his return to the narrative world, by a more pragmatic readiness to treat her (like any of his other women) as a mere object of financial exchange. The slight pause that Jourdan injects into the middle of this line just before saying 'business matter' and the subtle stress he places on these two words do imply a degree of self-consciousness on his part about the performative nature of the role he is putting on here as he signals to Mamita his willingness to take up the coded offer that she had previously made to him during her private chat with him in the previous scene (the implications of which his angry outburst had, on that occasion, seemed intent on evading). But overall Jourdan's delivery of this line is characterised by an easy confidence and brusque efficiency that suggests little sense of resistance to what he is about to do.

In using its verbal disclosures elsewhere to gesture towards an emotional life in Gaston that struggles to find expression through the lyrics of the title song, and in showing him to be unable to carry forward the more positive emotional momentum that *is* developed during the course of the number into the more prosaic, ordinary realm of speech and narrative, the film demonstrates its adeptness in foregrounding the difficulties for the male – and indeed for the musical genre itself – in escaping from the constraints of a patriarchally constructed form of language and society.

Given such a perspective, the implied challenge facing Minnelli and the composers, as the film moves towards its dénouement, is how to employ the musical elements in a way that is able to bring Gaston into a closer, more meaningful contact with his emotions and how, in turn, to translate the insights that *are* achieved into the more ideologically pressure-ridden world of the narrative.

The solution to this dilemma comes mainly through the decision to use orchestral, non-singing reworkings of the 'She is Not Thinking of Me' and 'Gigi' numbers during critical closing stages of the film. In adopting such an approach, Minnelli and the composers are therefore able to draw on the already established meanings that Gaston's earlier interior singing monologue and musical soliloquy had acquired but in a way that, by freeing this character from the need to put his feelings into words, now seems to facilitate the attainment of a much deeper state of self-reflection. This strategy of withholding the singing voice so as to suggest the discovery of an inner and more self-critical form of voice in Gaston finds its collective starting point just prior to the reprise of the first of these numbers. Hence, as Jourdan's character is shown arriving at Maxim's with

Gigi (following her decision to agree to become his mistress after all) the composers adopt their previous policy of suspending the music and having the other people in the room stop in their tracks and gaze at the newcomers as before only to then exclude, on this occasion, the sound of the guests' chanting voices accompanying this on the soundtrack. Far from mitigating the original effect, the suppression of these voices tends to heighten our sensitivity to the fact of the guests' gossiping as we are brought into an acute shared awareness with Gaston of Gigi's vulnerability in this environment. Unlike the looks of wide-eyed innocence that she casts around the restaurant, the anxious, resentful glances that Gaston throws around the room and the force with which he pushes his cane into the stand all serve to make clear his feelings of anger at the gossip that Gigi is being exposed to. The fact that we cannot actually hear what he seems able to at the same time endows these voices with a subjective quality, their inaudibility suggestive, on some deeper level, of how they have become internalised by Gaston as part of the responsibility and guilt that he must absorb and shoulder.

This process of internalising the voice to the point of inaudibility is developed in the next part of the scene where the orchestral reprise of the song 'She is Not Thinking of Me' is used to accentuate our awareness of the increasing discomfort that Gaston is feeling inside as he is forced to witness Gigi now carrying out the role of model courtesan that he had earlier seen Liane performing (in her case with greater duplicity) during the first rendition of that number. The music's ability to evoke his earlier line, 'Acting out her part', is especially telling in terms of what it implies about Gaston's resentment of Gigi's behaviour here as she is shown engaging in the courtesan's ritual of choosing the right cigar for him and pouring out the coffee in the way she has been trained to do, while repeating her aunt's phrases and expressions in comments on the significance of the 'dipped' jewellery that Madame Dunard is wearing and the beauty of the emerald bracelet that Gaston has given her. In suggesting the extent to which the male protagonist is unable to admit to what he is feeling, the withholding of Jourdan's singing voice throughout this sequence is also symptomatic of how the blame that had earlier been levelled by Gaston at Liane has now been turned inwardly on himself as he is forced to confront the implications of what he has done by making Gigi his courtesan and exposing her to the public scrutiny of Maxim's. His feelings of intense shame at turning her into another one of his bought women finds just one fleeting moment of acknowledgement within the dialogue itself when on hearing Gigi enquire about the present for her that he has hidden in his breast pocket, he responds not with a confident sense of his own benevolence but with the guilt-ridden voice of a man by now fully cognisant of what the giving of such a gift signifies: 'I'm sorry.'

Gaston's shame at what he has done becomes unbearable during the sequence where he is forced to listen to Honoré talking about Gigi according to the superficial male discourse that Jourdan's character had earlier been so comfortable with: 'Did you have to improve the arrangement? ... Oh, she looks adorable. So fresh, so eager, so young. It's the sophisticated women who get boring so quickly. What can they give you? Everything but surprise. But with someone like Gigi, she can amuse you for months', enthuses Chevalier in a manner that finally drives the younger man to abruptly terminate the couple's visit to the restaurant. The curt 'Good night. Good night' that he issues to his uncle as he gets up to leave with Gigi marks a key moment of rupture in his allegiance with Honoré and one that, in echoing and extending the earlier, more politely tempered, 'Goodbye, Honoré' that he had uttered on stopping the carriage and aborting his journey to their next social engagement during the initial version of 'It's a Bore', constitutes an important culmination of Gaston's previous attempts to break away from the kind of social world represented by Chavalier's character. In its rhyming inversion of the moment when Gigi was shown pulling Gaston as he in turn pulls a donkey along the beach at the end of the Trouville sequence, the next shot shows Gaston dragging a distraught, crying Gigi up the stairs to her grandmother's apartment. In reversing the structure of that original memorable shot in this way, Minnelli underlines the extent to which Gigi's ability to act as the driving life force in their relationship has now been invalidated and destroyed by the male protagonist's readiness to position her in the role of courtesan. Yet in choosing to evoke that earlier image, the director simultaneously points to an attempt by Gaston to retrieve the former conditions of the couple's relationship, the desire for which is also embodied in his act of restoring her to a space that had previously offered him such relief from the demands of Parisian society.

Having left Gigi with Mamita, Gaston is shown walking down the stairs in a dazed state and pausing briefly in the street below before striding away from the apartment, only to stop, turn back towards it and then, swiping his cane down from his shoulder, turn and walk off again in the opposite direction. The visual reworking that this sequence offers of Jourdan's earlier to-ing and fro-ing from Mamita's apartment following his return from Monte Carlo is aurally reinforced by the sound of the 'Gigi' theme music which strikes up at this point in a further highly evocative allusion to that earlier moment of crisis. Conrad Salinger's orchestration here broadly reprises the main stages of that original song as the score shifts from a more urgent, brass version of the initial angry section of the number (played during the sequence where Gaston walks out of the apartment and away down the street) to an intensely poignant string variation on its second part (which begins at the point where he arrives at the fountain he had earlier paused and sat in front of during the first rendition of the song). Yet in recalling the title number in this way it does so in a manner that is not simply reiterative but, rather, powerfully expressive of the now profound change taking place in Jourdan's character. The extent of the development that Gaston undergoes during the course of this orchestral reprise becomes evident when one compares the moment of crisis experienced by him here with that which Professor Higgins (Rex Harrison) undergoes during the final number, 'I've Grown Accustomed to Her Face', in *My Fair Lady* (George Cukor, 1964). Although that song also serves to articulate the male's sense of crisis (as Higgins is shown swinging, as Gaston had previously done during his earlier delivery of the 'Gigi' number, between angry denial and momentary acknowledgement of his feelings for the female protagonist), its positioning at such a late stage in the narrative and without any equivalent musical forerunner to the first rendition of the 'Gigi' number has the effect of severely closing down any possibility for following through the self-discovery and emotional awakening that are gestured at by it. Given that the *Gigi* film project followed on so soon after Lerner and Loewe's work on the stage production of *My Fair Lady* (which opened on Broadway in April 1956), one senses the composers actively learning from their earlier approach by now choosing to include two versions of this 'male in crisis' number and with the equivalent of the one sung by Harrison now positioned at a much earlier stage in the narrative. In adopting this strategy, they allow a far more extensive development to take place in Jourdan's character than in Harrison's as the moment of realisation achieved during that initial rendition is first challenged and interrogated within the narrative before then being re-explored and redefined during this reprise sequence as the male protagonist moves towards a deeper state of emotional maturity and self-discovery.

Having provided for this musical reworking of the film's title number, Lerner and Loewe's decision not to include a sung variation on its original lyric is also crucial in determining its overall effect. In adopting this strategy they are able to signal how Gaston has now reached a state of introspection so private and so oppositional to the patriarchal codes and values of the society he inhabits that it cannot be adequately expressed or represented through language. Freed from the demands of the lyric, he is thus able to achieve a more intense and meaningful connection with his inner self, the absence of any singing signalling not so much a withdrawal or invalidation of the voice as an internalisation of it so deep that only Gaston, having reached this state of communion with himself, can hear it. For a filmmaker noted for his verbal inarticulacy in discussing his work, and whose movies are so concerned with exploring the creative inner life of the individual, there is something extremely emblematic about this sequence in directorial terms, too. Shifting to a level of interiority so extreme (even for Minnelli) as to render Gaston's voice inaudible, we are left to infer what the male protagonist is feeling from the associative powers of the music and the visual richness of the *mise-en-scène*.

Thus, as Gaston stands looking despondently downwards and leaning inwardly in front of the fountain, his cane resting inactively on his shoulder, his bodily posture becomes indicative of a state of self-absorption so extreme that he never even notices when a carriage pulls up abruptly in front of him. The orchestral reprise, at this precise moment, of the music relating to the penultimate main verse of the title song immeasurably enhances this portrayal of Gaston's state of introspection. In movingly re-invoking his earlier admission of self-deception in the context of his more recent blinding of himself to the implications of making Gigi his courtesan ('Gigi, am I fool without a mind/Or have I merely been too blind/To realise?') its lush, deep violin strings serve to imbue his mood of self-reflection here with a profound sense of sadness, shame and loss. Then, as the music reaches what would (in the first rendition of the song) have been the line: 'Gigi, you're not at all that funny, awkward little girl I knew!', the intensity of these musical and performative elements combine to suggest Gaston's now much deeper comprehension of what has been lost. The contemplation of this seems to bring about the dramatic moment of epiphany that follows as, on walking towards the other side of the fountain, he suddenly starts back right in the midst of the musical section relating to the words 'little girl I knew'. The fountain setting itself helps endow his rejuvenation here with a heightened sense of conviction achieved both through its associations with youth and rebirth and its ability to evoke, via its water imagery, a more vibrant sense of the couple's idyllic time at Trouville than that which Gaston himself had been able to recall when sitting in the same spot during his first performance of the title number. In contrast to the tranquillity of the lake that had earlier formed such a gentle backdrop to his lyrical contemplation of Gigi's transformation (during the equivalent second phase of that initial rendition of the title song) the fountain is spurting white jets of water now lit up against the night sky, giving dramatic visual expression to his moment of self-illumination. Then,

as Gaston suddenly starts back and looks upward as he realises what he has to do, his silhouetted profile comes to emulate that of the stone statue of the horse rearing up behind him (Fig. 2.6). It is a mirroring of poses that contrasts with the earlier use of the swans to reflect the transformation then taking place in Gigi and as such, it is indicative of this musical sequence's heightened concern with

Fig. 2.6

exploring the male protagonist's own process of change and self-development. Indeed, as Gaston continues to move backwards in this more upright, alert stance before turning to face the other way, the music's evocation of Gigi's earlier transition ('Oh no! Overnight there's been a breathless change in you!') almost seems to rewrite itself in ways that become applicable to him too. And if the two stone horses positioned at either end of the fountain, facing in opposite directions, had earlier encapsulated Gaston's state of conflict and vacillation, as he stood immobilised by the competing pulls of ideology and instinct, then this moment – where he starts back in a manner that assumes the more active stance of the rearing horse behind him – marks the breaking of that tension as, turning in the direction of the other stone animal, he walks back to the apartment and up the stairs for the last time.

The extent of the transformation that Gaston undergoes during the course of this musical reworking of his earlier experience is evident, most crucially of all, in the contrast that its closing sequence offers with the one that followed on from the original rendition of the 'Gigi' number. Where Gaston's earlier performance of that song had been marked in the later stages by a romanticisation and celebration of his newfound feelings for Gigi that could not be sustained on his return to the convention-bound world of the narrative, in this instance the reprise of the title music during the fountain sequence gestures towards the possibility of a lasting inner change having taken place in him, the emotional charge of which, rather than being expended in the act of singing, is now able to be channelled quietly and undramatically into the ordinary world of speech and language. Thus, in contrast to the brusque confidence and coldly detached form of delivery that Jourdan had previously adopted when telling Mamita that he has 'an important business matter to discuss', on this occasion his voice becomes endowed with great emotional warmth and tenderness when, confounding the grandmother's expectations, he addresses her in the following manner: 'Madame ... will you do me the honour ... the favour ... give me the infinite joy of bestowing on me ... Gigi's hand in marriage?'

One could argue that the shift from number to narrative still requires the adoption of a more realist, pragmatic worldview since Gaston is shown containing any possibly more radical implications arising from his earlier unspoken thoughts within the conventional parameters of this request for Gigi's hand in marriage, the generic and ideological conformity of which also serves to confirm (rather than challenge) the predictability of the available destinies that Honoré had mapped out for Gigi and the other girls in the opening scene: 'Some day, each and every one of them will either be married or unmarried...' Yet far from coming across as anti-climactic in the wake of the musical and visual splendour of the fountain sequence, Gaston's request for Gigi's hand in marriage instead manages to offer a most moving fulfilment of that earlier commitment on the part of the film to finding a way of translating the utopian form of feeling generated during the course of the musical number into the quotidian realm of speech and narrative. The uplifting nature of Gaston's request owes much to the special qualities of Jourdan's voice. With its exquisitely soft pitch and gentle style of enunciation (all of which are so different from Chevalier's more heavily ornate French-accented kind), it is able to convey a considerable tenderness and progressiveness of feeling on his character's part for Gigi. The thoughtful pauses he injects before each of the main sections of this, his final line of dialogue, complement the gentle properties of the voice itself in a manner that is deeply expressive both of the care with which he now seeks to define Gigi's value to him and his own newfound lack of presumption about the likely outcome of his request.

In conveying such respect for Gigi and such a sense of humility about Gaston's own position as suitor, Jourdan's voice articulates his character's ability to now reject the system of values (so typified by Honoré) of treating women as mere objects of sexual pleasure to be bought and then discarded after their novelty value has worn off. At the same time, it also suggests a readiness on Gaston's part to eschew the patriarchal forms of dominance that, by contrast, had been hinted at as there in incipient form in Kay's marriage to Buckley in *Father of the Bride*, most notably through the suggestions provided of that male figure's attempts to impose Nova Scotia on her as a choice of honeymoon. In bringing out these more progressive tendencies to his character, Jourdan's voice is in turn able to complete an overall trajectory of meaning with regard to his own star persona that can be seen as stemming from his association with a certain kind of role in Minnelli's *Madame Bovary* (1949) and Max Ophuls' *Letter From an Unknown Woman* (1948). In both of these films, he played the part of an aristocratic/highly-cultured male lover figure who, unable to commit to a serious relationship, dissipates his youth in an endless series of superficial affairs with women, eventually engaging in a passionate affair with the female protagonist only to leave her abruptly when their relationship gets too intense. Earlier on in *Gigi*, such star associations helped invest Jourdan's expressions of dissatisfaction and boredom with an added depth and conviction, providing a level of intertextual motivation to his character's desire to break free from the predictability and superficiality of his current way of life. In establishing Gaston's disenchantment with all this at the outset, the film can therefore be understood as following through what was gestured at in the final section of *Letter From an Unknown Woman* when, during his last encounter with Lisa (Joan Fontaine), Jourdan's character, Stefan, expressed his disillusionment with his bachelor playboy existence and his longing to find the one ideal woman who will give his life meaning. In that film, the only redemption available to the male seems to come in the form of his decision to go to the duel after all (his reading of Lisa's letter having prompted him to face up to the confrontation – and the likely death that it involves – that he had earlier sought to escape). In the case of *Gigi*, its capacity for achieving a deeper state of male interiority through the music allows Gaston to discover a lyricism and emotional maturity to his voice that in those earlier films had often been compromised by its association with the more manipulative patter of the bachelor playboy's seduction rhetoric and a certain tendency towards aristocratic aloofness.[3] This is not something that Jourdan's character is allowed to arrive at easily, for, as we have already seen, a key mark of this film's achievement lies in its readiness to explore the difficulty for the male – weighed down as he is by the pressures and expectations of his position – of gaining access to the more utopian possibilities of music and song and, indeed, of finding a language of expression, musical or otherwise, that is able to do justice to his innermost feelings and desires. It is the enactment of this process of struggle, however, that in turn makes Jourdan's final line of dialogue all the more satisfying, given the extent of the change it registers in a character whose half-hearted style of singing had at the beginning of the film done much to convey his boredom and fatigue with the superficiality of his way of life and his inability to enjoy the utopian pleasures offered by the musical form but who, through the gentle, thoughtful phrasing of this closing request, is now finally able to move towards a recognition of 'the infinite *joy*' that marriage to Gigi will bring him. Indeed, if one were to construe the significance of Gaston's overall trajectory within the film in vocal terms, one could say that, having initially been in a state of mind that prevents him from singing without sounding as though he were still speaking, he finally arrives at a point where he is now able to speak with the emotionality and commitment of one who sings.

2. Male trauma, vocal impairment and the rejuvenating power of the soothing/nurturing/crooning voice

So far I have deliberately not broached the gender-based work that has been carried out on the voice in cinema as, in line with this study's overall aims, I wanted the films to be allowed to speak for themselves without the analysis of them being too pre-determined by some of the theoretical assumptions and priorities that have tended to drive this field. With the notable exception of Maria DiBattista's book *Fast Talking Dames* (2001), much of the feminist-based writing on the cinematic voice has, of course, been understandably concerned with the difficulties associated with the woman's attempt to speak in main-stream film. This is a problem that has generally been explained in terms of cinema's structuring of its auditory dimension in ways that serve the needs of a male subjectivity. As such, much of the work in this area has tended to regard cinema's treatment of the woman's voice as very much consistent with its use of her image. The argument here is that in both cases the female figure in film acts as a site of displacement for what is ultimately construed (drawing on theories of castration anxiety) as a fear in the male subjectivity of his own inadequacy and lack. Thus, in posing the question: 'How does classic cinema engender sound?', Kaja Silverman writes in the prologue to her book *The Acoustic Mirror*:

> I will attempt to demonstrate that Hollywood requires the female voice to assume simi-
> lar responsibilities to those it confers upon the female body. The former, like the latter,
> functions as a fetish within dominant cinema, filling in for and covering over what is
> unspeakable within male subjectivity. In her vocal, as in her corporeal, capacity, woman-
> as-fetish may be asked to represent that phenomenal plenitude which is lost to the male
> subject with his entry into language. However, the female voice, like the female body, is
> more frequently obliged to display than to conceal lack – to protect the male subject from
> knowledge of his own castration by absorbing his losses as well as those that structure
> female subjectivity. (1988: 38–9)

According to Silverman, this desire to project the male's own sense of lack onto the fe-male (a lack that, challenging Freud, she sees as preceding the male child's discovery of the female's lack of a penis) finds its solution, in auditory terms, in mainstream cinema's use of a range of defensive mechanisms aimed at invalidating and rendering inadequate the woman's ability to speak in film. While questioning whether the 'bleak picture' (Law-rence 1991: 10) that Silverman puts forward 'holds true for every representation of the speaking woman in classical film' (ibid.), Amy Lawrence shares that theorist's concern with the attempts made by such cinema to contain the woman's voice. It is something that she explores in relation, among other things, to the use of sound technology itself which, she argues, 'frequently exposes itself in its effort to repress' women when they 'challenge the status quo' (1991: 5). For Lawrence, though, 'the speaking woman' remains (in the films she studies) a source of disruption to 'the dominant order' and one that 'provokes increasingly severe methods of repression because she refuses to be silenced. Attempts to stop her from speaking rupture classical conventions of representation, however, and expose the way patriarchy uses language, image, sound and narrative to construct and contain "woman"' (1991: 32). Because of the greater emphasis she places on the disruptive potential of the female speaking voice, I find myself in closer affinity with Lawrence than Silverman (who is prone to make much more absolutist claims about classical cinema). Indeed, I would argue that when one takes into account the female singing voice – particularly the voice of the great female singer (as I do in my book on the musical) – the possibilities for gender disturbance take on another interesting dimension. While the power of the great female singer's voice does undoubtedly tend to provoke some extreme, and at times very violent, attempts at suppression and control on the male protagonist's part, the films themselves are notable for the considerable value that they invest in the enduring strength and importance of the woman's voice in enabling her to rearticulate and redefine her sense of selfhood by the end of the narrative. In dealing with the phenomenon of the great female singer, these films also consistently reveal the ability of such a voice to expose the very kind of anxieties and insecurities in the male's own identity that Silverman argues classical cinema seeks to cover over and deny (for an analysis of these various aspects to such films, see Smith 2005: 54–116). Because of the emphasis that these backstage musicals place on the unique talent of the great female singer it could be argued that they constitute an exception to the general rule governing the treatment of the female voice in mainstream film. Yet, as we will explore later in this chapter in relation to the actress Greer Garson, there are instances in which even the quieter, more unassuming form of female speaking voice may become endowed with a very active, independent strength and in a way that finds its most interesting realisation in two films of hers that were made right in the midst of the classical Hollywood period. This is not to dismiss Silverman's work out of hand, of course, as there are certain aspects to her approach that, as we shall see, are particularly helpful in alerting us to the psychological significance of Garson's vocal performance in *Random Harvest* (Mervyn LeRoy, 1942). However, as the forthcoming analysis will also explore, there are a number of meanings and effects arising from the use of Garson's voice both in that film and *Goodbye, Mr Chips* (Sam Wood, 1939) that substantially challenge and outstrip some of the key assumptions and claims that Silverman makes.

If all of this is to suggest that there may be complexities to the use of the female voice in film that are not altogether explainable in terms of the kind of theoretical frameworks adopted by Silverman and others, then the analysis of *Father of the Bride* and *Gigi* in chapter one can also be understood as opening up an aspect to do with the articulation of the *male* voice in cinema that is even less well catered for by such approaches. Whereas a major part of Silverman's argument is predicated upon the idea of classical cinema using the female as a site onto which the male subject's own sense of lack can be projected and thereby disowned, *Father of the Bride* and *Gigi* offer two significant instances of films that are, by contrast, wholeheartedly committed to celebrating the strength of selfhood and fullness of spirit that the female embodies in both her child and adolescent forms. In doing so, not only do such films in turn refuse to define the female according to some psychoanalytic notion of innate biological lack, but they also attribute the subsequent diminution or suppression of her subversive vitality on growing up to the social and ideological workings of patriarchy itself. The actualisation of this process is presented in each of these films as involving an immense loss for the male, too, and one that brings him to a state of intense crisis with regard to his own position as upholder of the patriarchal order and its values.

As we explored in that chapter, these films' ability to articulate such a position is due in large part to their use of the male voice in ways that allow for the emergence of a deeper form of character interiority – an aspect of classical cinema that Silverman argues has (because of its potential for containment and entrapment) usually been made synonymous with femininity (1988: 63). Arguing that 'diegetic interiority' is equated 'with discursive impotence and lack of control, thereby rendering that situation culturally un-acceptable for the "normal" male subject' (1988: 54), Silverman states that:

> Interiority has a very different status in classic cinema from the one that it enjoys in the literary and philosophical tradition which Derrida critiques. Far from being a privi-leged condition, synonymous with soul, spirit or consciousness, interiority in Hollywood films implies linguistic constraint and physical confinement – confinement to the body, to claustral spaces, and to inner narratives. (1988: 5)

Yet as already observed, it is Minnelli's preoccupation with the inner, creative life of the individual and his use of the voice as a means of exploring this that are what allow these two films to articulate such a resistant male perspective on the conventionalising of the female as she grows up. This is especially true when combined (as in *Gigi*'s case) with the heightened mode of expressivity associated with the musical genre. In exploring the complexity of this relationship between masculinity and the voice yet further, I want to begin by considering the question of what happens when the male is faced not so much with an internalisation of his voice but, rather, with the threatened loss of it altogether. While the study of this in relation to the first two films covered in this chapter offers a logical point of continuity from chapter one – given the concern in *Father of the Bride* and *Gigi* with the male protagonist's search to find a voice capable of giving expression to his innermost feelings – what I am particularly interested in exploring here are the additional creative possibilities and effects that may arise in those cases where the male's struggle to speak manifests itself in the form of some quite literal impairment to his voice.

Mr Smith Goes to Washington (Frank Capra, 1939)

> Senator Smith has now talked for 23 hours and 16 minutes. It is the most unusual and spectacular thing in the senate annals. One lone and simple American holding the great-

est floor in the land. What he lacked in experience, he's made up in fight. But those tired boy-ranger legs are buckling, bleary eyed, voice gone, he can't go on much longer. And all official Washington is here to be in on the kill. (CBS reporter commenting on Jefferson Smith's performance during the filibuster in *Mr Smith Goes to Washington*)

James Stewart's performance as Jefferson Smith, the naïve young senator who uses the democratic right of the filibuster to fight back against the corrupt business forces at work within the senate, is justly regarded as one of the most memorable in cinema history and did much to push this actor into the front rank of Hollywood's male stars. Yet while the extreme efforts that Stewart went to in order to achieve the necessary effect of hoarseness for the closing section of the filibuster speech have often attracted commentary (see this actor's biographer Donald Dewey, for example, on how Stewart sought out medical help from a doctor who 'applied a dichloride of mercury compound that produced the requested inflammation and a more persuasive rasp, then hung around the set in case reapplications were needed during the day' (2003: 194), there has been, so far as I am aware, little academic consideration given to the creative ways in which this film makes use of Stewart's voice and the crucial importance of this actor's vocal performance in helping to establish and articulate the full complexity of his star persona.

In seeking to explore this, it is worth beginning by considering the significance of Capra's decision to cast Stewart – not Gary Cooper – in the lead role. In doing so the director was able to capitalise not just on a greater degree of emotionality in Stewart's performance style (Dewey 2003: 193–4) but also on certain qualities and tendencies inherent in his voice, the full potential of which had not been creatively exploited in Stewart's career thus far. His habit of speaking in a slow, stumbling, hesitant way had certainly already become a recognised part of his performance repertoire by this time. Indeed, it is something that in his early films had often been used to underscore his popular persona as the decent, ordinary all-American guy whose manner of speaking was earnest and humble and, in its ability to evoke the sense of thoughts just breaking through into consciousness as he speaks, remarkably free from the kind of manipulation more frequently associated with a faster style of talking (of the kind adopted in such extreme form, say, by Cary Grant in *His Girl Friday* (Howard Hawks, 1940)). In the case of the filibuster sequence in *Mr Smith Goes to Washington*, however, the propensity towards attenuation in Stewart's vocal delivery was extended and dramatically integrated in ways that took it to another level of conceptual realisation entirely as the political survival of his character now becomes wholly dependent on Jeff/Stewart's ability to stretch out his entire speech (not just individual words or sentences) for as long as possible: 'Read them Constitution next very slow' advises Saunders (Jean Arthur) in a note written to him at one point.[1] Although Gary Cooper was himself noted for his slow, somewhat ponderous style of delivery, with him there was a recalcitrance to his use of words that seemed less in tune with the film's need for its central character to keep on talking. In Stewart's case, moreover, Capra was able to exploit a feeling of vulnerability arising out of the tremulous nature of this actor's voice and the hesitant manner of his phrasing. And this, in feeding into the whole suspense surrounding whether Jefferson Smith will manage to hold out for long enough to be able to clear his name, is something that finds its most extreme form of realisation in the closing sequence where Stewart's character finds himself on the verge of both vocal and physical collapse.

It is possible to detect signs of this creative use of Stewart's voice emerging much earlier on in the film during the scene where a nervous Smith tries to read out his new bill proposing a national camp for boys during his debut speech in the senate. On that occasion, his reading of the bill in an extremely unsteady voice (matched only by the shaking of his hands which fail to stop the papers he is holding from flopping back as he tries to read from them) prompted the chair of the senate (Harry Carey Sr) to comment: 'Our young senator will make a good orator once his voice stops changing.' At this point, the senate chamber, already moved to laughter, is shown dissolving into an even greater mood of hilarity. In one sense, Carey's joke here about the young senator's lack of experience as an orator is quite ironic in star performance terms given the considerable degree of manipulation and control that must have been required on Stewart's part in order to achieve this effect of intense nervousness. Yet as an implied commentary on Stewart's (not just his character's) vocal performance, Carey's remark is nevertheless interesting for the way that it manages to draw attention to a certain instability of effect that this actor was capable of producing through his distinctive style of delivery, the quavering nature of which, together with its tendency to slip at times out of a bass register and into a higher, more 'feminine' key, are here given comic scope for amplification and exaggeration. In equating Stewart's voice with that of an adolescent boy whose breaking voice is indicative of an incipient but not yet fully attained state of manhood, Carey's comment derives additional significance from its ability to link this quality of instability to a more specifically masculine form of insecurity.

In showing Jeff going on to pull off a spectacular feat of oratory via the filibuster, the film on one level allows Stewart's character to fulfil the manly potential alluded to so playfully by Carey in that earlier scene. Yet while the condition of hoarseness does help to eliminate his voice's earlier, boyish register, it also conveys a sense of the immense strain involved in trying to achieve and maintain this more adult state of 'political manhood' (to use DiBattista's term (2001: 157)). In coming to signify not so much Carey's notion of the adolescent male moving towards manhood but more the threat of impairment and loss that may accompany its attainment, this near 'breaking' of Stewart's voice in the closing stages of the filibuster sequence thus manages to bring out a much more fraught, pressure-ridden side to the actor's star persona that is strikingly anticipatory of some of his later, darker work. In his brief but illuminating analysis of this actor's star persona in his book on Katharine Hepburn, Andrew Britton has maintained that Stewart's overall persona is marked by a certain duality, whereby the popular image of him as 'an embodiment of homely, middle-American integrity and moral earnestness' (1995: 14) is countered in some of his post-war films for Capra, Mann and Hitchcock by the emergence of a much darker, more neurotic side, the compulsive drives and barely-contained violence of which seem symptomatic of the repressions and frustrations arising from the need to fulfil the role of normative male hero. This being the case, then, in the unrelenting pressure it places on Stewart's voice during the second part of its narrative, *Mr Smith Goes to Washington* is notable for its ability to utilise this aspect of the actor's performance in a manner that (at times outstripping the film's more limited ideological agenda) manages to give early expression to such tendencies.[2] And if, as Britton has also argued, 'the meaning of the Stewart persona might be said to be: "if you are the perfect, middle-class, heterosexual American male, you go mad"' (1995: 14), then nowhere is this signifying potential of the star articulated more clearly or presciently than during that moment in the film where Jeff, frustrated by the other senators' lack of response to a particularly impassioned, idealistic passage of his speech, cries out in exasperation: 'Either I'm dead right or I'm crazy!' (on this see also Dewey 2003: 194–5). Although the impact of this outburst is quickly defused through the use of humour, it is nevertheless uncannily prophetic in the potential for neurosis that it admits to in the Stewart persona as the strain of trying to uphold the kind of moral integrity so associated with his popular image leads to the momentary contemplation of another – much darker – possibility.

This use of Stewart's voice in ways that manage to bring out a more troubled complexity in his persona is something that is compounded by the narrative emphasis that is placed on the attempts by Senator Paine (Claude Rains) and the corrupt businessman Taylor (Edward Arnold) to silence and invalidate Jeff's attempts to speak both within the senate chamber and beyond. In stressing the persistent nature of such acts of vocal suppression, the film intensifies this sense of frustration and powerlessness in the Stewart protagonist in ways that seem particularly prophetic of the actor's later work for Hitchcock. The scene where Jeff has to sit and witness the false testimonies and forged papers produced during the committee's investigation into his supposedly corrupt dealings interestingly prefigures, for example, the humiliation and anguish that Stewart's character is forced to endure during the inquest into Madeleine's 'suicide' in *Vertigo* (1958). Similarly, Jeff's refusal to stay and speak out in his own defence also initiates a form of self-induced vocal withdrawal that finds its much bleaker culmination during the scene at the sanatorium in *Vertigo* where Scottie, now in a state of mental breakdown, is shown losing his capacity for speech altogether. The greater idealism inherent in *Mr Smith Goes to Washington* helps bring about a more optimistic form of resolution by allowing Jeff to find both solace and renewed motivation in the words of encouragement that Saunders gives him during her encounter with him at the Lincoln memorial. This can be contrasted with the situation in *Vertigo* where Scottie is rendered completely incapable of responding to the attempts by Midge (Barbara Bel Geddes) to bring him out of his mental breakdown. However, in demonstrating Saunders' ability to inspire Jeff to go back and stand up to the Taylor machine,[3] Capra's film nevertheless reinforces an extensive reliance by Stewart's character on the female throughout its narrative that was itself to become a significant feature of some of his work for Hitchcock.

Jeff's repeatedly foregrounded reliance on Saunders' whispered instructions from the gallery at crucial points during his performances in the senate chamber can, for example, be seen as pointing forward to the Stewart protagonist's dependency on Jo's (Doris Day) voice during the scenes at the Royal Albert Hall and the foreign embassy in Hitchcock's American version of *The Man Who Knew Too Much* (1955). Such a connection is strengthened when one considers how it is left to Jean Arthur to emit a triumphant whoop of delight at the very end of Capra's film as Stewart's character lies unconscious on the floor. In giving vent to a female voice otherwise marginalised and denied by the male-dominated world of politics, it prefigures the even more cathartic scream of protest that Jo gives out during the scene at the Royal Albert Hall (for an analysis of the use of Day's voice in that scene, see Smith 2000: 104–15). In privileging Arthur's vocal response at the very end of the narrative, Capra's film is also interesting for the way that it anticipates Hitchcock's foregrounding of Lisa's (Grace Kelly) active gaze in the final scene of *Rear Window*, the Stewart protagonist once again having been rendered unconscious by this stage in the story. The *Mr Smith Goes to Washington*/*Rear Window* connection is also evident, of course, in the physical containment of the Stewart character's active masculinity throughout some or all of these narratives, with Jeff's requirement to stay within the senate chamber for the entire duration of the filibuster sequence finding its more extreme counterpart in Jeffries' confinement within his apartment and wheelchair for almost the whole of *Rear Window*. Although the physical containment that Stewart's character endures in Hitchcock's film is much more severe than in Capra's, the rule that requires Jeff not to leave the chamber or stop talking if he is to continue to hold the floor does tend to make the strain on his voice all the more intense and unremitting and without the compensating form of potency that his namesake is able to achieve in *Rear Window* through the assertion of the voyeuristic look.

The sense of helplessness and strain that are generated by this combination of Stewart's own vocal performance, the various attempts made by certain figures within the narrative to suppress his character's attempts to speak and the heightened pressure that is placed on his voice as a result of the physical containment that Jeff is required to endure within the senate chamber during the filibuster sequence, have led some commentators to express scepticism about the adequacy of the resolution offered at the end of the film. In his account of *Mr Smith Goes to Washington*, Stewart's biographer Donald Dewey comments on the implausibility of Paine's attempted suicide and subsequent confession in the closing stages of the filibuster, observing that his sudden, narratively unprepared, hysterical outburst 'comes almost as a deus ex machina' (2003: 199). In his biographical study of Frank Capra, moreover, Joseph McBride cites the screenwriter, Sidney Buchman, as having loathed Capra's adoption of the suicide device (1992: 416).[4] Such charges of implausibility certainly seem to be partly borne out by the physical helplessness of Jeff's situation at this point, his earlier collapse onto the senate floor – only moments after vowing that he will 'stay right here and fight for this lost cause' – having rendered him oblivious to the narrative dénouement that follows and requiring his reliance on this drastic turn of events to bring about a resolution to his problems. As Dewey remarks, 'he and all his ideals are unconscious when the Rains character admits the truth of everything. He has to be awoken and *told* that his obstinacy has won the day'

(2003: 197). The precise manner of Jeff's collapse – as he faints on the unfinished line, 'Somebody'll listen to me. Some…' – compounds this sense of desperation, especially prefiguring, as it does, the moment in *It's a Wonderful Life* (Frank Capra, 1946) when, faced with bankruptcy and on the verge of suicide, Stewart's character George Bailey stands alone in Martini's bar and prays to God to show him the way. In both cases, the appeal for help (construed in Jeff's case more in terms of an assertion of faith in the possibility of someone being able to rescue him from his situation rather than as an actual prayer) finds its response in the act of intervention that follows, with Paine's suicide attempt and confession anticipating Capra's use of Clarence the angel (Henry Travers) to avert what has now become, in that later film, the Stewart protagonist's own attempt to kill himself.

Yet to focus solely on these aspects would be to overlook a central paradox that is raised by Stewart's performance during the filibuster sequence – namely that it is at the very point where his voice is physically at its weakest and most vulnerable that it is able to achieve its most compelling auditory power. This is signalled right at the start of the closing part of the filibuster when, as the CBS reporter finishes his report (quoted at the beginning of this section), Capra cuts to a high-level viewpoint looking down over the senate chamber. In emphasising the grandeur of the setting and reducing Stewart to an almost indiscernible figure in its midst, this shot tends to visually reinforce the reporter's preceding emphasis on Jeff's position of helplessness at this point, the bird's-eye view adopted here even going so far as to evoke his reference to the predatoriness of the eyes of 'official Washington' as they gather 'to be in on the kill'. Yet, as we take in such a view, it is Stewart's voice that can be heard transcending the considerable spatial reaches of the senate chamber. The hoarse, croaking tones that he employs – which seem in danger of disintegrating even as he speaks – manage to invest his words ('No sir, there's no compromise with truth. That's all I got up on this floor to say…') with a most moving power of expression at the very point where his voice seems to be on the verge of almost total collapse. This is confirmed in the very next shot when, as Saunders returns to the gallery and tells her journalist friend Diz (Thomas Mitchell) that she has to stop Jeff as 'terrible things are happening' back in his home state, the engrossed reporter deters her from doing so with the words: 'They're listening to him. Anything might happen now.'

The observation embodied in Mitchell's first line of dialogue here is immediately borne out by the ensuing series of shots showing the senators (in marked contrast to their earlier displays of indifference) now turned towards Stewart and listening in rapt attention to what he is saying. The prediction inherent in his second sentence arguably finds *its* moment of realisation during the sequence where Jeff, demoralised by the sight of the baskets of telegrams demanding that he yield the floor, but buoyed up by the compassionate smile that Carey's President of the Senate gives him, turns towards Paine and addresses him very directly. 'I guess this is just another lost cause, Mr Paine', says Stewart as Capra frames him in side profile from his position at the front of the chamber. His act of then turning around and explaining to the rest of the senate – 'All you people don't know about lost causes. Mr Paine does' – is quickly followed by a

Fig. 3.1

Fig. 3.2

Fig. 3.3

Fig. 3.4

return to this more private mode of address: 'He said once they were the only causes worth fighting for', insists Stewart before walking across towards the older senator while continuing with his commentary. 'And he fought for them once for the only reason any man ever fights for them', he says, only to lean over Paine's desk, one hand on either side of it, and assert in an even more strained, whispering tone of voice: 'Because of just one plain, simple rule: Love thy neighbour' (Fig. 3.1). The transition to a medium shot showing Paine looking downwards with an intently serious expression on his face (Fig. 3.2) captures the difficulty inherent in his attempt to maintain a sense of emotional detachment from Smith at this point. This shot composition is returned to with some significant variation a few moments later. Having first shifted to a lower camera position from the desk, looking up at Jeff as he says, 'And in this world today full of hatred a man who knows that one rule has a great trust. You know that rule, Mr Paine. And I loved you for it, just as my father did. And you know that you fight for the lost causes harder than for any others' (Fig. 3.3), Capra reverts to this previous view of Paine who can now be seen looking directly at Stewart as the latter concludes in a yet more rasping, highly-charged whisper: 'Yes, you even die for them. Like a man we both knew, Mr Paine' (Fig. 3.4).

The moral impact of Stewart's speech here lies partly in the appeal that his words make to Paine's bond of kinship with Jeff's dead father, whose ideals of sticking up for the ordinary people and fighting for their 'lost causes' Paine himself used to so believe in. Yet, as the earlier scene showing Jeff's frustration at the senators' collective lack of response to a particularly impassioned piece of rhetoric by him made clear, it is not simply the words themselves but the changed 'grain' (to use Barthes' term (1977)) of the voice itself which, in registering the wear and tear wrought on the male protagonist's body by Taylor's corrupt business tactics, is what is able to bring about this intent and direct state of listening in Paine at this point. The effect of Stewart's speech is heightened by his tendency to lower his voice at certain key moments. In modulating his voice in this way he is able to carve out a much more private, intimate emotional arena for his character's encounter with Paine and in a way that makes the moral weight and intensity of his words all the harder to avoid.

In granting such space to this performance by Stewart, Capra's film therefore has the distinction of being the first to fully recognise and exploit the expressive power of this actor's voice when reduced to a quieter, more hushed form of speech. It is something that Hitchcock would of course go on to exploit so effectively in *Rear Window* where the physical impairment and confinement to which both character and actor are subjected seems to license even more intense – at times quite menacing, even perverse – bouts of whispering by Stewart. The provocative moral force that Stewart's voice is able to assume during the closing filibuster sequence in *Mr Smith Goes to Washington* also owes much, of course, to the condition of hoarseness itself. In depriving this actor's voice of its broader tonal range and colouring, and in making the sheer physical effort of trying to speak all the more fraught and difficult (as evidenced by the coughs and sharp gasps of breath that punctuate the various stages of his delivery), it does much to convey the sense of a self stripped of all artifice and pretence and exposing itself in its raw, elemental form. The effect of this is enhanced all the more when one considers it in relation to Barthes' notion of the voice as the ultimate site of intersection and negotiation between the body and language – or, as Silverman puts it, 'between meaning and materiality' (1988: 44). For in the physical effort and struggle that Stewart's rasping, forced-through-the-throat style of delivery conveys, one could argue that much of the significance of the actor's performance lies in its ability to restore a sense of the *bodily* origins and integrity of the voice to the *discursive* realm of the senate chamber as Jeff proceeds to expose a congressman so habituated to using his own voice in the service of linguistic manipulation and cover-up to a more emotionally direct, visceral way of speaking and feeling.

Operating rather like an aural equivalent of sandpaper, this actor's hoarse voice scratches and scrapes away at Paine's outer armour, breaking down his façade of cynicism and deceit and forcing him to confront a moral side to himself that he seems to have buried and denied following the death of his best friend. In doing so, Stewart's performance here poses a challenge to the idea (advanced by Dewey) that Paine's confession comes suddenly from nowhere for, in using the emotional, moral force of this actor's voice to unlock the older senator's inner, guilt-ridden state, this act of direct vocal address can be understood as paving the way for the hysterical revelation that follows (Fig. 3.5). Indeed, in acquiring this provocative force, Jeff's passionate appeal to Paine can be considered as forming part of a broader coherent pattern of vocal disturbance and disruption that began with his

Fig. 3.5

debut speech in the senate. Here his reference to Willet Creek (as the site he plans to use for his proposed national boys' camp but which, unbeknownst to him, has already been earmarked by Taylor and Paine for their corrupt dam project) during his reading out of his new bill had the effect of disturbing Paine's normally suave, unruffled exterior. This pattern finds further scope for inflection during the sequence where a now wised-up Jeff sets out to expose the fact that Section 40 of the deficiency bill (which stipulates Willet Creek as the location for the new dam) is being misused by Taylor and Paine for their own personal financial gain; his intense assertions of the truth on that occasion managing to bring out an emotional turbulence to Paine's performance that was to prove even more prophetic of his later hysterical confession. In the first of these cases it was only the revelatory effect of the words themselves (in specifying Willet Creek as the proposed site for Jeff's boys' camp) rather than the voice itself that was able to provoke such a disturbance in Paine (the volatile unsteadiness of Stewart's voice having prompted merely laughter and amusement in both him and the other senators). Yet, in demonstrating an ability to wipe the smile off Paine's face, this moment of vocal intervention can nevertheless be understood as initiating a process of disruption that, culminating in Jeff's face-to-face encounter with Paine in the closing scene, is marked on all three occasions by the older senator having to make a hasty departure from the senate chamber.

In seeking to account for this ambivalent aspect of Stewart's vocal performance during the filibuster sequence, it is possible to understand its combination of vulnerability and power partly in terms of that duality referred to earlier between the darker and homelier sides to the actor's star persona. However, in exposing the male insecurities and instabilities that Silverman argues it is the psychic impulse of classical Hollywood cinema to try to deny and efface while at the same time raising the possibility of an alternative, more emotionally expressive masculinity emerging out of the condition of vocal impairment, this performance by Stewart is also significant in revealing some of the surprising effects that may arise, more broadly, when the cinematic male voice is deprived of its habitually more secure relationship to speech and language. And it is this twin potential to the male voice when it finds itself in this liminal state between speech and silence that we are now going to explore further in relation to our next film – *Random Harvest.*

Random Harvest (Mervyn LeRoy, 1942)

> Our story takes you down this shadowed path to a remote and guarded building in the English Midlands: Melbridge County Asylum. Grimly proud of its new military wing which barely suffices in this autumn of 1918 to house the shattered minds of the war that was to end war.

In beginning its story with this opening commentary by a disembodied male narrator whose voice, while never formally identified or heard again in the narrative, is actually that of James Hilton, the author of the English novel on which the film is based,[5] *Ran-*

dom Harvest starts in a way that would seem to bear out Silverman's view: 'Hollywood's soundtrack is engendered through a complex system of displacements which locate the male voice at the point of apparent textual origin, while establishing the diegetic containment of the female voice' (1988: 45). Silverman regards such strategies as working to evade the male subject's fears of dependency and lack, yet this opening voice-over narration by Hilton is of interest precisely because of the way that it uses its position of discursive authority to foreground a much repressed history of male trauma and loss arising from the experience of the Great War. The bleak legacy of this finds its most poignant acknowledgement of all in the form of Ronald Colman's hauntingly sensitive portrayal of Smith, the shell-shocked amnesiac whose experience of fighting in the trenches in France has completely deprived him of *his* claims to vocal mastery. The association of the male narrator's voice with discursive authority does find some form of diegetic continuation in the scene where the psychiatrist (Philip Dorn) is shown recounting (during his meeting with an elderly couple who have come to visit Smith in the hope that he may be their missing son) how Smith was retrieved from the trenches in France and brought back to England. Yet in following through Hilton's narration in this way the film begins its narrative in a manner that ultimately seems designed to accentuate the vocally disadvantaged state of Smith as he is forced to rely on these two authoritative, fluent male voices to tell what is known of his story.

The pathos of Smith's condition is greatly intensified by the casting of Ronald Colman for, as he proceeds to give expression to his character's traumatised situation during this opening sequence, we are forced to witness an actor so noted for his richly eloquent voice being reduced to using a broken, halting form of speech. In requiring Colman to suppress the velvety flow of his voice, LeRoy's use of this aspect of the actor's performance seems quite different, in one sense, from Capra's deployment of Stewart's voice in *Mr Smith Goes to Washington* where the filibuster sequence in particular offered so many opportunities for exaggerating certain tendencies already inherent in Stewart's voice. The contrast just outlined may not be quite so stark as it initially appears, however, for with Colman there was also, albeit more subtly than in Stewart's case, a quality of vulnerability arising from the sensitive timbre and phrasing of his voice – what R. Dixon Smith refers to as 'the indefinable fragility of that famous, exquisitely modulated voice' (1991: 1). This is something that, when combined with a certain haunted, lost look in his eyes, he was able to put to such memorable creative use in his realisation of this character. Colman's occasional habit of injecting slight pauses and hesitations into his delivery consequently finds much more extensive outlet for expression in his sensitive execution here of his character's very slow, halting form of speech. This is especially true during those moments where he summons up the effort to speak the words 'my ... my parents' on first hearing the news of the Lloyd couple's (Elisabeth Risdon and Charles Waldron) visit from the psychiatrist and when trying to ask one of the male attendants what will happen if they turn out to be his father and mother. His inability in the latter case to get beyond a stumbling repetition of 'If... If...' on that occasion prompted the staff member concerned to finish the first part of his sentence for him. The attendant's response – 'If they are your parents?' – in turn provides Smith with the vocal and verbal help he needs to falteringly complete his earlier line of enquiry: 'They … would … t… take me out of … here?' During the sequence where he does finally meet up with the Lloyd couple, this quality of fragility to Colman's voice finds its logical extension (rather like Stewart's voice at certain moments of crisis in *Mr Smith Goes to Washington* and *Vertigo*) in a complete withdrawal of the voice altogether. Thus, as they enter the room where he has been waiting for them (Fig. 4.1) Colman stands up and, in a re-version to the kind of understated style of silent film acting that he had become so noted for during his accomplished career in cinema prior to the arrival of talking pictures, looks pleadingly at them without uttering a word. The slight, tentative reaching outward of his right arm and excited yet apprehensive look in his eyes as he tries to smile at them, perfectly encapsulate the emotional tension in his character here as his longing to be recognised is held in check by an accompanying fear of rejection. On hearing the husband confirm that Smith is not their son, Colman registers his character's pain and despair, not by making any dramatic movements or exaggerated stuttering sounds but through a subtle intensification of his previous gestures as his arm reaches out just that degree more intently, his highly expressive eyes now more widened and fearful than before (Fig. 4.2).

Fig. 4.1

Fig. 4.2

Given the crucial importance that psychoanalytic theory has often attached to the acquisition of language – as that point in a child's life where their subjectivity and cultural identity are formed and their sense of oneness with the object ('the breast, the faeces, the mother's voice, a loved blanket' (Silverman 1988: 7)) is lost – *Random Harvest*'s opening scenario is additionally fascinating. This is due to the way that it seems to enact a return to this more liminal condition as Smith, deprived of all memory of his social identity and struggling to regain his speech, finds himself hovering somewhere on the boundary between these pre-subjective and subjective states (or between what Jacques Lacan refers to as the imaginary and symbolic realms).[6] This psychological dimension to the film is encouraged by the initial view we are given of Smith standing alone by the window like a lonely, disconsolate child (Fig. 4.3) and cut off spatially from

Fig. 4.3

the other adult male patients who were seen in a previous shot. Then, as the psychiatrist and doctor move forward towards him, LeRoy frames all three of them in a triangular configuration that is suggestive of the surrogate parent/child nature of this relationship (Fig. 4.4). As they continue to stand in this formation, Dorn can also be heard revealing to Smith the news of the Lloyd couple's visit and thus the possibility that his real parents may have been found.

Fig. 4.4

While the male-ordered world of the asylum and the kind but authoritative figure of the psychiatrist might seem to associate this attempt to reintegrate Smith back into language as a return also to the world of patriarchy – and, more particularly, an acceptance, in the form of Dorn's character, of the 'Law of the Father' – a key part of *Random Harvest*'s significance lies in its readiness to reject the Oedipal male trajectory implied by such a process. This is something that it manages to achieve by making Smith's escape from this institution and his entry into an alternative feminine realm, governed by principles of nurturing warmth and compassion, a prerequisite for his recovery. In this context, it is perhaps significant that it is Mr Lloyd who shakes his head and utters a firm 'No' in response to the psychiatrist's question, 'He is not your son, then?', for it is this rejection of the son's identity by the 'father' that seems to trigger the process of release and movement away from the patriarchal order. Thus, after the initial despair and isolation brought on by this rejection, Smith is shown emerging from the asylum building in the very next shot, and walking through its grounds amidst a heavy blanket of fog that, despite its cold, clammy nature, seems to offer him a degree of protection and relief from the oppressiveness of that institution. On being greeted by one of the guards who comments on his hardiness in being out in such weather he is then shown walking away and beginning to talk with growing confidence to himself as he picks up the strands of conversation previously broached by that figure. The sudden noise of the factory siren, followed by the sound of first one then several guards shouting out in excitement at the news that the war is over, facilitates

a more complete break away from the patriarchal order represented by the asylum as Smith, seizing the opportunity created by the guards' desertion of their posts, escapes through the main gate and into the anonymity of the fog-filled night (Fig. 4.5).

This re-entry into the outer adult world at first proves too much for Smith who, on finding himself jostled by the jubilant crowds of people as he walks through the town of Melbridge and on becoming overpowered by the sound of their cheering and singing, eventually seeks refuge in a little tobac-

Fig. 4.5

Fig. 4.6

Fig. 4.7

Fig. 4.8

conist shop just off the main street. Initially flustered by the abrasive manner of the small, waspish shopkeeper (Una O'Connor) who emerges from the back room there ('Well? Well, what is it you want? Oh come on, I haven't got all night', she says to him impatiently (Fig. 4.6)) it is nevertheless in this secluded, otherwise tranquil little space that Smith first encounters Greer Garson's character, Paula. This moment of their first meeting follows on directly from the sequence showing the shopkeeper's frightened reaction on realising that Smith is an escaped inmate from the asylum. 'Why, you're from the asylum. You're … It's alright, dear. You take your time. Have a nice look round, see. I'll be back in a jiffy', she says before scurrying back into the room behind her, clearly intent on phoning the authorities for help. As the camera then switches to a medium view of Colman's bewildered face, his attention is suddenly distracted by the sound of Garson's voice striking up for the first time (Fig. 4.7). 'You are from the asylum, aren't you?', she asks from a position somewhere off-screen to the left of frame. Then as Colman turns in the direction of the voice's source, the camera moves slightly forward then left towards the door to show her, walking towards him, as she asks the question, 'Aren't you?' (Fig. 4.8).

In a manner that seems quite unlike the more threatening potential that Michel Chion (1999) accords to the off-screen voice in cinema, Garson's voice here seems to float almost magically from nowhere into the narrative world (there having been no prior indication of her having entered the shop), its soft, hushed tones suffusing the screen with its warm emotional colours and caressing Smith in the protectiveness of its soothing aural embrace. In doing so, it introduces itself into this fictional universe in a way that is not only tenderly romantic but also evocative of the enveloping quality that has often been associated in psychoanalytic theory with the maternal voice. As Silverman points out:

> It has become something of a theoretical commonplace to characterise the maternal voice as a blanket of sound, extending on all sides of the newborn infant. For Guy Rosolato and Mary Ann Doane, the maternal voice is a 'sonorous envelope' which 'surrounds, sustains, and cherishes the child'. (1988: 72)

She goes on to argue that

> the trope of the maternal voice as sonorous envelope grows out of a powerful cultural fantasy, a fantasy which recent psychoanalytic theory shares with classic cinema. The fantasy in question turns upon the image of infantile containment – upon the image of a child held within the environment or sphere of the mother's voice. (Ibid.)

According to Silverman, the '"appearances"' of this trope 'are always charged with either intensely positive or intensely negative affect' and 'the fantasy of the maternal-voice-as-sonorous-envelope takes on a different meaning depending upon the psychic "lookout point"; viewed from the site of the unconscious, the image of the infant held within the environment or sphere of the mother's voice is an emblem of infantile plenitude and bliss', while 'viewed from the site of the preconscious/conscious system it is an emblem of impotence and entrapment' (1988: 72–3).

Considered in the light of such theoretical work, it is possible to regard *Random Harvest* as partly investing in this maternal voice fantasy as Smith is shown being drawn to Paula by the soothing, protective qualities of her voice. The reassuring, all-enveloping sound of this – in managing to conjure up some imagined state of 'infantile plenitude and bliss' and oneness with the mother – is able to offer him immediate relief from his present-day concerns about his lack of identity. The decision to stage Garson's introduction in a manner that requires Smith to become aware of her in the form of a voice whose source begins outside of his perceptual field of view, seems especially significant in this context given the way that it re-evokes aspects of the foetus's first auditory perceptions of the mother. The tobacconist shop setting tends to enrich this psychoanalytic dimension to their initial encounter all the more by offering a sequestered space cut off from the outside world that is quite womb-like in nature. The scenes that follow help to develop this reading by showing Smith first finding protection in Paula's readiness to speak for him during their visit to the Melbridge Arms, and then being lulled to sleep later on by her soothing words of comfort as he lies ill in bed, agitating about what will happen to him if he goes back to the asylum. In doing so, this opening section of the film places Colman's character in a position that can also be seen as re-enacting the male infant's reliance on the maternal voice in the early post-birth phases of life. Given all this, it seems quite telling that it is shortly after the birth of their own son that the idyllic nature of their married time together in the Devon countryside is broken. This rupture to their romance is overtly triggered by the job offer that Smith receives, the news of which, in prompting him to journey to Liverpool the very next day, is what brings about his accident, the subsequent recovery of his former memory and the loss of all recollection of his time with Paula. Yet it is a narrative upheaval that can also be seen to be motivated by a desire to deflect attention away from the psychological conflict that the son's presence poses to Smith's unconscious construction of his own relationship to Paula in infant/mother terms.

The possibility of utilising Garson's voice in ways that are suggestive of this maternal voice fantasy is something that one can find more explicitly at work in this actress's previous film, *Mrs Miniver* (William Wyler, 1942), most notably during the scene where the Miniver family takes refuge in the air-raid shelter during a heavy German bombing raid. On that occasion, Garson's character was shown sending her two youngest children to sleep by reading them part of the closing passage from Lewis Carroll's *Alice's Adventures in Wonderland* before resuming her recital just as her husband's (Walter Pidgeon) attempt to read out the same passage is interrupted by the noise of the bombs falling. Although the basic motivation of this scene is unmistakeably propagandist in nature (like the one later on where Garson is shown standing up to the harsh Nazi rhetoric of the stray German paratrooper) it is nevertheless interesting for what it reveals once again about the ability of this actress's voice to carve out a feminine realm of nurturing feeling that is quite different from the hostility and aggression that are associated with the masculinist arena of war. With her soothing tones, Garson thus manages to transform the air-raid shelter into another 'womb-like' enclosure set off from the world outside, the serene beauty of her voice (as she now recites the words without the aid of the book and while continuing with her knitting) serving to imbue this space with an air of tranquillity amidst even the most terrifying stages of the bombing attack.

While *Random Harvest* also uses Garson's voice as a reassuring counterpoint to the noise and chaos of war, it is, arguably, a measure of this film's greater interest and significance that it should choose to place her voice's compassionate qualities not in opposition to the threat of some foreign enemy (as in *Mrs Miniver*) but in contrast to English society's own prejudiced treatment of its shell-shocked soldiers. Regarded by some as 'loonies' (to use the term invoked by the guard during the scene in the Melbridge Arms where he refers to how he 'blotted [his] copybook' by allowing one of the inmates to escape) these victims of the Great War are locked away in an institution whose bleak isolation from ordinary society was evoked so vividly by Hilton's use of words such as 'shadowed', 'remote' and 'guarded' during his opening voice-over narration. Indeed, one could perhaps sum up the difference in outlook of these two films by saying that whereas in *Mrs Miniver* Garson's voice served quite unambiguously to provide reassurance and comfort to a country at war,[7] in *Random Harvest* it functions in ways that imply the nation's own need to adopt a more nurturing, compassionate approach towards its traumatised soldiers. Significantly, it is the ex-boxing champion known as 'the Biffer' (Reginald Owen) who – as someone who is more astutely attuned to the realities of fighting – remains most steadfast in support of Paula's attempt to help Smith by taking him away from the asylum. This is in contrast to her boss, Sam (Rhys Williams), who quickly capitulates on hearing the guard speak of Smith's dangerous potential during his visit one night to the bar, and to the shopkeeper whose prejudiced fears on discovering that Smith is from the asylum prompt her to act in a manner that constitutes, if anything, a betrayal of the nurturing instinct. The film even goes so far as to acknowledge Paula's own vulnerability to such attitudes during the scene where she returns to Smith's room in the inn and tells him of her reluctant agreement with Sam that it is perhaps best after all if he returned to the asylum. This in turn prompts Colman to lapse back into a worrying state of vocal withdrawal, as he registers, through his faltering 'I ... I ...', and ensuing silence, the breaking of the earlier bond of reassurance that her words now denote.

It is significant that the only occasion where Garson's voice prompts a relapse of this kind in Smith is when she broaches the 'wisdom' of returning to the asylum. In all other respects the film values her voice precisely for its ability to open up an alternative realm of female feeling and experience that lies outside of the traditional patriarchal order that it is the aim of that institution to rehabilitate him back into. In doing so, *Random Harvest* departs crucially from the maternal voice fantasy that Kaja Silverman critiques. For whereas this trope works, she argues, to disavow the male's own position of infantile lack and helplessness 'by reversing the respective positions of the mother and the infant subject' (1988: 99) in ways that have the effect of 'stripping her of all linguistic capabilities' (1988: 105) and 'by moving her to the interior of the sonorous envelope' (1988: 99), in *Random Harvest* it is precisely Garson's ease with language and the calm, articulate flow of her voice that are such a source of reassurance to Smith. According to Silverman, the maternal voice fantasy also works to disavow the mother's 'crucial role during the subject's early history' (1988: 100), thereby denying the fact that 'she is traditionally the first language teacher, commentator and storyteller – the one who first organises the world linguistically for the child, and first presents it to the Other' (ibid.). Yet in *Random Harvest* it is precisely this tutelary role that Garson's voice is so adept at performing as Paula is shown sitting with Smith and using her own confidence with speech and language to bring him out of himself in a manner that the male psychiatrist could not.

Her ability to enable Smith to discover, in turn, a more distinctive voice of his own is reflected not just in the empowering effect that she has on his speech initially but also in his discovery later on (during the Devon countryside section of the narrative) of a talent for writing. Although the possibilities arising from this find their more quotidian outlet in the form of the offer of a job writing for a Liverpool newspaper, it is symptomatic of Paula's ability to recognise and elicit a more creative side in Smith that she should choose to equate his writing status with that of one of the great English Romantic poets. Thus, on checking over the items he has packed in his suitcase just before he leaves for his job interview in Liverpool, she remarks, 'This cuff's a bit frayed' only to then add, 'but, there, I don't suppose Keats was very dressy.' Far, then, from associating the nurturing aspects of Garson's voice with a state of interiority prior to language or a condition of inarticulate sound, it is the ability of her voice to display a discursive mastery of its own, together with its capacity to unlock a more creative use of language in Smith, that the film presents as so crucial in bringing about this rehabilitation in Colman's character. The fact that Paula first announces herself to Smith in the form of an off-screen voice that prompts him to turn and look in her direction consequently acquires another level of significance in this context. As well as carrying evocations of the unborn infant's auditory experience of the mother in the womb it is indicative of the power of Garson's voice to emulate the more guiding tutelary aspects of the maternal role as she uses it to draw Smith out of his withdrawn state of interiority here and into a relationship with, and awareness of, the outside world.

If part of *Random Harvest*'s significance, therefore, derives from its ability to utilise Garson's voice in ways that, while making clear the attractiveness of its nurturing qualities to Smith, nevertheless challenge and contest some of the reductive, distorting tendencies that Silverman has argued underpin the construction of the maternal voice fantasy in both classical film and psychoanalytic theory, then this is complicated yet further by the film's deployment of such a voice within a highly romantic context. In addressing this key aspect of the film, it is possible, in one sense, to understand the properties of Garson's voice as helping to counter and contain any more threatening potential arising from her romantic pursuit of Smith, the active nature of which was alluded to quite openly by Paula during the idyllic scene later on in Devon where Smith proposes to her. 'I've run after you from the very beginning. You know I have. I've never let you out of my sight since I first saw you in that little shop…', she said then in confirmation of her feelings for him before going on to rebuke him gently for not taking it upon himself to kiss her: 'Smithy, do I always have to take the initiative?'

The important role that her voice plays in tempering this active aspect to her desire is evident during her first appearance in the tobacconist shop. On that occasion, its soft tones and gentle rhythms had the effect of reassuring him even as she uses her voice to draw him to her. In exuding such qualities, Garson's voice also manages to defuse any more intimidating effect arising from Paula's initial question, the directness of which ('You are from the asylum, aren't you? Aren't you?') is consequently able to pro-

Fig. 4.9

voke not confusion and insecurity in Smith (as the shopkeeper's fearful utterance of words similar to these had done) but, rather, his outright honesty and trust: 'Yes, but I, I'm all right, really…' (Fig. 4.9). This comforting aspect to her voice similarly helps offset (along with the compassionate beauty of Garson's image) any more threatening potential inherent in her initial act of walking towards him. The forward motion of this, while on the one hand confirming the active nature of her desire, simultaneously affirms her associations with directness and openness in a way that contrasts refreshingly with the previous gestures of rejection performed first by the Lloyd couple and then by the shopkeeper. Far from appearing threatening, then, the gliding nature of her movement towards him, coupled with the soothing, caressing qualities of her voice, create an overall impact to her initial appearance, that, in being active and open yet reassuring, have the effect of drawing Smith out of himself almost immediately, enabling him to talk more freely to another person than he has at any point in the film so far.

In view of all this, it is significant that it is on hearing Garson sing, in her character's role as a music-hall artist, the old Harry Lauder song 'She's Ma Daisy' in front of a jubilant crowd of soldiers and civilians in the local theatre, that Colman's character is shown eventually succumbing to the effects of 'flu (Fig. 4.10). For, in watching her perform this number in a gruff and increasingly croaky Scottish accent he is forced to witness a removal of the very properties that had earlier been so comforting in her voice. The destabilising effect arising from this change is rendered all the more acute (from Smith's point of view) by Garson's use of her voice to sing of the man's desire for Daisy: in taking on this active male singing role she is able to express her performing identity in ways that act out, in co-medically anarchic form, the unconventional nature of her relationship with Colman's character. In tim-

Fig. 4.10

ing the feverish Smith's collapse so that it occurs immediately after he has watched her perform this song from his seat outside her dressing room (the shot showing him lying unconscious on the floor while everyone else is celebrating down on stage comes right at the end of her performance) the film gestures towards the possibility of a much more threatening aspect to this strong, independent woman's voice. It is a potential that invites comparison (up to a point) with certain tendencies that I have explored elsewhere on the Hollywood musical's fascination with the great female singer (see Smith 2005: 54–116). Indeed it is, arguably, a measure of the disruptive energy generated by Garson's vocal performance here that *Random Harvest*'s romance narrative requires Paula to give up her singing career almost immediately in order to help Smith escape. However, while this relinquishing of Paula's performing identity is suggestive of the film's unwillingness to go as far as those backstage musicals do in giving vent to the disruptive possibilities of the female singing voice, in making this change (which feels like less of a loss than might have been the case had Garson been noted as a singer) *Random Harvest* is able to restore a fluid dialectic between the romantic and nurturing aspects to this actress's voice that is itself capable of exerting a quietly subversive charge.

It is a dialectic that her previous film, *Mrs Miniver*, had sought to separate out in more safely and clearly delineated ways through casting her in the dual role of devoted mother and loyal, beautiful young wife. However, even here the potential for the nurturing and romantic sides to her persona to interact in more fluid, disruptive ways is suggested extra-textually by Garson's controversial off-screen romance with (and eventual marriage to) Richard Ney, the actor who (15 years her junior) had played her eldest son in the film. MGM head Louis B. Mayer's attempts to stop the couple from continuing with their affair for fear of the adverse publicity it would generate at the time of the film's release (Troyan 1999: 146–7) is indicative of the unease provoked in conservative circles by this slippage between the maternal and romantic elements in Garson's persona.[8] The disruptive possibilities of this can be seen to find their more subtle on-screen coalescence in Garson's role as nursemaid and lover to Colman's character in *Random Harvest*. Unlike the older woman/younger man scenario inherent in Garson's relationship with Richard Ney, however, Colman's greater age (he was, at the time of the film's production, in his early fifties), coupled with the Garson character's associations with a very youthful, active form of romantic desire, tend to work in ways that pull against the idea of there being any more implied Oedipal dimension to Smith's attraction to Paula.

In terms of Garson's voice, it is perhaps appropriate to understand this fluidity between the nurturing and romantic aspects as providing Smith with an aural bridge that enables him to negotiate a transition between his current child-like state of vulnerability and the world of adult romantic experience. This is evident most of all during the sequence where they are shown arriving at the Devon countryside. At this point they are still unsure of the fate of Paula's boss Sam, whose attempt to intervene and stop Smith from leaving the Melbridge Arms had earlier resulted in that character's fall and black out and their worried departure from the scene. As they stand looking out at the dreamy rural vista that first greets them, Paula can be heard commenting on this landscape in a manner that invites its insulating properties to be read as a specially transformed, romantic extension of the protectiveness offered by the maternal womb, the special qualities of which also find their spatial realisation in the highly romantic yet still womb-like enclosure of the country cottage that the couple move into on getting married. 'It's the end of the world. Lonely and lovely. We'll be safe here, even if...', she remarks in a voice whose soft, hushed tones seem to find a natural point of extension in the serenity of the setting that she describes. Garson's ability to infuse not just the landscape but the film's central romance with this protective quality may also help to explain why Colman's character does not appear as threatened by the birth of his son as one might expect given the implied infant/mother aspect to his own relationship with Paula. For while, as suggested earlier, their baby boy's arrival introduces a potential source of conflict that the film seems keen to avoid through its removal of Smith to Liverpool, in all other respects this infant comes to serve as an affirmation of the tender, nurturing principle on which their marriage is founded.

If this nurturing aspect to Garson's voice is crucial in accounting for the regenerative power that she is able to exert over Smith then this also has to be considered alongside the contribution that Colman's own voice makes to the blossoming of the couple's relationship. It is possible to illustrate this by comparing *Random Harvest*'s central romantic relationship with its counterpart in the musicals about the great female singer where the male's possession of some form of impairment often tends to signal a vulnerability and insecurity to his identity that the woman's singing voice ultimately serves to intensify and compound. This is quite different from the situation in *Random Harvest* where Smith's halting form of speech is construed much more positively as something that can be repaired by the healing properties of Garson's voice. Not only that but it is also viewed as being capable of shaping the development of their romance in its own right through the opportunities it affords for slowing down the pace of their exchanges and giving time for their feelings and insights about each other to emerge and breathe. This is displayed most touchingly of all during the scene in Paula's theatre dressing room where she is shown sitting astride a chair in front of him, dressed in her kilt costume and shifting nearer to him as she becomes especially impassioned by her desire to bring him out of his state of despondency (Fig. 4.11). On this occasion, the moving nature of their encounter derives not just from seeing Smith respond with growing confidence to the intimacy and directness of her manner but from the way that the slow, yet thoughtful, nature of his delivery allows her the opportunity to discover an emotional complexity and depth in him too, as curbing her end-of-war effusiveness, she responds with growing empathy and tenderness to the sadness of his situation (Figs 4.12 and 4.13). The expressive possibilities that this slow, minimalist form of delivery offer Colman had first been gestured at during the opening sequence in the asylum, most notably during the scene where, as he sits in the reception room waiting for the elderly couple to arrive, he utters their name 'Lloyd' twice in slow succession. In one sense, the unmistakeable texture of this actor's voice – so richly bass in tone yet marked by a great gentleness and quiet earnestness – has the effect of considerably heightening the pathos of this moment, evoking as it does the notion of a highly cultured, genteel kind of man now cut adrift from his social moorings and desperately trying to find some form of meaning and clue to his identity in this word. Yet, through the emotional resonance of his voice, Colman manages to endow Smith with a depth of substance and integrity of character that resists this threatened annihilation of his sense of self. The rich expressivity that he is able to bring to his utterance of this word serves to assure us – as it does Paula later – that there is a genuine core to his inner being that cannot be eroded or blotted out.

Fig. 4.11

Fig. 4.12

Fig. 4.13

In exploiting the creative potential inherent in this form of delivery during the later scene in Paula's theatre dressing room – as Colman invests each available word with a remarkable degree of emotional colouring – the film allows a most touching form of vocal chemistry to emerge between Smith and Paula. The poetic qualities of this, in setting a tone and rhythm so different from the madcap, frenetic verbal pace of the screwball comedies of the 1930s and 1940s (especially those centred around the fast-talking dame's bewildering of the hapless male), do much to suggest the special harmony and tenderness of their romantic union. The emergence of this is also linked quite precisely (through Paula's renaming of Colman's character as 'Smithy' in that same scene) with the discovery in this male figure of a new sense of identity.[9] This use of the voice to shape the rhythm and pace of the couple's relationship manifested itself as well during that earlier sequence (directly after their initial encounter in the tobacconist shop) where Paula follows Smith to a darkened corner of the main street as he stands resting against some railings, overwhelmed once again by the noise of the crowds and unsure where to go. On that occasion, he was shown responding to her earnest display of concern ('Can I help you? I thought you weren't feeling too fit, so I followed you. You don't mind, do you?') by shaking his head and staring at her as if transfixed, his lack of confidence with his speech allowing him the time to take in her serene beauty and compassionate qualities in much greater detail than would otherwise be the case. As such, it offers a moment of male contemplation of the woman's face that invites comparison with the one that occurs at the end of Norman Maine's (James Mason) and Esther's (Judy Garland) first dialogue-based encounter in *A Star is Born* (George Cukor, 1954) where Maine was shown calling Esther back so as 'to take another look at' her. In that film it is the strength of the singer's voice (following Mason's experience of hearing Garland sing 'The Man That Got Away') that seems to bring about this emotionally mature way of looking at the woman's image (Smith 2005: 92–3). In *Random Harvest*, though, it is the gentle, becalming qualities of Garson's voice, coupled with Smith's own vocally-impaired state, that (in depriving him, in the latter case, of the verbal assurance and eloquence more typically expected of the male seducer) affords him the opportunity to engage in such a deeply appreciative study of her character.

A major part of *Random Harvest*'s achievement, then, lies in its readiness to show how, when stripped of his former patriarchally-constructed identity and mastery of speech and when removed from his family ties and social setting, the male protagonist finds himself able, in this relatively raw and unmarked state, to respond to the humanity of this woman's influence and thus discover in the process a new and more profound sense of self worth. This is borne out even more in the second half of the narrative when, on recovering the memory of his past life as Charles Rainier, a military captain and eldest son of a wealthy business family based at the imposing Random Hall in Surrey, Colman's character is shown becoming caught up by the demands and expectations of that very traditional upper-class world and no longer able to respond to Paula (who now names herself Margaret) when she comes to work for him as his secretary. (Interestingly, this restoration of his social standing is also reflected, in cinematic terms, by his sudden acquisition of the status of voice-over narrator as he walks through the streets of Liverpool shortly after his accident.) The fact that he returns to Random Hall on the day of his father's funeral reinforces the symbolic impact of this return to upper-class patriarchy and, on stepping back into this world, he immediately proceeds to inherit the family home and take on a leading role in the running of the business. The loss and suppression that this involves is made clear soon afterwards, as the long-held ambition to write that he had been able to express during his time with Paula and which he admits (to his butler) wanting to 'take a fling at' on moving in to Random Hall, is quickly stifled by his growing sense of obligation to the family business. On hearing his sister's stepdaughter Kitty (Susan Peters) remind him (during their conversation at a restaurant) that 'You used to say that you hated business ... You were just going to whip things into shape and then get out quickly', he proceeds to justify his decision to stay on in terms of an even broader sense of social duty and conscience: 'I found that Rainiers kept other families going, too. Little families in little homes. Thousands of them, all over England', the burden of which responsibility is then registered by his young female companion who remarks wryly in response, 'I see. Uncle Atlas, eh?'

Despite the earnestness of Charles' demeanour here, and the overall gentlemanly nature of Colman's star persona, it is possible to detect in Rainier's attempt to define himself in the role of the benevolent upper-class patriarch a certain tone of condescension that hints at another negative consequence arising from his return to his former life and identity. Indeed, it is this sense of condescension (and the assumption of class superiority it involves) that seems, most crucially of all, to blind him to the significance of the

suitcase of clothes he left behind in a hotel on the day of his accident and which he is led to by Paula when she follows him to Liverpool several years later, intent on helping him to reclaim his memory of their time together. 'John Smith. Highly unimaginative incognito. And what could be more anonymous than these poor rags?', he remarks with a note of disparagement in his voice as he looks at the name on the luggage label (Fig. 4.14). His clinical dismissal of this crucial clue to his former identity prompts yet more silent distress in Paula who, as he leaves the room, lingers behind and lovingly touches the shirt that, with its frayed cuffs, had earlier invoked her romantic comparison of Smith with the poet Keats (Fig. 4.15). This ingrained class attitude in turn goes some way towards explaining Rainier's unresponsiveness to Paula when she comes to work for him. Unlike Kitty, whose place in that upper-class milieu gives her the opportunity (and confidence) to pursue and be considered as a full romantic partner for Charles despite the considerable gulf that exists between them in age, in Paula/Margaret's case her role as secretary (albeit private secretary) to Rainier

Fig. 4.14

Fig. 4.15

seems to render her invisible to him outside of that function. The active yet compassionate voice that he had formerly been so enraptured and soothed by, and which had played such a leading role in their relationship, thus becomes reduced for much of the time to a disembodied sound issuing from the office intercom machine and subject to the formal authority of his instructions.

The effect of these class and gender hierarchies in preventing him from regaining emotional contact with Paula/Margaret becomes most apparent when one compares the scene in the office, where they discuss the possible purchase of the Melbridge cable-works and then his marriage to Kitty, with the one earlier on in her theatre dressing room where she gets the shell-shocked Smithy to talk about himself. In contrast to the open-

Fig. 4.16

ness and mutual responsiveness of that earlier encounter, here he sits behind his desk, detached and cut off from her by the formality of the set-up and only intermittently engaging in any form of face-to-face contact with her (Fig. 4.16). In view of this, it is significant that it is only when she admits to an interest in the male-dominated, upper-class world of politics – during their conversation at the Houses of Parliament following his election as an MP – that he begins to take notice of her. Even here, however, the romantic potential arising from his observation of how her hair 'is bright red in the sunshine' is countered by his construal of his marriage proposal to her as a business venture – 'a merger' as he puts it. This suppression and distortion of the male's more tender inclinations towards the female is something that invites comparison with the moment in *Gigi* where Gaston, on returning to Mamita's apartment after the first rendition of the title number, announces brusquely to her grandmother that he has 'an important business matter to discuss'. In both cases, the significance of such a moment derives from the way that it serves to expose the male's inability to express a more authentic sense of self through language as he is shown trying to cloak his feelings for the female within the defensively cold, matter-of-fact terms of the business offer. In *Gigi*, the sense of disjuncture we feel at this point arises from Gaston's inability to translate into the ordinary realm of speech and language the romantic feelings for Caron's character that he had earlier managed to discover through the heightened medium of song. In *Random Harvest*, however, the effect is much more ironic given how it stems from our realisation that it is only when Smith is placed at the opposite end of the spectrum – that is, *when he finds himself in a vocally-impaired state of being barely capable of speaking* – that he is able to discover an emotional expressivity to his voice that is then lost on his recovery of his discursive mastery. Having said that, it is during this same encounter between Rainier and Paula at the Houses of Parliament (following on from his intent staring at her face and his admiring comment about her hair) that Colman's character admits to how he experienced a strong sensation of having known her before on seeing her the first day she came into his office. But, the possibility of a more intimate connection being achieved with her is once again thwarted by his act of immediately looking downwards while brushing some cigarette ash from his jacket.

Given the vital role that Garson's voice played in the first part of the story, it seems quite implausible, on one level, that Rainier's memory would not be triggered at least by this, if not by her image. This is particularly the case when one considers the proximity of contact offered first by their close working relationship and then by their marriage, not to mention the jolting effect that the merest fleeting sound of the male psychiatrist's voice had on him, by contrast, during his visit to the restaurant with Kitty. Yet it is precisely the active, leading role played by her voice in the first part of the narrative that makes Rainier's persistent unresponsiveness to Garson so highly suggestive on a psychoanalytic level. Indeed, when considered along the latter lines, his habit of barely looking at her during their conversation in his office, coupled with his later instinctive reaction of looking downwards and brushing the cigarette ash from his jacket at the first admission of having had recollections of having known her before, could be seen as symptomatic of some form of psychological blocking or denial on his part. In carrying out these actions it is as if he seeks to disavow the extent of his former dependency on this woman whose compassionate nurturing of him in that initial phase of the narrative may also have served to reawaken earlier repressed fears of infantile reliance by him on the mother figure. Rainier's unacknowledged desire for Garson's character consequently becomes displaced instead onto Kitty, whose role as stand-in for the lost object of his desire is suggested both by her own acknowledgement at one point that sometimes, in their closest moments of intimacy, she 'had a curious feeling that [she] reminds [him] of someone else' and by the consistently strong parallels that the film itself invokes between her and Paula. Thus, in an echo of Paula's romantic equation of Smith with the poet Keats, Kitty can be heard commenting during the scene where she reads out a letter written by her to Charles: 'Dear Charles, so you've left Cambridge and gone into the business. What a shame. I know you hated to leave your books in that quiet corner of the river where Rupert Brooke used to dream.' During their later encounter at the restaurant she confesses (in a manner reminiscent of Paula's earlier assertion of having run after Smithy from the start): 'It's no secret, is it? I've always been mad about you. Even as a schoolgirl.'[10]

This strategy of displacement is ruptured, however, during the wedding rehearsal scene in the church when Kitty, on witnessing him lapse into a trance-like state of distant reverie on hearing the song 'Oh Perfect Love', originally played at his wedding to Paula being performed once again here by the organist, decides to call off their marriage because she is 'not the one'. This in turn prompts Rainier's return to Liverpool in an attempt to retrieve his memory of those lost three years of his life, and his subsequent request for Garson's character to become his wife. His parting from Margaret at the train station as she sets off for her trip abroad contributes to this breakdown of the displacement process yet further, reawakening as it does his earlier experience of being separated from Paula by his trip to Liverpool. All of this then culminates in the scene depicting his return to Melbridge when he makes what turns out to be a successful attempt to resolve the workers' strike at the Cable Works factory that his family now own there. LeRoy charges this scene with echoes of the earlier sequence set in the same town: the opening shot shows the wrought-iron sign above the Melbridge Cable Works factory and initiates a chain of association that continues with the evocative sights and sounds of the cheering workers celebrating their industrial dispute victory, and the heavy fog that descends over the town as Rainier and his work colleague walk through the streets. Colman's return to this setting is therefore dramatised in ways that construe it not just as a physical retracing of his earlier steps but as a journey back to a forgotten psychological

Fig. 4.17

landscape, the rediscovery of which also involves him regaining contact with his former emotional self and the more sensitive, vulnerable masculinity that it entailed (Fig. 4.17). Within a setting so redolent of his earlier experiences, it is highly significant that it is the tobacconist shop that Colman's character first remembers. As the quiet, 'womb-like' space wherein Paula had first met and rescued him from impending reincarceration, it marks not just the point of origin in his relationship with Garson's character but also the start of his psychic rebirth ('My life began with you' as he tells her later). It is the retrieval of this memory that in turn enables him to confront his buried recollections of the asylum and his feelings of disorientation and fear at the time of his escape.

As he exclaims, 'There was a girl. There was a girl. Yes, there was a girl!' on walking down the path from the asylum with one of his business colleagues, the fog that once again enshrouds that building (as on the night of his escape) suddenly begins to fill the foreground of the screen only to be replaced, following the transition to the next

Fig. 4.18

scene, by a white blanket of mist that rolls across the frame. Then, in a romantic, dream-like image that beautifully evokes this gradual coming back to life of Paula in Smith's memory, the curling wisps of mist eventually clear to reveal Paula's face at the window of the old inn where she and Smith first stayed years before on their arrival in the Devon countryside (Fig. 4.18). Her observation to the female innkeeper moments later – 'The mist is lifting' – continues this chain of poetic association as she now verbally gestures towards this clearing of the male protagonist's inner fog and the magical

dénouement and reconciliation that is about to take place on his return to the cottage where they spent their newly-married life together. The sequence where Colman arrives at the cottage and opens the still-creaking gate, walks down the path past the overhanging bough of cherry blossom and opens the front door with the key he has kept on his person since the time of the accident, only for Paula to appear at the gate herself and call out to him, is greatly cherished by lovers of this movie. For such viewers, Smith's retracing of his steps to this idyllic retreat that seems to exist in a fantasy space outside of the normal parameters of time may come to express something about the capacity of film itself to offer us, as audiences, highly evocative sites of recollection and return.

Precisely what is being returned to here is also extremely crucial, of course, in accounting for the memorable nature of *Random Harvest*'s romantic resolution. In staging the couple's reunion at the very site most associated with the idyllic nature of their former marriage, LeRoy and his screenwriters (Claudine West, George Froeschel and Arthur Wimperis) manage to construe the coming together of these two characters in ways that allow for a reaffirmation of the more positive values and meanings that their earlier relationship had embodied. This is encapsulated most of all by the decision to have Garson call out the name 'Smithy' to Colman as she arrives at the cottage and stands by the gate. In choosing to reactivate the couple's romance in this way the filmmakers allow the reunion to be achieved in a manner that involves a most moving re-empowerment of Paula's voice. The exact staging of this part of the closing sequence is especially important in understanding the regenerative force with which Garson's voice becomes endowed at this point. For while we as an audience are now privileged with a shot showing her arriving at the gate and calling out 'Smithy?' (Fig. 4.19), the cut to a shot showing Colman standing at the doorway of the cottage with his back to Garson, then turning around on hearing her refer to him by his former name, makes clear the ability of this moment to re-enact for him the earlier nature of their first encounter, as he once again becomes aware of her in the form of a voice whose bodily source lies somewhere outside his frame of vision (Fig. 4.20 and Fig. 4.21). In announcing herself in this way, Garson thus manages to reactivate Smith's memory in ways that evoke both the actively desiring nature of Paula's character and her associations with the nurturing, maternal figure. The combined psychological effect of this tends to heighten the significance of Colman's initial moment of hesitation all the more, as he is shown visibly stiffening on hearing her first utterance of his former name, before then turning around and relaxing on seeing who is standing before him. As well as managing to reassert the active strength and deeper psychic connotations that her voice had exerted during the first phase of their relationship, her calling out of 'Smithy' (Fig. 4.22) also signals a stripping away of the upper-class status that had so contributed to the constraining nature of the Rainier marriage. The

Fig. 4.19

Fig. 4.20

Fig. 4.21

feeling she puts into this word invests it with a special quality of individuality that contrasts so markedly with his earlier disparaging view of the banality of the name 'Smith' as a 'highly unimaginative incognito'.

Fig. 4.22

In becoming endowed with a regenerative charge capable of bringing Smithy out of the emotional death of his former existence (her three utterances of 'Smithy? … Oh, Smithy! … Oh darling!', being eventually followed by Colman's single but intense calling out of 'Paula!', as he finally pieces this woman's voice, image and identity together), Garson's voice thus acquires an affirmative strength that is comparable in its emotional impact to the kind to be found at the end of those musicals dealing with the phenomenon of the great female singer. Rather than using her voice to renegotiate her relationship with the male protagonist in some changed way that reflects (as it does in those other films) the threatening effect that it has come to exert over him, in Garson's case the emotionally-charged nature of her utterance functions more as a way of restoring her bond with Colman's character to some former highly-valued, even ideal state. Given the vital role that Garson played earlier in allowing Smith to discover a new sense of self at a time of great crisis in his identity, this film's overall significance therefore derives much from the creativity with which it uses that special combination of active and soothing, romantic and nurturing qualities in her voice to bring about a two-fold regeneration in this male figure. While *Random Harvest* is quite distinctive in this respect, it does have one interesting precursor in the form of *Goodbye, Mr Chips*, the film that marked Greer Garson's debut appearance in American cinema and which was adapted from another James Hilton story.

Goodbye, Mr Chips (Sam Wood, 1939)

As with *Random Harvest*, the ability of *Goodbye, Mr Chips* to recognise a complex potential to Garson's voice is evidenced right away in the director and screenwriter's decision to introduce her in the form of an off-screen voice. This occurs during the Austrian walking holiday section of the narrative when, as Chipping (Robert Donat) finds himself stranded alone up on a mountainside amidst a heavy blanket of mist, it is Garson's voice calling out, 'Hello-o-o! Hello-o-o!', from somewhere further up on another ridge that has the effect of drawing him out of his emotionally withdrawn state and, in prompting him to climb up and 'rescue' her, bringing him into a life-changing romantic involvement with her. As with Garson's performance of the song 'She's Ma Daisy' in *Random Harvest*, this independent assertion of her voice (which turns out not, as Chipping thought, to be a call of distress but the utterance of a modern young suffragist woman sufficiently uninhibited enough to feel able to 'let out a shout at random') *is* presented as having a more dangerous, threatening potential to it during the sequence where Donat is shown precariously clambering around a ridge and almost falling from it as he climbs up to the mountain to reach Garson's character, Katherine Ellis. Yet, while the wooden sign dedicated to the memory of 'One who lost his life here' that Chipping comes across during this dangerous climb of his might seem to confirm such a potential, ultimately its words demand to be read quite ironically given the emotional renewal that the schoolmaster proceeds to undergo as a result of responding to her call.

In demonstrating this ability to cut through the otherwise impenetrable mist, and draw the timid schoolmaster Chipping up to her, Garson's voice invites comparison, to some extent, with those ubiquitous off-screen female – especially benevolent maternal – voices that Michel Chion writes about in his book *The Voice in Cinema*. Indeed, in view of how Garson's voice is able to alert Chipping to her presence despite the heavy blanket of mist that cloaks the Austrian mountainside, it seems particularly appropriate to invoke that critic's discussion of the role played by the woman's voice in John Carpenter's horror film *The Fog* (1980). As Chion observes, much of that film's interest lies in the way that it dramatises the benevolent power of the voice of the female protagonist (Adrienne Barbeau) in guiding the local people (from her position as broadcaster in a remote radio station located at the top of a lighthouse) away from the monstrous clutches of the ghost-ridden fog that travels in from the sea and envelops their small coastal town. In doing so, Chion suggests, the film is able to gesture, even more fascinatingly, towards some form of underlying affinity between these two main forces within the narrative: 'Here the voice does battle with formlessness, and with what is formless in it; it confronts the fog as a sort of embodiment of the voice itself' (1999: 119).

Chion's construing of the fog as a visual manifestation of the more uncontainable aspects of the female voice is certainly something that seems both relevant and helpful when seeking to understand the association of Garson's voice with the mist in *Goodbye, Mr Chips* – and, indeed, with the heavy fog that also serves as a backdrop to her first appearance in *Random Harvest*. In accounting for the full significance of such elements, though, one would have to bear in mind their importance, as well, in acting as external embodiments of the male protagonist's own inner state. The fog's role in giving visual expression to Smith's mental disorientation and loss of memory in *Random Harvest* is something that finds its counterpart in *Goodbye, Mr. Chips* through the use of the mist to evoke Chipping's situation as a middle-aged, emotionally unfulfilled man who feels he has lost his way in life. But just as the fog in *Random Harvest* also performed (unlike its counterpart in Carpenter's film) a rather more benevolent function in helping to mask Smith's escape from the asylum, in *Goodbye, Mr Chips* the mist fulfils a similarly protective role for Chipping. In his case it creates a blanketing effect that, in impairing his vision and cutting him off from the world below, provides him with an environment within which he is able to gain a distance and freedom from his habitual outlook and way of life. In insulating the male protagonists in this way, the fog and mist also invite further comparison with Garson's voice, although, unlike the cold, clammy nature of such inclement environmental elements, her vocal tones are distinguished by their warm, caressing qualities.

In the case of *Goodbye, Mr Chips*, the special features of Garson's voice can be discerned almost immediately on Donat's arrival on the upper ridge when, still unable to hear her, he lets out an unnecessarily loud shout of 'Hello!' only to be surprised to hear a much gentler, calmer 'Hello' coming from somewhere around the corner of an adjacent rock. As he walks in her direction and calls out, 'I can't see you', she can then be heard saying, 'Here I am', in a quietly relaxed manner before finally appearing amidst (significantly) a swirl of mist, the image of which interestingly prefigures that moment towards the end of *Random Harvest* where Garson's character Paula emerges out of the wisps of mist that sweep across the frame as she sits by the window of the old inn. This aspect to Garson's voice becomes even more prominent during the sequence where Chipping expresses his dislike of the new phenomenon of bicycles. 'Ladies riding bicycles. I don't approve of all this rushing around on wheels. The other day a man passed me in a cloud of dust, he must have been doing 15 miles an hour! You know, human beings were never intended to go at that speed!', exclaims Donat, with a frenetic pace to his voice and a tense shaking of his head that so ably manages to convey the very uptight, emotionally

Fig. 5.1

repressed nature of his character. On hearing this, Garson responds not with words of her own but by staring at him for a while with a mixture of amusement and fascination on her face. The sense of stillness and calm created by this meditative pause of hers has the effect of slowing down the pace of their encounter to something more comparable to the rhythm of her relationship with Colman's character in *Random Harvest* and allows him time to reflect on his behaviour: 'I suppose you think I'm old-fashioned…' (Fig. 5.1).

During the second, more intimate, part of their encounter, Kathy's growing influence over Chipping is reflected in Donat's adoption of a more wistful tone of voice as he begins to comment quite openly on the emotionally unfulfilled nature of his life. Thus, he confides how, on meeting her, he has realised what he has been missing in terms of female company and how, in more ordinary circumstances (away from the protective, insulating cover of the mist), he probably would have been too frightened to speak to someone who is 'so very nice-looking … and charming'. On hearing this, she reassures him with the words: 'So are you, Mr Chipping, frankly', his incredulous reply of 'Good heavens, no one has ever called me that!', being subsequently met by her with a comforting (not ridiculing) trill of laughter. Responding to this, Donat's voice suddenly becomes much more animated as, breaking out into a hearty burst of laughter, he engages in a lyrical exchange with Garson that testifies – in its gently alternating rhythm and flow – to the growing romantic harmony between their characters.

Chipping:	Oh! What extraordinary ideas come into one's head up here.
Kathy:	It's the altitude.
Chipping:	Do you experience a sort of exhilaration?
Kathy:	Definitely.
Chipping:	As though we owned the mountain?

Kathy:	To put it mildly.
Chipping:	We're pretty superior persons.
Kathy:	We're gods!
Chipping:	Up here there's no time, no growing old, nothing lost.
Kathy:	We're young.
Chipping:	We believe in ourselves.
Kathy:	We have faith in the future.

As Chipping becomes more pensive again, the film shifts to a closer shot of the pair as Donat exclaims with a deepening ache to his voice: 'It must be the altitude!' On hearing him ask, 'Do you suppose a person in middle-age could start life over again and make a go of it?', the animating power of Garson's voice comes even more fully into its own as she first reassures him with 'I'm sure of it. Quite sure', before proceeding, in a tone of hushed serenity, to re-inspire him with a belief in the value of his work:

Kathy:	It must be tremendously interesting to be a schoolmaster.
Chipping:	I thought so once.
Kathy:	To watch boys grow up and help them along, see their characters develop and, and what they be-come when they leave school and the world gets hold of them. I don't see how you could ever get old in a world that's always young.
Chipping:	I never really thought of it that way. When you talk about it, you make it sound exciting and heroic!
Kathy:	It is. (Fig. 5.2)

Fig. 5.2

Then, just at the point where their encounter reaches its closest point of intimacy, Kathy looks around and, anticipating the exact line that Garson's character speaks in the pen-ultimate scene of *Random Harvest*, remarks, 'Oh, look! *The mist is lifting!*' Uttered in a pleasantly surprised, uplifting way that endows this observation of hers (as in *Random Harvest*) with a sense of hope and new beginning, Garson's words thus gesture towards the liberating, transformative effect that Chipping's encounter with Kathy has had on him. As such, the lifting of the mist comes to signify both the possibility of him gain-ing release from the repressive cloud of old-fashioned values previously constraining his behaviour, and of him now being able to find his way out of his state of emotional stagnation and isolation.

In bringing about this transformation in the male protagonist, part of the poetic legacy of Garson's voice can be measured (both before and long after her character's premature death) by its effect of drawing out a natural musicality in Donat's own speaking voice, the distinctive qualities of which, having earlier been held in check by this actor during the section of the narrative dealing with the schoolmaster's emotionally repressed state, are now able to find much greater scope for creative expression. This is instantly noticeable on his arrival back at Brookfield when, on appearing at the doorway of the staff common room – now dressed in a more modern cut of suit and with his formerly overgrown moustache trimmed in a way that reveals the handsome charm of his smile – he responds to the other schoolmasters' congratulations at the news of his marriage in a delightfully sing-song kind of way. 'Thank you. My wife would so like to meet you. May I bring her in? We'll only stay a moment. Kathy!', he says in a lyrically lilting form of voice, the gentle rise and fall in pitch as he moves effortlessly and without a pause through his sentences helping to confirm the emergence of a much more emotionally assured, revitalised form of masculinity.

If Chips's rejuvenation in this scene partly bears out his own earlier commentary on Kathy's ability to invest his role as a teacher with a greater sense of virility ('When you talk about it you make it sound exciting and heroic…'), then the sing-song quality that emerges in Donat's voice here at the same time points to her capacity to bring out a less conventional form of masculinity in him. In this sense, *Goodbye, Mr Chips* invites further comparison with *Random Harvest* where Garson's vocal influence also seemed to allow for the emergence of a less patriarchally-bound form of identity in Colman's character. However, what makes the earlier film of additional interest is the way that it goes on to construe her legacy in terms of a discovery within the male himself of a more tender, nurturing potential. It is an aspect to Donat's character that – as evidenced later on by his abhorrence of the military ethic that comes to dominate Brookfield during World War One – makes him far removed from the patriarchal authority represented by the gruff, bearded headmaster who was in post when Chips first arrived at the school as a young man. It finds its fullest and most endearing expression during the sections of the narrative dealing with Chips's life as an old man, for it is there that Donat, capitalising on the license that his character's ageing affords him, is able to combine the rich, warm tones and cello-like timbre of his voice with a much higher, more musically ascending key.

The kind of effect arising from this vocal combination is demonstrated most notably of all near the end of the film during the scene where Chips, thwarting an attempt by two

of the older boys to play a trick on a new starter by having him knock on the old schoolmaster's door, takes pity on the scared young boy by inviting him in for tea. On discovering that the boy in question is none other than Peter Colley (Terry Kilburn), the son of a former pupil of his (played by John Mills) who was killed in action during the Great War, Donat's already kindly voice and overall manner become marked by even greater tenderness and compassion as, on pouring out the tea and giving Colley an extra large slice of walnut cake, he sits the boy

Fig. 5.3

down by the hearth and comforts him with words of reassurance and heartfelt empathy (Fig. 5.3). This culminates in the sequence where Chips, on hearing the boy talk about his mother and his wish for the schoolmaster to visit them both some day, shifts into a meditation on the time (unbeknown to the boy himself) when he visited the Colley household in the autumn of 1918. 'I know those hills of yours quite well. I was there ... one autumn when the leaves were turning. Beautiful colours. Green and red and gold', remarks Donat slowly in the rich, musical tones of 'a voice made more beautiful in timbre by the trace of a Northern quality it never quite lost' (Barrow 1985: 12). Inflecting the lilting rhythm and higher, upward end of his notes here with wistful pauses and cadences, this actor consequently utilises his voice in ways that manage to capture something of both the optimism and poignancy of his character's parting exchange with the boy's mother, when she commented on the 'marvellous' nature of the colours that autumn and her hopes (subsequently thwarted) of her husband being back 'before the leaves fall'. In recalling this earlier moment from the film, using a depth and shifting variety of emotional shading to his voice that becomes so poetically expressive of the beauty of the changing leaves he is describing, Donat thus reaches out to his young pupil in the narrative present in ways that privately attest to the longevity of his own presence as an alternative protective influence in the boy's life. It is an influence that first arose as a result of the John Mills character's request for Chips to stand in for him by looking after his wife and infant child while he is away fighting in the war but is something that also becomes linked to the maternal figure through Donat's invocation here of Helen's (Jill Furse) previously-voiced hopes for peace. In alluding to that earlier moment, Donat therefore manages to invest the schoolmaster's words with a wonderfully composite gender-nurturing quality and using a voice itself suggestive, through its complex tone and texture, of this embracing of male and female parental roles.

The emotionally enriching nature of this form of masculinity finds its ultimate validation, of course, in the boy's affectionate farewell of 'Goodbye, Mr Chips' on leaving the schoolmaster's house, the touching valedictory nature of which is confirmed all the more through the film's reinvocation of this moment in its closing shot. In using the abbreviated nickname that was originally applied to Donat's character as a term of endearment by Kathy, the boy's farewell also closes the film in a way that seems designed to remind us of the transformative impact of this woman's sensibility in bringing about such a deepening bond of friendship between Chips and his pupils. It is an influence that finds its most moving confirmation of all in the closing scene when, as Chips lies dying in bed while the doctor and headmaster stand over him, commenting on what a lonely life he must have had and how it was a pity that he did not have any children, the film allows him to intervene and challenge this attempt to impose such a pityingly bleak reading on him. 'But you're wrong. I have. Thousands of them. Thousands of them. And all boys...', he says in a voice that, now construing himself quite explicitly as some form of all nurturing alma mater/pater figure, redefines his years at Brookfield in terms of plenitude and meaning instead. The last word of this final line is stretched out masterfully by Donat in the form of a slow, contented sigh that testifies, even at the moment of death, to

Fig. 5.4

the lasting effect of Garson's vocal rhythms on his character (Fig. 5.4).

In drawing back from the bleaker reading of Chips's life that is put forward by the doctor and headmaster (the sombre tone of which hearkens back to those other sections of the narrative dealing with the wasted years endured by Chips prior to Kathy's arrival, and the overall loss of life incurred by Brookfield during World War One), *Goodbye, Mr Chips* could be accused of lapsing into sentimentality in its closing celebration of its male protagonist and the tradition of public-school life that he comes to embody. Yet it is precisely its readiness to invest in this emotionalisation of the male and his ability to discover a nurturing side to himself that enables the film to make such a significant departure from traditional depictions of masculinity. The extent of this achievement can be seen as finding external validation in the fact that it was Donat's sensitive embodiment of the kindly schoolmaster, not Clark Gable's performance as Rhett Butler in *Gone With the Wind* (Victor Fleming, 1939), that earned the award of Best Actor at the 1940 Academy Awards.[11] Elsewhere, the possibility of the male voice acting in this way is something that remains quite rare in both American and British cinema. This tends to be reflected in academic writing on the voice in film where critics like Michel Chion have concentrated more on instances involving the male's ability to appropriate the maternal voice in monstrous fashion while also noting the capacity of the maternal voice to act as a protective counterpoint to the aggressive male voice on certain occasions (on the off-screen voice of 'Mrs Bates' in *Psycho* (Alfred Hitchcock, 1960) and the climactic confrontation between Lillian Gish and Robert Mitchum's characters near the end of *The Night of the Hunter* (Charles Laughton, 1955), see Chion 1999: 140–51 and 118). Yet as we have already explored, there are some memorable instances of the nurturing male voice to be found in cinema and it is to another notable example of this that we shall now turn.

Going My Way (Leo McCarey, 1944)

In its story about an old priest, Father Fitzgibbon (Barry Fitzgerald), whose church is in dire financial straits and who, burdened by the responsibility of being in charge, has grown tired and set in his ways only to be challenged and, ultimately, renewed by the progressive approach of a young priest, Father Chuck O'Malley (Bing Crosby), *Going My Way* offers an interesting all-male variation on *Goodbye, Mr Chips*. In shifting from the romantic scenario involving Kathy and Chips to a relationship based on the tensions and eventual friendship between two priests, *Going My Way* also offers a significant reworking of the initially fraught and then loving bond of affection that develops between schoolmaster and male pupil in that film. The latter's emphasis, in its opening and closing sections, on the ability of Chips to connect in old age with the young boys thus finds its inverse reflection here in the young priest's eventual overcoming of the inter-generational conflicts between him and Fitzgibbon, and his success in forging a closer rapport with his formerly sceptical older colleague. In exploring how this relationship develops, we will focus on one key scene in that film, the achievement of which can be understood to lie centrally in its creative use of Crosby's singing voice.

The scene in question follows on from that point in the narrative where the old priest undergoes a major crisis. This happens as a result of him going to see the bishop with a view to asking for O'Malley to be transferred only to discover that the young priest has in fact been placed unofficially in charge of his church. Deeply shocked and disorientated by this news, he packs his bag and leaves that night in the pouring rain only to be then found and brought back home by a local policeman. In using both the pathos and humour of this incident to construe Fitzgibbon's behaviour as like that of a young child who runs away from home only to return meekly and with some degree of embarrassment to his anxious 'parents', McCarey skilfully paves the way for the touching encounter that ensues between the two priests in the old man's bedroom. This begins when Fitzgibbon, having finished the supper provided by his housekeeper and on being asked by O'Malley if he has 'a wee drop of the "crature" about?' to warm him up after his venture out into the rain, directs the young priest (after some initial reluctance) to his bookcase wherein lies hidden ('behind *The Life of General Grant*') a box containing a bottle of whiskey. On being given the box by O'Malley, the old priest lifts up the lid and, as the Irish folk lullaby 'Too Ra Loo Ra Loo Ral' begins to play, a child-like smile of recognition and delight lights up on his face as he glances over at the younger man. On hearing O'Malley comment affectionately on the source of the tune ('A bit of old Ireland, huh?'), Fitzgibbon proceeds to offer the following explanation with regard to the bottle of whiskey as he pours out a drink for each of them: 'Every Christmas since I left, my old mother sends me one of these. With a degree of abstinence, it becomes me calendar. I get a little behind during Lent, but it comes out even over Christmas.'

On closing the box and handing it back to O'Malley, who puts it on the table next to him, the old priest points up to the wall on his right and says, 'That's, that's me mother', as McCarey cuts to a shot of a portrait of a young woman. 'Oh, she's very beautiful', responds O'Malley as he follows the old priest's glance. 'Of course, that was taken some time ago. She's ninety now', adds Fitzgibbon as the camera returns to its previous view of the two men. 'Let's drink to your mother. Hope you'll be seeing her soon, Father', O'Malley replies tenderly as he raises his glass in a toast, the compassionate nature of his response prompting the old priest to enquire in return, 'Er, what about your mother?' 'Well, I don't remember much about her. She died when I was quite young', O'Malley confides quietly as he looks downwards rather pensively for a moment. Nodding his head slowly in response, Fitzgibbon himself becomes more reflective at this point as he suggests, both by way of solace and in a spirit of mutual understanding, 'Well, let's drink to the two of them, anyway.' 'Thank you, Father', says O'Malley gently and appreciatively as the two men proceed to down their glasses in memory of their mothers. Resting back on his pillow, Fitzgibbon continues his earlier train of thought: 'You know,

Father O'Malley, I always planned that as soon as I got a few dollars ahead, I'd go back to the old country and see my mother. Now, would you believe it, that was 45 years ago. And every time I get a few dollars ahead, I...' 'There's always somebody that seems to need it more than you do', intervenes the young priest in a further display of empathy. 'Ah you'd like her. She'd like you, too. She always had a song in her heart', asserts Fizgibbon and, looking upwards in deep thought, he continues: 'I, I, I can almost hear her now.' Responding to this reminiscing, O'Malley reopens the music box and, as the lullaby begins to play again, Fitzgibbon turns to the young priest and asks, 'My boy, do you, do you know "Too Ra Loo Ra Loo?"' As Crosby begins to sing the tune, McCarey alternates between shots of him and the older actor as the latter is shown casting another glance upwards at the portrait on the wall before nestling down contentedly in his bed. On seeing him fall asleep, Crosby moves into a gentle humming of the tune as he returns the music box to its place in the bookcase and switches off the light, only to then laugh in amusement on hearing Fitzgerald calling out, 'Goodnight', just as he is about to leave the room.

In demonstrating this capacity to assuage the old priest's worries and send him into a peaceful reverie, Crosby's singing displays a quality that is strongly reminiscent of Garson's speaking voice in *Goodbye, Mr Chips* and *Random Harvest*. The unmistakeable properties of that actress's speaking voice thus find their male musical counterpart here in Crosby's crooning which (as well as complementing through its apparent artlessness the unadorned nature of the music box's tinkling accompaniment) seems to wrap each note that he sings in a soft, cocooning warmth. Unlike some of his crooning predecessors, though, Crosby also brings a rich, baritone quality to his singing.[12] The deep masculine tones of his voice thus tend to create their own distinctive effect of reassurance here through the lush bass range that he exhibits on lines such as 'Hush, now don't you cry', and through the sureness of his timbre and pitch as he both holds and extends the opening, 'Too', of each line, moving from deep, to mid-, to high notes as the song goes on. In demonstrating the possibility of the male voice acting in this way, Crosby's singing fulfils a potential that we had already begun to explore in relation to Robert Donat's speaking voice in *Goodbye, Mr Chips*, particularly during the scene where his character comforts the scared new boy Colley as they sit in the schoolmaster's lodging house by the fire. The prominence of the glowing hearth just behind Crosby as he sits talking and singing by the old priest's bedside provides another point of connection with that endearing moment of male tenderness in *Goodbye, Mr Chips*. In a reversal of the scenario that plays out there, however, here it is the more virile baritone voice of the *younger male* that is now shown becoming endowed with the capacity to soothe and assuage the *old man*'s anxieties.

In allowing Crosby to comfort the older man by singing a lullaby that rekindles the old priest's childhood memories of his mother's protective influence (not to mention his nostalgic love for the Irish motherland itself), this scene is striking for the openness with which it construes the male singing voice as equivalent to that of the maternal figure. In doing so it develops what had also been gestured at in *Goodbye, Mr Chips* through

Donat's implied invocation of the boy's mother's words. Crosby's ability to stand in for the long-absent mother is visually confirmed by the sequence of shots showing Fitzgerald first looking up at the portrait of his mother shortly after the singer begins his rendition of the lullaby and then gazing fondly at the younger man, his act of taking off his spectacles just as he looks at Crosby suggesting the extent to which these two figures have now blurred together in his character's mind (Figs 6.1, 6.2, 6.3 and 6.4). This aspect to the younger man's voice is also articulated, of course, through the lullaby itself, the restful qualities of which are so exquisitely brought out by Crosby's gently alternating movement between bass and higher notes, all of which complements, in turn, the 'cradle rocking' effect that is already inherent in the rhythms of the lyrics and music:

Fig. 6.1

> Too-ra-loo-ra-loo-ral,
> Too-ra-loo-ra-*li*,
> Too-ra-*loo*-ra-loo-ral,
> Hush, now don't you *cry*!
> Too-ra-loo-ra-loo-ral,
> Too-ra-loo-ra-*li*,
> Too-ra-loo-ra-loo-ral,
> That's an Irish *lullaby*.

Fig. 6.2

Amidst the otherwise steady vibrato and the assured phrasing, Crosby occasionally breaks the unadorned nature of the delivery by introducing a slightly wavering quality into some of his higher-note renditions of certain syllables and words (shown above in italics). Known as the 'upper mordent', this technique is a well-recognised hallmark of Crosby's singing style and one that, in revealing something of this singer's Irish immigrant roots, finds what is surely one of its most lyrically apposite and poignant expressions here. In his study of Crosby's early years as an entertainer, Gary Giddins regards the upper mordent as 'the primary semblance of Irishness in his [Crosby's] work' and refers to this 'signature vocal technique' of his as 'a

Fig. 6.3

Fig. 6.4

broken-note adornment imported from Ireland and Scotland that became known as the Crosby cry.' (2001: 11). He goes on to explain that:

> The mordent – a fast wavering from one note to another and back, a fleeting undulation that suggests a mournful cry – was a vestige of the Byzantine influence that dominated European music in the Middle Ages. That influence vanished from most of Europe but endured in the plaintive folk music of Scotland and Ireland, owing to their economic and geographical isolation from the modernising impact of the Reformation and Renaissance. A 1950s edition of *Chambers' Encyclopaedia* defines the mordent as a 'certain oscillation or catch in the voice as it comes to rest momentarily upon a sustained sound'… and goes on to qualify it as a basic attribute of 'crooning'. (2001: 18)

In introducing this tremulous, wavering quality into the song at certain points, Crosby thus invests the Irish nature of the lullaby with considerable authenticity, his most pronounced application of the upper mordent being reserved, appropriately, for the final word of the last line: 'That's an Irish lu-ull-aby.' In using it in the context of this particular song, Crosby at the same time manages both to reinforce and add greater complexity to his identification with the nurturing role. For if the crooning properties of his voice help compensate elsewhere in the number for the absence of the mother herself, then in making use at certain key points of a technique noted for its ability to suggest 'a mournful cry' he is also able to articulate a more poignant sense of the mother's grief at being separated from her son. Hence, while this lullaby-like quality to Crosby's voice is also inherent, up to a point, in his singing of the title number to the homesick troops and his serenading of Rosemary Clooney's character with the song 'Count Your Blessings' in *White Christmas* (Michael Curtiz, 1954), nowhere was it employed with greater depth of coherence and insight than in this particular sequence from *Going My Way*. By providing a therapeutic moment of pause and meditation, Crosby's moving evocation of the mother's act of singing to the infant son thus marks a vital point of transition in the film that enables both a closer bond of affection and understanding to emerge between O'Malley and Fitzgibbon, and a significant process of rejuvenation to take place in the old priest himself as he proceeds to respond to the younger man's investment in music and sport with renewed interest and vitality: 'Shades of me childhood. You know, I feel ten years younger', he exclaims with a chuckle and little tap dance on returning reinvigorated from his first game of golf with O'Malley and the priest of a neighbouring parish, Father O'Dowd (Frank McHugh).

The rejuvenating influence of Crosby's voice also manifests itself elsewhere in O'Malley's transformation of the local boys from street urchins and petty criminals into a harmonious choir. This process is reflected in musical terms by their gravitation from a basic rendition of the nursery rhyme 'Three Blind Mice' to their sublime performance of 'Ave Maria', as they accompany first Crosby and then Rise Stevens (in her role as O'Malley's opera-singing friend) during a practice session down in the church basement. These two strands to Crosby's musical influence beautifully coalesce in the final scene where O'Malley prepares to leave the church and move on to his next assignment (having also managed to transform the previously uncharitable mortgage lender into a reformed Scrooge and thus ensure the financial security of the church). In what is one of the loveliest sequences in the entire film, Fitzgibbon is shown beginning to speak in praise of the younger man's virtues to his congregation only to have his eulogy softly broken by the sound of the choirboys' gentle singing of 'Too Ra Loo Ra Loo Ral' which strikes up just as his frail old mother (sent for from Ireland by O'Malley) appears at the doorway and, stretching out her trembling hands, begins to walk towards him (Figs 6.5 and 6.6). In having the choir reprise the lullaby at this point, McCarey on the one hand allows the music to signal the conclusion of the boys' own emotional transformation as, in a final relinquishing of their earlier tough-guy images, their voices now become enlisted in a moving celebration of this reunion between mother and son. At the same time, the boys' singing of the lullaby also marks the fulfilment of O'Malley's role towards Fitzgibbon for it is on watching this event with evident pleasure from his now marginalised position at the doorway, that Crosby then turns and departs into the snow-filled night, on seeing this personal aspect to his work at St Dominics complete (Fig. 6.7).

Fig. 6.5

Fig. 6.6

Fig. 6.7

There is a delightful aptness to ending with an analysis of a male lullaby since it encapsulates this study's overall concern with exploring some of the distinctive uses to which certain actors' voices have been put in individual films. The richly expressive effects of these uses seem (as in this case) so deeply at odds with what has often been construed as classical/mainstream cinema's attempts to deploy the voice in ways designed to shore up patriarchal norms of sexual difference. In allowing Crosby's voice to fulfil its caring potential, this moment from *Going My Way* thus constitutes an important culmination of what we have been exploring elsewhere in other films central to this study where the strategy (in those cases) of internalising the voice or subjecting it to some form of literal impairment had the effect – in freeing the male figure from his habitual ties to language and giving greater scope to the visceral texture and bodily grain of his voice – of allowing for a more expressive, resistant, less patriarchally hidebound form of masculinity to emerge.

NOTES

chapter 1

1   Commenting in his book, *The Films of Vincente Minnelli*, on the miscasting of Steve Martin in the Spencer Tracy role – a role that, if Dore Schary, the head of MGM at the time of the original film's production, had had his way would have gone to the comedian Jack Benny, not Tracy (the director and producer's first choice) – James Naremore observes that: 'The Disney company made the same decision that Schary almost made: it chose a standup comic rather than a dramatic realist. At various points in the 1991 film, Steve Martin tries to behave in a subdued fashion, but at bottom he remains a professional wise guy, a specialist in send-ups of square characters. An expert at winking at the audience from behind his mask, he seems unconvincing or flat in the serious moments, and he overplays everything that calls for a delicate response' (1993: 93).

2   Referring to Stanley's 'man-to-man' talk with his future son-in-law, Naremore states that: 'Caught off guard [by Buckley's 'rigid, military posture' and by his 'politely offering to answer any questions'], Stanley covers his nervousness by launching into a monologue about his own marriage and early struggles. A dissolve shows the ashtray beside his chair filling up with matches, an hour has passed [sic: actually half an hour], and we see Buckley struggling to stay awake while Stanley drones on, accounting for every penny he ever earned' (1993: 100).

3   One thinks, especially, of the moment at the ball in *Madame Bovary* where, on being told who Emma's husband is, Jourdan sneeringly remarks: 'Oh, yes, that peasant.'

chapter 2

1   In capitalising on this tendency towards attenuation in Stewart's vocal delivery, Capra thus anticipates Hitchcock's use of that same actor's voice within a thriller context – particularly in *Rope* (1948) and *Rear Window* (1954) where Stewart's slow, tremulous style of speaking plays such a central role in shaping the tone and pace of the suspense during certain key scenes.

2   In his insightful discussion of Stewart's persona, Andrew Britton himself acknowledges that 'Stewart's early work occasionally anticipates its subsequent trajectory (most fascinatingly, in *Mr Smith Goes to Washington*)...' (1995: 15).

3   Maria DiBattista regards this speech where Jean Arthur's character, Clarissa Saunders, outlines her vision of Jeff's role in democratic history as the 'making of a political manhood [that] is one of the most consequential Pygmalion acts in American screen comedy' (2001: 157–8).

4   Buchman is noted as saying: 'When I watch the film again, I always leave before the end. I detest the [attempted] suicide of Claude Rains; it was an idiotic idea and I fought against it, without success' (quoted in McBride 1992: 416).

5   According to Greer Garson's biographer Michael Troyan, 'James Hilton was so pleased with the casting and the screenplay treatment that he agreed to deliver the opening narration in the film' (1999: 139).

6   As Silverman also puts it: 'The entry into language is the juncture at which the object is definitively and irretrievably lost, and the subject is definitively and almost as irretrievably found. It
is also the occasion for a further sacrifice, that of the subject's own being' (1988: 8).

7   In his discussion of how Garson's portrayal of the war-time heroine Mrs Miniver 'had inspired
audiences on an unparalleled international scale', Michael Troyan refers to how the Queen of
England wrote to Garson thanking her in the following terms: 'You made us feel more brave
than we actually were by your performance. To you, we will all be eternally grateful' (1999:
1–2).

8   Troyan also recounts how resistant Garson was to the idea of playing mother to a 20-year-old
and quotes her as saying that: 'I continued to be cool and distant to Mr Ney throughout *Mrs
Miniver* ... which was a ridiculous piece of feminine pique on my part since, obviously, he had
no more to say about the casting than I. So perhaps it was a form of retribution that when the
picture was finished and our roles of mother and son safely canned and jelled, I went dancing
with Mr Ney and had a most beautiful time' (quoted in Troyan 1999: 146).

9   Commenting on the vocal harmony between Garson and Colman, the director Mervyn LeRoy
is quoted as follows: 'It [*Random Harvest*] could have been written for them. Between the two
of them, the English language was never spoken more beautifully on film' (quoted in Troyan
1999: 139).

10 According to the producer Sidney Franklin, this parallel between Kitty and Paula was quite
deliberate and would have been heightened even further if another promising actress, Ann
Richards (who ended up taking a more minor role in the film), had got the part. According to
Troyan, Franklin 'told [that] actress: "If you had come to the lot earlier, you would have gotten
the much more important role of Colman's fiancée, which Susan Peters is already signed to
play. She is supposed to remind him of his first love, Greer Garson, whom you resemble more
than Susan does"' (1999: 139).

11 In his biography of Donat, Kenneth Barrow highlights a number of glowing responses that
this actor's performance as Chips earned him from his peers, a few key examples of which
are cited here: Spencer Tracy: 'May I say without reservation that your Mr Chips is the finest
performance I have ever seen on the screen. I should like someday to give one remotely approaching it. All of the awards of former years must now be melted and one moulded for you.
In deepest respect...'; James Stewart: 'Every screen actor in the world should go and study
Robert Donat as Mr Chips. There is something so magnificent in this character study and performance that it seems almost a miracle that it could happen. I have seen it twice and intend
to see it three or four more times'; Paul Muni: 'That is the most magnificent performance I've
seen on any screen. Not a false [e]motion [sic] – not a wasted gesture. He is the greatest actor we have today' (1985: 111). Barrow also refers to a cable sent by Alfred Hitchcock asking
Donat to star in his next project, *Rebecca* (1985: 120).

12 As Gary Giddins observes, 'Bing's singing was nothing if not virile ... After Bing achieved his
breakthrough, the word *crooner* would usually be used descriptively or with admiration' (2001:
203).

BIBLIOGRAPHY

Barrow, Kenneth (1985) *Mr. Chips: The Life of Robert Donat*. London: Methuen.

Barthes, Roland (1977) 'The Grain of the Voice', in *Image-Music-Text*, selected and trans. Stephen Heath. London: Fontana Press, 179–89.

Britton, Andrew (1995 [1984]) *Katharine Hepburn: Star as Feminist*. London: Studio Vista.

Chion, Michel (1999) *The Voice in Cinema*, ed. and trans. Claudia Gorbman. New York: Columbia University Press.

Colette (2003 [1944]) *Gigi and The Cat*. London: Vintage.

Dewey, Donald (2003) *James Stewart: A Biography*. London: Time Warner Paperbacks.

DiBattista, Maria (2001) *Fast Talking Dames*. New Haven and London: Yale University Press.

Doane, Mary Ann (1985) 'The Voice in Cinema: The Articulation of Body and Space', in Elisabeth Weis and John Belton (eds) *Film Sound: Theory and Practice*. New York: Columbia University Press.

Dunn, Lesley C. and Nancy A. Jones (1994) *Embodied Voices: Representing Female Vocality in Western Culture*. Cambridge: Cambridge University Press.

Giddins, Gary (2001) *Bing Crosby: A Pocketful of Dreams – The Early Years 1903–1940*. London: Little, Brown.

Hilton, James (1941) *Random Harvest*. London: MacMillan.

___ (2001 [1934]) *Good-bye, Mr Chips*. London: Hodder and Stoughton.

Kozloff, Sarah (1988) *Invisible Storytellers: Voice-Over Narration in American Fiction Film*. London: University of California Press.

Lawrence, Amy (1991) *Echo and Narcissus*. Oxford: University of California Press.

Lerner, Alan Jay (1978) *The Street Where I Live*. London: Hodder and Stoughton.

McBride, Joseph (1992) *Frank Capra: The Catastrophe of Success*. London: Faber and Faber.

Minnelli, Vincente with Hector Arce (1990 [1974]) *Vincente Minnelli: I Remember It Well*. Hollywood: Samuel French Trade.

Naremore, James (1993) *The Films of Vincente Minnelli*. Cambridge: Cambridge University Press.

Silverman, Kaja (1988) *The Acoustic Mirror: The Female Voice in Psychoanalysis and Cinema*. Bloomington: Indiana University Press.

Smith, R. Dixon (1991) *Ronald Colman: Gentleman of the Cinema*. London: McFarland.

Smith, Susan (2000) *Hitchcock: Suspense, Humour and Tone*. London: British Film Institute.

___ (2005) *The Musical: Race, Gender and Performance*. London: Wallflower Press.

Telotte, J. P. (1989) *Voices in the Dark: The Narrative Patterns of Film Noir*. Urbana and Chicago: University of Illinois Press.

Troyan, Michael (1999) *A Rose for Mrs Miniver: The Life of Greer Garson*. Kentucky: University Press of Kentucky.